The Development of Autobiographical Memory

Autobiographical memory constitutes an essential part of our personality, giving us the ability to distinguish ourselves as individuals with a past, present and future. This book reveals how the development of a conscious self, an integrated personality and an autobiographical memory are all intertwined, highlighting the parallel development of the brain, memory and personality.

Focusing strongly on developmental aspects of memory and integrating evolutionary and anthropological perspectives, areas of discussion include:

- why nonhuman animals lack autobiographical memory
- development of the speech areas in the brain
- prenatal and transnatal development of memory
- autobiographical memory in young children.

The Development of Autobiographical Memory offers a unique approach through combining both neuroscientific and social scientific viewpoints and as such will be of great interest to all those wanting to broaden their knowledge of the development and acquisition of memory and the conscious self.

Hans J. Markowitsch is Professor of Physiological Psychology and Director of the Centre for Interdisciplinary Research at Bielefeld University, Germany.

Harald Welzer is Director of the Center for Interdisciplinary Memory Research in Essen and Research Professor of Social Psychology at the University of Witten/Herdecke. He also teaches at the University of Hannover, Germany, and at Emory University in Atlanta, Georgia, USA.

The Development of Autobiographical Memory

Hans J. Markowitsch and Harald Welzer

Translated by David Emmans

Psychology Press
Taylor & Francis Group
HOVE AND NEW YORK

First published in 2005 as *Das autobiographische Gedächtnis*
by Klett-Cotta

This translation first published 2010
by Psychology Press
27 Church Road, Hove, East Sussex BN3 2FA

Simultaneously published in the USA and Canada
by Psychology Press
270 Madison Avenue, New York, NY 10016

*Psychology Press is an imprint of the Taylor & Francis Group,
an Informa business*

© 2010 Psychology Press

Typeset in Times New Roman by
RefineCatch Limited, Bungay, Suffolk
Printed and bound in Great Britain by
TJ International Ltd, Padstow, Cornwall
Cover design by Hybert Design

British Library Cataloguing in Publication Data
A catalogue record for this book is available from the British Library

Library of Congress Cataloging-in-Publication Data
Markowitsch, Hans J., 1949–
  [Autobiographische Gedächtnis. English]
  The development of autobiographical memory /
  Hans J. Markowitsch and Harald Welzer.
    p. cm.
  Includes bibliographical references.
  1. Autobiographical memory.   I. Welzer, Harald.   II. Title.
  BF378.A87M2713 2010
  153.1′3—dc22

                                                    2009019002

ISBN 978–1–84872–020–6 (hbk)

Contents

Acknowledgements

Work on this book was done while our joint interdisciplinary research project "Remembering and Memory" was being supported by the Volkswagen Foundation. We are greatly indebted to them for their support, especially Dr Vera Szoelloesi-Brenig and Professor Axel Horstmann. The Institute for Advanced Study in the Humanities at Essen housed our project and has helped us extensively. We would particularly like to thank the former President of the Institute, Professor Jörn Rüsen; the Managing Director, Dr Norbert Jegelka; and the Director of Administration, Harald Watermann.

This book could not have been finished without the work of our coworkers Dr Anja Lemke, Dr Olaf Jensen, Silvia Oddo and Anne Schwab. Silke Matura conducted the study on photos with children, and she and Dr Karoline Tschuggnall wrote early sketches on prenatal, transnatal and early memory. We are very grateful for their help. We also thank Oliver Eller for thoroughly checking the completed manuscript. We are especially indebted to our English copy-editor, Dr Joe Garver, for his competent and very careful attention to detail.

David Emmans was an ideal choice as translator. After earning a degree in classical philology in his native New York, and a diploma in psychology in Germany, he was a long-time coworker in the neuropsychological research group of Hans Markowitsch. He is now earning a degree in archaeology in Germany. Many thanks to him for his excellent translation.

Section I

An interdisciplinary view of memory

1 A new approach to viewing memory

Human memory is what distinguishes our mind from that of other primates and all the more from other mammalian species. Put more precisely, autobiographical memory is what makes humans "human" beings, giving them the ability to say "I" or "me" so as to distinguish a single, unique person who has his or her own life history, a present and an expectable future. On a yet higher level of abstraction, autobiographical memory enables individuals to position their personal lives along a continuum of space and time, and to look back to a past that preceded the present. This ability to undertake "mental time travel" (Endel Tulving) directly subserves the purpose of developing a sense of orientation for future actions. What was once experienced and learned thereby becomes the foundation for planning and conducting activity in the future.

In order to make such orientation possible, autobiographical memory has to fulfill three prerequisites. First, memories have to preserve a personal reference to the subject so as to become useful for that person. For example, a child readily avoids fire only if he or she was burned and remembers it. Second, and directly related to this point, is the necessity for autobiographical memories to have an emotional index, that is, that they be coupled with a positive or negative evaluative feeling that clearly indicates just which events are fairly logically deducible for the future from those memories or from going through the same experience again. Third, autobiographical memories must be "autonoetic": with the help of this quality we do not just remember something, but we are also very aware of the fact that we are remembering. This ability of autonoetic memory supplies us with the invaluable advantage of having conscious, *explicit* recall of memories. A person can thus deliberately replay long-past situations so as, for example, to review an action and then see whatever alternatives were not thought of during the original event, with the benefit that, if the event repeats itself later, it will be responded to this time with a broader spectrum of actions, with decisions now being better founded.

From an evolutionary perspective, possessing an autobiographical memory offers an enormous advantage, allowing an organism to think in a conscious and self-reflective way on what has occurred in the past and what the reaction to it was then. Animals demonstrate this ability to a certain degree when, for example, they "remember" either a place where food can best be found, or which other animals are rivals for food or which situations are just too dangerous for them. To this extent, memory is fundamental for life at all, in a specially relevant sense. Even the simplest life forms live in an external environment and can only survive there successfully when they internalize certain demands of the environment into their system of reactions. Interestingly, many of the decisive advances in memory research were made by investigating how the neuronal connectivity of very simple organisms develops and changes (such as the sea slug *Aplysia*; compare, for example, Bailey & Kandel, 1995) depending on experience in their respective environments. Thus, memory is first of all a mechanism for converting an organism's experience with its environment into the structure of the nervous system. And seen in this way, memory is essentially related to the development of an organism within a specific environment, and this development in turn unfolds depending on either experience or usage.

Basal memory functions are the same for humans as for other organisms. But as we will show further on in this book, in addition to these functions, which evolved in common with other mammals and especially with the primates, humans phylogenetically and ontogenetically developed a unique system of memory with a decisive evolutionary advantage: the ability for elevating their memories up to a functionally more efficient level, in two respects.

First, the ability for positioning one's self along a continuum of space and time means that the environment can be systematically examined as well as evaluated. Without such a self-reflective memory that reviews stimuli and reactions, demands, and responses, all reactions merely occur in sequence without any direct relationship to each other. The ability of conscious memory, on the other hand, opens up a basically unlimited number of delays between one challenging situation and the possible reactions to it. A self-reflective memory introduces the chance for waiting for better conditions before responding, for persevering through difficult times, and for developing more efficient strategies and solutions. Put briefly, a memory system that reflects on its own contents allows for actions that are based on choices and considerations of timing. Such a memory system creates room for action, and releases the person from the immediate pressure of the moment for prompt action, and this is very different from mere activity and mere reactions, so that we can speak of purposeful action.

A second point, and one which is directly associated with the first, is that a self-reflective memory creates the capability to externalize the contents of memory, to shift them outside the original organism. In a long line of evolutionary steps, from simply marking a hidden source of food all the way up to the development of symbolic forms of exchange through linguistic communication and the use of written language, humans have created unique forms of representing the different contents of their memories that permit not only further release from the immediate necessity to react, but also the social transmission of their memories. Humans can preserve and communicate this information, and once writing had been invented, they could pass it on to others who did not need to be in any way directly connected in time or place with them. In this way a wealth of stored knowledge radically overcomes the limitations inherent in needing direct physical channels for effective communication. Working in the field of comparative infant and primate research, a developmental psychologist, Michael Tomasello (2002), advanced the theory that the development of symbolic communication had a decisive evolutionary advantage: Creating the possibility of cultural transmission of experience, through the media of linguistic communication, in fact makes use of social means to accelerate an evolution that would otherwise be much slower. The speed of evolution in human life forms, breath-taking and apparently constantly intensifying, thus intensifies its own momentum. Humans can pass on their individual progress in coping with the demands of their environment far over space and time, so that following generations expand their developmental options on the basis of previous social practices, elevating these options to a higher level of experience.[1]

This enormous increase in developmental possibilities is mainly due to the technique of externalizing memory and making it accessible to an extended social context. Thus, the surprisingly rapid technological and cultural progress of *Homo sapiens sapiens* took place in the extremely short evolutionary period of but 200,000 years, a progress that we can still witness, in fact, day by day with an ever increasing speed of transfer. This progress is directly related to the developmental "leap" that a self-reflective memory system made possible, and one of the subjects we will treat in greater detail later is how this memory arises ontogenetically. When humans successfully relate to one another not only across considerable differences in space and time but also throughout various social settings, they are organisms with specific biological equipment that influences their own further developmental course over time and their further potentiality. Nonetheless, human pregnancy still usually takes place only over a period of 9 months, and individual development still passes through certain stages that are the same no matter how different the various historical or intellectual contexts are. Although it is a fact that memory can already be demonstrated in the fetal stage, autobiographical memory develops ontogenetically rather late. It is this form of memory that distinguishes the various time zones of past and present from the future and that sets one's own personal self in relation to these zones.

---

1 This line of thinking is not quite so recent as Tomasello thought: theoretical speculations were already published on this in the 1940s, 1950s and 1990s (Huxley, 1953; Elias, 1991), but only had negligible influence on research concerned with the brain, consciousness, memory, etc. At present, however, with increasing convergence in the results from several fields of work, undertaking further studies on the social or cultural acceleration of biological evolution could very well be an intriguing and promising line of research.

The first signs of a developing autobiographical memory – the use of personal pronouns and recognizing one's own face in a mirror – appear at the age of approximately 2 years, but the start of a functional level does not occur until somewhere between 3 and 5 years, at the age when our earliest personal memories are first established. The months and years before that period are not recollected or even "rememberable" at all, something that has been called "childhood amnesia", a term which, it should be noted, does not designate amnesia occurring in small children, who at that age can of course very well remember events which happened in the past. The term is reserved rather for the failure of adults to remember events from their early years. The developmental age for autobiographical memory coincides with the acquisition of language. Obviously, certain specific levels in brain maturity are a prerequisite for acquiring language, and we will be treating these relationships in detail later in the book. But the origin of autobiographical memory is a developmental task that continues into late adolescence and even early adulthood. It requires an exceptionally long period to develop, indicating that a highly complex process is involved, dependent just as much on biological as on sociocultural conditions.

However obvious and relevant it may be to us that we are in possession of an autobiography and can thus relate episodic or narrative information from our own lives, we should not forget that this is not an inherently necessary ontogenetic development, and even less is it phylogenetically self-explanatory. In fact, almost all forms of memory treated in this book need a certain amount of time until they become functional, and in the final analysis they are thus acquired capacities, not inherent ones. It is precisely the ability of autobiographical memory and of relating details of one's own life history that requires the longest period of time for maturing and is thus the very last such development to achieve competency. It is probably the most complex form of memory of all because it has functions that are specifically relevant only for one individual organism, and because it also matures in dependence on other memory functions. It is the one form of memory that creates the impression of a lifelong continuity, making it possible to claim "I am the person I am", and in strongly individualized societies, this is the basis for synchronicity, communication and reliability.

With its present characteristics, autobiographical memory is itself a product of the modern period. The feeling for autobiography and for individuality is far less pronounced in societies with a static hierarchy of power and an apparently undisputed sense of order, in which people's position in the society is not defined by their own ambitions or achievements, but rather by the social position and circumstances they are born into. The development of more modern societies and a more personal, dynamic and individualistic course of life leads to that form of autobiographical memory that today we consider "normal". Sociological theories, in particular the theory of civilization that Norbert Elias put forward (1969), have shown how general historical change can manifest itself in the behavior of individuals: for example, how changes in the larger context of power structures, economics, etc., are related to changes in the individuals, their habitus and their concept of themselves as persons. A central idea of Elias is that when societies become more advanced, the chain of possible behaviors in that society necessarily becomes longer through division of labor as well as through specialization or differentiation of functions, meaning that the interdependence between the different members of society is augmented in quantitative and qualitative ways.

Elias illustrated this idea in the strategy that was developed within courtly society which called for both an increase in the time allowed for certain sequences of formalized behavior as well as for deliberate delays between one action and the subsequent reactions, all for the purpose of giving time to anticipate the long-term consequences. The foresight that was necessary for this strategy automatically led to a different kind of communication style, with more self-control and deliberation than had previously been the case. (As an interesting sidelight, we may note the derivation of the word "courteous", from "courtly".) Elias explained the basic principle thus: "The behavior of more and more people has to be aligned to that of others; the 'fabric' of their actions has to be organized more and more precisely and strictly so that each and every action fulfills a social function. The individual person is obligated to regulate behavior in a way that is increasingly differentiated, consistent and stable" (Elias, 1969, p. 317).

The person is of course not aware of the functioning of this process. Such regulatory behaviors are more an aspect of habitual practice than of conscious intention, and they very effectively express themselves in the long term through changes in habitus which entail a substantial reformation in the internal state, the psychology, of the members of that society in the course of civilization over time. The theory put forward by Elias (1996) describes a continuous change in the relationship between one's own demands and those of others. For example, in a feudal society, order is preserved when an opponent is first threatened verbally and only then directly attacked, whereas modern societies are characterized by a constant reduction in the level of direct aggression, that is, by a reduction in external force. At the same time, however, internal demands and expectations become more relevant, so that a person lives up to and fulfills regulations without having been subjected to any external force. This can be seen in another example, the process that enabled a daily working style to finally prevail in the industrial age: Edward P. Thompson (1987) recalled graphic descriptions of how workers in the early phase of industrialization had to be coerced with clubs and whips to stay in the factories for 12 hours, and how they regularly failed to come to work on Mondays so that they often had to be physically forced, literally thrashed, to return to work. Subsequently, the working day was slowly reduced to a rhythmical period of but 8 hours, and by now it appears as a natural matter of course in which all members of society, from the young to the retired, take their daily working hours or their sleeping periods and their recreation simultaneously, in step with one another. The original external demand has mutated into an internal one, and this is the point Elias was making: socio-genesis and psychogenesis are two aspects of the same process. Changes in social systems generate psychologically different human beings in whom the rise of feelings of shame and embarrassment indicates the birth of a self-identity that is highly aware of the fact that their prosperity and success in life are not dependent upon other people or divine powers, but on themselves, exquisitely so.

Persons who are guided by their own internal principles will have a similar style of education for their children, and support their sense of self-discipline, ambitions and achievements, etc. When disciplinary practices, such as a very early and rigid toilet training, are begun even in the infant stage, it becomes apparent how close the relationship is between social, psychological and biological aspects of ontogeny.

In addition, when interdependence among the members of a society increases, the need for calibration of their complex social and communication relations becomes a much longer-lasting task, and this explains why a differentiation has been made between childhood, adolescence and adulthood with a corresponding differentiation in the behavioral standards throughout history. The phases before adulthood, at least in Western societies, are allowed to take up more and more time because rehearsing the habitual and defining standards of the social environment requires an ever increasing amount of time.

Elias explained this by pointing to the fact that children "in a relatively short period of growth prematurely reach the stage of shame and embarrass-ment which took many centuries to unfold. Their impulses still have to be subjugated to the strict rulings and the specific models which typify our societies and which, in history, developed very slowly. Parents are actually only the instruments, although often insufficient, or the primary executors for conditioning, but through these parents and through thousands of other instruments is always the society as a whole and the entire fabric of human-ity that puts pressure on the coming generation and fashions them more or less successfully" (Elias, 1969, pp. 198ff.).

This view is an indication that Elias, who published his theory in the 1930s, accepted the biogenetic principle that ontogeny recapitulates phylogeny, as if in quick motion. But Julian Huxley (1953) had already pointed out that this principle in no way explains all development, but rather only the initial stages, which then go through further differentiation, and their expression in turn depends on experience and the organism's environment. This argument can be illustrated in what we described above on the cultural acceleration of biological evolution. In humans, ontogeny takes place in a sociocultural environment which has been shaped by whatever stage of progress was attained by preceeding generations. In the ideal case, every generation begins its own development on a level that is higher than that of the generation before. This process has recently been given the metaphorical term "ratchet effect" (similar to using a jack to lift a car), but it must not be forgotten that there are fundamental biological steps in development which, at least up to now, cannot be replaced by any cultural innovations, however impressive these may be.

The ratchet effect is made possible by the fact that the human brain is uniquely plastic. Compared to that of other mammals, its development, maturation and morphology depend to a great degree on influences from the environment during childhood and adolescence. More than half a century ago, this fact was already recognized by a zoologist, Adolf Portmann (1956/1995), who called the first year of an infant's life the "premature extrauterine year" to emphasize that humans, as opposed to other mammals, are born prematurely in respect to their developmental status, which is in no way sufficient for an infant to survive on its own. Infants are incapable of obtaining their own nourishment, defending themselves or else having recourse to flight. They require, for a relatively lengthy amount of time, external protection and assistance in obtaining the most elementary necessities of life, and they require this until their organic growth is advanced far enough that they can, at least theoretically, survive on their own.

The fact that humans are born prematurely, with their organic development still incomplete, means that genetically programmed processes of maturation occur together with social processes of maturation. Organic and social development takes place concurrently, as was already the case before birth, but is more apparent postnatally. The development of the human brain directly reflects this fact. No other organism has a similar degree of neuroplasticity; no other brain is so inherently incomplete as is the human; or, in other words, no other organism has a comparable developmental potential for adaptation to such different and changing environmental conditions.

We mentioned earlier that, basically, memory is the transformation of experience of the environment into the self-organizing neuronal structures in a developing organism. And, of course, this principle also holds for the organism with the most complex neuronal structure of all, the human. The central organ for expertise in the world is in many ways already astonishingly well-developed at the moment of birth. Mammals can, for example, hear, see, smell, feel, taste and communicate, but, compared to a mature adult's brain or even to those of other primates, the brain of a newborn human is nonetheless markedly immature.

At birth, the human brain weighs approximately only one-fourth that of an adult's (Figure 1.1). In the newborn chimpanzee, genetically the closest relative of humans, it has already reached almost 60 percent of its later weight. And only in humans does the number of connections continue to grow after birth at the original fetal rate and magnitude.

Up to the age of around 6 years, an amazing total of 30 synapses is formed every second under every square centimeter of the surface of the brain (Rose, 1998, p. 17). On the other hand, we also observe phases of rapid reduction in the number of synapses during childhood. This is indeed a highly intriguing process, brought about by the fact that only those synapses are retained that

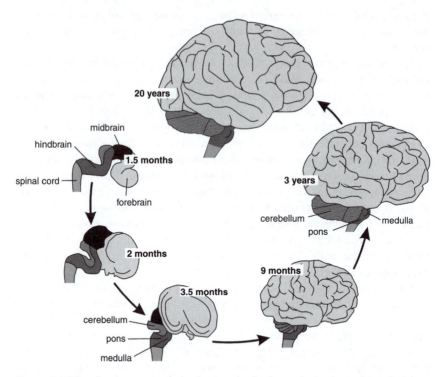

Figure 1.1 The development of the human brain from the embryonic period into adulthood.

become a part of a behavioral pattern still in use. These connections originate while stimuli and information are being processed. Synapses which do not continue to be used during certain time windows for development disappear, a process which is termed "pruning".

But changes take place over a long period of time not only at the level of synaptogenesis and pruning. Some brain areas and their organs do not attain their final maturation until adolescence (such as the frontal lobe), and others, such as the temporal lobe, are only completed at the end of adolescence (Welzer & Markowitsch, 2001).

These processes which take such a surprisingly long time are precisely the ones that are apparently so necessary for developing a mature personality, capable of clearly realizing the distinction between self and others and for finally working out autobiographical memory. Although still a matter of some debate, there is increasing evidence that new neurons are in fact generated throughout life, something that was held impossible until recently. In summary, in the human brain, we have an organ that remains exceptionally incomplete for an exceptionally long time. Whatever humans can perform long before their final maturation, and in fact whatever capabilities humans have from the day of their birth, it all underscores the perfection of this organ, the one most susceptible to developmental alterations, the most flexible organ that evolution has brought forth, a fascinating continuum of metamorphosis.

The explanation for the survival advantage of humans as a species lies in their potential for development and their ability to be receptive to the formative influences from the natural and social environments. No other organism can adapt so well to such different and vacillating environmental conditions as humans do. In other, more precise terms, the human species constitutes the organism that creates the very environment in which it can exist and evolve. As far as the general evolution of any one species is concerned, that ability is a characteristic of high-caliber robustness, but as far as the individual is concerned, there is no organism that is so little robust and in fact so unfit for survival as the human. This high degree of vulnerability is the price that the human brain pays for developing and then improving on its capacities over the whole course of its life. Such a development and improvement are only possible because, with its basic structure and principles of organization, it has evolved precisely for making use of potentialities and is genetically determined only in its original structures at birth. As infants we are capable of so very little because later we have to be capable of so very much.

The human abilities that are formed epigenetically all require a period of time for development. As we will treat in more detail later in the book, for the task of learning fundamental skills such as seeing, speaking, etc., certain "time windows" are fixed within which the acquisition of the skills has to take place. Neglecting these windows leads to an irreversible loss. Tragic examples from the past show that children who are born blind, due to specific deficits, and who later are operated upon so that, technically, they then have a basically intact visual system, are nonetheless incapable of learning to sort out and structure the visual information they are successfully receiving. They cannot differentiate the foreground from the background, that is, they fail to process what they actually see. In these patients, the window was definitively closed a long time previously, the window that a small child normally makes use of by the age of 2 years in order to perfect the gift of sight as a genuine ability for experiencing things, and thereby enabling the brain to establish the necessary neuronal structures.

This is also the case in speech acquisition, for which critical phases have also been identified. Language is of essential importance for the development of autobiographical memory because it is the medium which permits symbolic exchange and the externalization of experience, and to that extent creates the possibility of defining oneself relative to all others. Autobiographical memory depends on the change that takes place when a child learns to have first a passive and then an active control over a representative language, allowing the child to imagine itself outside the immediate, actual present, as for example, when a child remembers having had an accident at kindergarten a week previously. This stage of distinguishing the past, the present and the future is usually attained some time between the third and the fifth years, which in the West coincides with the end of so-called childhood amnesia.

The ability of autobiographical memories is a distinct social skill, inasmuch as it is subject to training effects in social communication together with other persons by means of "memory talk" (K. Nelson, 1993) and "conversational remembering" (Middleton & Edwards, 1990). It is social also for another reason: it provides a stable point of reference for orientation amid all the myriad fluctuations in roles and situations and so furnishes the assurance for oneself and others as well that over different times, places, and personal histories, we are still one and the same "I", the same person, and that this will still be the case in the future.

To a certain extent, autobiographical memory is not something that "belongs to" the individual person alone; it is rather a social institution that guarantees the basic demands for synchronization within modern society. We mentioned above how modern societies are substantially different when compared functionally to others throughout history, and have to provide more and more extended time for development and schooling for the next younger generations, and these considerations show that the level of development a society finally attains to becomes more and more diverse and versatile. This means that a person's own autobiographical project has access to fewer and fewer fixed points of reference, and this, in turn, makes working on that autobiography far more complex. For this reason it is not until early adulthood that a person finally assumes the mature autobiographical position that can convince himself or herself, as well as others, that this is one and the same person now, as in the past, and will be the very same person in the future, supertemporally and diachronically.

In a review article on the surprisingly poor level of the developmental psychology of childhood and adolescence, Habermas and Bluck (2000) came to the similar conclusion that the ability to relate a consistent life narrative is not complete until the end of adolescence, showing that the developmental span of autobiographical memory concurs directly with childhood and adolescence. The ability to remember autobiographical information is a competence that requires a substantial amount of time for successful learning, and such an "apprenticeship" relies on influences from manifold social, cultural and biological determinants. As a case in point, a recent study (Romeo et al., 2002) discussed decisive processes of change occurring in adolescence, supporting our conclusion that essential developmental steps for attaining new personal and social capabilities always correlate with developments at the level of the brain (Markowitsch, 2002a).

The brain and memory (as part of the central nervous system) make up an organ whose structure organizes itself and develops in direct communication with the physical and social surroundings, and for this reason their development is principally not an autonomous biological process, but rather one which is influenced by social and cultural determinants and receives its final form within social interactions. By precisely viewing brain development from the aspect of its experiential dependency, we see why it is impossible to understand the brain, memory or even consciousness as something intrinsically adhering only to the individual person alone. Viewing the brain this way, we can conceptualize the social form of human existence itself as a supranatural adaptive environment in which each of the coming generations begins its own course of development socially on the level that the previous ones established and cultivated beforehand. Unlike in other mammals, this permits a completely different quality of dynamics, made possible through storing and then sharing experience, knowledge and tradition.

And that means that when we discuss human phylogenesis and onto-genesis, natural and cultural histories converge. Recognizing this will avoid, in our view, two of the major obstacles to progress in modern scientific thought. The first is Descartes' body–soul dualism, which still attracts many philo-sophers, psychologists, cultural sociologists and historians as well as natural scientists, and the second is the dichotomy between nature and culture, between heredity and environment, or between instinct and learning, all of which presume that, for humans, any one of the two aspects could be considered completely without the other. By referring instead to the experiential dependency of brain development, on the one hand, and, on the other hand, to the biocultural dependency of cognition, we are able to concentrate on identifying fields of convergence in the approaches and the findings of different disciplines studying memory, and then make these results even more fruitful for further research.

Such fields of convergence are difficult to observe when only the high-end product, the brain of adults, is taken into consideration, that is, the brain of the fully socialized individual, who is capable of relating mature, autobiographical material. Limiting attention only to the adult brain leads inevitably to the dichotomies mentioned above that make it appear impossible to establish a bridge between the biochemical and electrophysiological processes in the brain of an autobiographical narrator and the contents of his narration, without any direct structural correspondence between, say, a

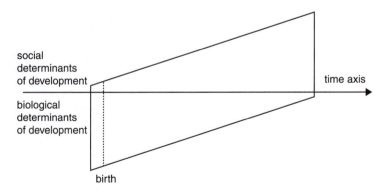

Figure 1.2 Schematic model of development.

moving experience of love and some specific brain activity responsible for the experience.

We can avoid the pitfalls involved in these dichotomous preconceptions by focusing on the process by which the brain develops and memory originates. This perspective reconciles the misleading contrasts in these dichotomies and also shows that, in the development of memory, self-identity and auto-biography, organic and psychological maturation, social interaction, and the cultural context are simply different aspects of the same process. In other words, to understand how memory, autobiography and self-identity originate, we need a biopsychosocial model that is based on a continuum of balanced biological and social determinants of development. The smaller and more immature a child is, the more prevailing the role is for prior biological default settings; and, vice versa, the more advanced the child is, the more relevant the role is for the factor of social interaction in the environment that the child has been born into or belongs to. Figure 1.2 shows this process schematically.

As we have sketched it up to now, this model is rather schematic and linear, although we well appreciate that ontogenetic development does not progress continuously but in jumps or sudden transitions in which the role of different factors can vary strongly in various phases. Nevertheless, the model aptly demonstrates our central argument: At no stage in human development can we speak of a purely biological course of events, independent of the social context or social conditions. Similarly, we cannot identify a stage in develop-ment which completely lacks biological factors for maturation. On the contrary, it is becoming more and more evident how important the social, cultural and historical influences are in the formation of memory and the personal identity of children and adolescents, and this directly implies that autobiographical memory (which, as we pointed out, only begins unfolding, at the earliest, at the age of 3 years) is the most social form of memory, defined to a striking degree by society, culture and history.

2 Zones of convergence between different sciences

> The human brain is the only brain in the biosphere whose potential cannot be realized on its own. It needs to become part of a network before its design features can be expressed.
>
> Merlin Donald

Memory and remembering have been the subject of considerable and broad interest for some two decades now, involving both the natural sciences and the humanities, and becoming a topic of everyday concern, for many reasons. The contingencies and pressure to perform adequately in a modern, highly industrialized society make it necessary to keep adapting one's personal past to external exigencies. This is also the case when societies make constant reference to living up to the norms of the past. The systemic transformations at the end of the twentieth century particularly seem to have evoked a growing need for confirming our historical roots and at the same time finding orientation in the new world. The interest in memory and remembering has also increased due to substantial age-related changes in demographics in the majority of Western countries. There are increasing numbers of people who have more to look back upon than to look forward to, and disturbances in memory, correlating with greater age, as in cases of dementia, Alzheimer's disease, etc., are becoming a major concern for health and social programs. In addition, medical technology developed methods of cerebral imaging that made it possible to directly view brain activity, and this gave memory research a tremendous boost. Whereas before we could only rely on testing, animal experimentation and brain-damaged patients to distinguish various memory systems and functions, modern-day imaging techniques have made such progress in showing task-related activity patterns in the living brain that the last decade (1990–2000) was named the "decade of the brain". The neurosciences at times seemed to succumb to the hubris of claiming to be the sole means to explain questions of consciousness, the will and memory.

Progress in neuroscientific research on memory has been impressive. Using methods of cerebral imaging we can now distinguish different forms of processing in memory activities, as, for example, between emotional and neutral memories; we have identified a number of different memory systems with completely different functions; and we can distinguish the processing of memories of stories in a person's mother tongue from those told in a foreign language learned later on. More recently, brain imaging has been applied to detect differences between lies and true memories (Ganis et al., 2003; Kozel et al., 2004; Markowitsch, Kessler, Weber-Luxenburger, Van der Ven, & Heiss, 2000; Spence et al., 2001). Today, we understand much better than before the role of different brain organs such as the hippocampus, the amygdala and the thalamus in storing, preserving and recalling memories, and – one of the main topics of this book – we can now distinguish the processing of memory content according to the age of the person remembering. This is not only of interest for theoretical scientific research, but it also offers numerous practical possibilities of application for medical intervention from microsurgery to specific treatments for Alzheimer's disease and epileptic patients.

The findings of neuroscientific research are furthermore of vital interest for the picture we make of ourselves, as, for example, when it turns out that memories of events which we are completely convinced of as having actually happened, are in fact false, coming from some source other than our real historical past. Memory is apparently fully capable of constructing associations that have nothing, or very little, to do with the actual events. A case in point: the victims of extreme traumas do not necessarily remember exactly what happened to them, but rather what they were most afraid of (the "greatest fear vision", Schacter, 1996, p. 207).

In general, autobiographical memories are susceptible to confusing the particular circumstances of an event and the sources of the event. This confusion goes so far as to create cryptomnestic memories, that is, memories of events that never took place. This has been corroborated by a number of experiments with persons who were told of events that had not happened to them, but who were given the strong suggestive hint that they would later certainly remember the details themselves (Hyman et al., 1995; Loftus & Pickrell, 1995; Loftus et al., 1995). The experiment that has gained the most recognition is the "lost in the shopping mall" experiment (Loftus & Pickrell, 1995), in which the subjects were told events from their own childhood that only their close relatives had in fact remembered. One of the episodes, however, was purely made up, relating how the child had gotten lost in a supermarket. In the first trial of the experiment, a total of 29 percent of the participants already "remembered" the event as told, although they had not in reality experienced it with the particular details. What is especially intriguing about this experiment is the fact that when the trials were repeated, even more of the subjects succeeded in "remembering" the occurrence. Apparently, even mentioning the event in the first trial was sufficient to establish an association within the subjects' real life history, an association which functioned as an import gateway into their personal biography. In addition, the subjects "remembered" more and more individual details from the event, which seems to have become a definite part of their biography in the course of the experiment. Their false remembrances felt just like real ones. Analogous experiences were found in experiments using made-up events in the emergency ward of a hospital at night, and highly embarrassing events such as upsetting the punch bowl onto the expensive apparel of the bride and groom during a wedding reception (Hyman et al., 1995).

In one of our own experiments, conducted by Sina Kühnel as part of her doctoral dissertation, we showed the subjects films in which certain short sequences were excluded, such as what happened between having just gotten out of bed and then standing next to the bed fully dressed. Another incomplete sequence showed a woman in a store picking up a bottle of perfume and then abruptly wiping it off her wrist, while the logical scene in between of her actually spraying the perfume was left out. When we later showed the subjects picture material which portrayed the missing scenes, they were falsely but regularly identified as having been seen. There were further distortions of memory of various kinds (compare Schacter's "Seven Sins of Memory", Box 2.1) with the final result that more than 40 percent of the memories documented were in fact "false memories", a result that none of the subjects thought could be possible.

Box 2.1   True and false memories

It is obvious that, depending on their age, people show different ways of accessing their memories and also that these memories themselves are subject to highly different reinterpretations, new structural analysis and additions, etc. A review of the literature on "false memories" reveals that even memories of one's own life history can be relied on only with considerable reservation. For example, in a review article, Daniel Schacter listed the following frequent mistakes or problems in remembering ("Seven Sins of Memory", 1999):

1   Fading of memories. We can assume that memories disappear when they are no longer put to use. Conceivably, the synaptic connections for the corresponding engrams decompose when the memories are never recalled again (Schacter, 1999, p. 184).
2   An additional problem for memory arises at the very moment of encoding/storage because our perception itself is highly selective in every situation that we experience. In fact, the only aspects of any situation which are conducted into long-term memory at all are those which are within the range of attention. We can see this easily in the case of tricks performed by magicians on the stage, which succeed only because our attention has been so focused onto one particular visual aspect of the whole situation that the actual

manipulation does not strike us at all even when it is actually performed in full view. Another convincing case of selective perception can be seen in an experiment done by Simons and Levin (1998). The person conducting the experiment asked individual students the way to a particular building on the campus and in that moment two workers carried a large door between the student and the person asking the question. In the brief moment when the person was fully hidden from view, he was replaced by another person. Surprisingly, only 7 of the 15 subjects noticed they were then talking to someone different. What is apparently involved here is the fact that persons are perceived according to categories, meaning that usually it is not of any importance to remember the characteristics of a person who asks the way and who will probably never be seen again. Law enforcement personnel can give an endless list of analogous cases of mistakes in memory from eyewitness reports.

3   The recall of memories often appears somehow blocked. Usually, this involves a temporary difficulty in remembering something clearly: one has the impression that something is on the "tip of the tongue", the "TOT phenomenon". This is usually explained by assuming that other elements in memory storage interfere with the specific remembrance that one intends to recall. Interestingly, in such situations one is quite sure of actually knowing the right word or the right name that one is searching for, without being able at the moment to recover it. Because recall of a memory apparently consists of activating an associative pattern, interference from other associations would in fact impede a correct activation. This would explain why the name being sought for suddenly occurs to the mind later when completely different things are being attended to (Schacter, 1999, p. 188).

4   A considerable number of examples of false memories consist of simple errors, mistakes concerning the origin of particular memories, etc. An unintended, ingenuous import of "false" memories into storage occurs when we do remember a fact or relationship correctly, but erroneously attribute it to a wrong source, such as a book or a film, which was in fact the origin of the memory. Such thoughts about the source of the memory also become part of the memory. The most drastic form of such source confusion came, unwittingly, from a memory researcher himself, Donald Thompson, who was described in detail and later identified as the perpetrator by a victim of rape. Thompson fortunately had a convincing alibi: at the moment the crime was committed, he had just been interviewed live on television on the topic of memory warping. Although it sounds unbelievable, the victim had just seen this

interview moments before being attacked and falsely gave Thompson's description as that of the attacker (Thompson, 1987; compare Schacter, 1999). Similar cases of source confusion and source amnesia play a role occasionally in copyright disputes, such as when the melody of one hit song is claimed to have been stolen from another. Even in such cases of "unintentional plagiarism", the actual cause can be source confusion in a composer who, completely without intention, sees his melody as his own creation although in reality he originally heard it somewhere else. Another aspect of source confusion can be seen in the relevance of visual representation to memories. When a person feels that "I can see it right before my very eyes", and believes that literally every detail can be recalled at will, this feeling evokes the firm (but often unfounded) conviction that what is remembered actually took place. What is all the more astonishing and very difficult to understand is the fact that such subjective conviction is not dependent on the event's first having actually passed through the retina on to the brain for accurate storage. It is rather unsettling to realize that the neuronal systems for processing both visual perceptions and imaginative contents do in fact overlap, with the result that purely imagined events can "reappear" later "right before my very eyes" with convincing visual accuracy. The discrepancy between the subjective conviction of remembering something perfectly and the actual artifactual nature of this memory can be demonstrated best in such cases.

5   An interesting aspect of false memories due to source amnesia and confusion is seen in a person's degree of suggestibility, which can play a significant role in specific situations such as therapeutic settings. It can generate whole memories that have no correspondence in actual life events. A rather spectacular case was that of the author Binjamin Wilkomirski, who described his memories as a child in a concentration camp in a book that became quite well known. But it was soon discovered that Wilkomirski's real name was Bruno Dössekker, that he had been raised as an adopted child in Switzerland, and that he had had nothing to do with the Holocaust. In fact, he had frequently visited former concentration camps, read extensively on the conditions there, and, under the influence of suggestive feedback during several therapy sessions, he had slowly developed an identity as a victim, which he was apparently thoroughly convinced of himself (Assmann, 2001; Koch, 2001).

6   The problem of memory distortion was mentioned above as related to the process of categorization. Strong convictions and attitudes

to other people have a basic tendency to induce selective perceptions and memories in conjunction with our preferred categories. One of the early workers in the field of memory, Frederic Bartlett, published a classic study in which he presented British students with a somewhat exotic story from an ethnological report, which they were to read and then retell. There were two experimental settings. In the first, the subject heard the story and then had to tell it to another person, who in turn was to tell it to a third person, and so forth, similar to the children's game of chain whispering, only with far more complex details. This condition Bartlett termed "serial reproduction". In the second setting, the same subject was asked just to repeat the story after a certain interval, the condition for "repeated reproduction". Bartlett recorded the differences with extreme care and found that under the condition of repeated reproduction, even the second retelling, after 20 hours' delay, amassed significant changes from the original story. First of all, the story became noticeably shorter; second, the narrative style in retelling became "more modern" than the original; and third, the story now had, from the viewpoint of Western culture, a more logical and coherent structure (Bartlett, 1932/1997, p. 66). These tendencies remained even when, some years later, the subjects were once again asked to repeat the story. Bartlett concluded that cultural schemata, once they are generally effective in a society, help form perception and thus the later memories to such an extent that extraneous material, which did not happen, can easily become one's own material, in a very subtle way not even noticed by the person. Thus, his original story was bereft of all the surprising, unaccountable and illogical elements, while other characteristics, such as names and objects fitting the cultural expectations of the subject, were freely imported into the narrative (1932/1997, pp. 86ff.). In the other condition, serial reproduction, there were similar effects, so that again the original story now appeared abbreviated, compressed, with free imports, and more rational. Bartlett's results showed not only that perception, storage and recall are influenced by cultural attitudes, but also that, to a high degree, memory is itself a very constructive, creative process which conforms to one's own personal and cultural sensory needs while remembering many things in everyday life. Recent studies have also confirmed how different information about the conclusion to a story influences the retelling of the whole story (e.g., Conway & Ross, 1984; Spiro, 1980), so that the final reproductions are "warped" in the direction of the final scene. This has been called "retrospective bias".

7   A further basic problem can be seen in the persistence of memories, when something "just won't get out of my mind", although the person certainly wants to forget. This phenomenon is often seen after traumatic experiences or in depressive states when such patients even constantly brood over negative or unfortunate events. A further tendency in these cases is for the patient to overgeneralize the memories and thus extend the emotion or mood for a longer period in the light of the one, very unfortunate but central event (Williams, 1997).

What Wolfgang Hell said about memory is an apt summary of these different points: "An emotional preference in any one field, repeated questioning, suggestions and a good many other things are capable of inducing a false memory which can appear to the person remembering just as real as any correct memory and even seem completely reliable to someone else who is led to believing it simply because of the liveliness of the narrative. In children this effect is even stronger than in adults" (Hell, 1998, p. 274).

We have grown accustomed to thinking of apparent dysfunctions in memory such as forgetting, confusion, etc., as something principally negative. But much of what occurs in everyday life and appears as a frustrating failure in memory is actually highly functional, when judged on the inherent reason for forgetting: the ability to forget is an essential constituent of the ability to remember at all. If we did remember everything that we perceive in the course of events or even all the many more things that make up the background of our immediate environment, and if these memories were to remain "rememberable" at all times, we would not have the slightest chance of orienting ourselves or deciding what to do next. Forgetting is in reality a highly functional and adaptive ability. Even the phenomena of memory blocks can probably be best seen as an adaptive ability, namely as an inhibition which serves to help in sorting out which memories we really require from all the background noise even though some blocks may be unfortunate, minor accidents in an otherwise well-functioning system of recalling. The same is also true for the selectivity of perception: We see primarily whatever occupies our momentary attention, while all other details disappear at the unsharp boundaries of our attention. Everybody knows how narrowly attention is focused when we are looking for a particular object, such as a piece of paper with, say, an important telephone number, in the drawer of a desk full of papers, notes, business cards, etc. But this is the case generally, and so only very few characteristics of any one event ever find their way into our working memory, and from that storage, again, only very little progresses into long-term storage (compare pp. 66ff.). Even the precursors of encoding, storage, recall and renewed encoding undergo the effects of selection: Engrams, the neuronal representations of memories, may disintegrate if they are not activated. Situations demanding recall often involve but a single aspect of an otherwise quite complex context. And whenever renewed encoding occurs, information about this new situation of recalling the original memory will now be stored as well. In short, the content of our memories is particularly subject to use-dependent changes in that content. This means that our autobiographical memory itself is encased within constant processes of change. This explains why, as explained earlier, we can integrate events and experiences that we have actually only heard or read about into autobiographical memory. The original source of what we heard or read about has been lost somewhere along the line, but the event nonetheless survived and has been imported into the context of our own personal life history.

But, as can be expected, this is only possible for events that have sufficient similarities to the real course of our biographies which we can look back upon. Such events which have survived the loss of their source have to appear at least sufficiently probable within our biography to find an acceptable place in that biography. Once again it can be seen how much the social element plays a role here. For example, in the retelling of wartime events, we can detect a surprising similarity in the supposedly highly personal stories of many different people. Something like a narrative standard for recapturing experiential relations seems to be at work here, relations in which a good number of people were in fact involved, so that in the long run group-specific or generation-specific experiences are formulated and condensed in a standardized narrative form. And vice versa, the individual narrators, or autobiographers in this case, make use of appropriate stories from a standard repertoire and integrate one or the other detail into their own life history, without ever noticing what they have done. Although this may sound somewhat impracticable, we did in fact did a study of wartime reports and made the surprising discovery that numerous events that were originally reported in the newspapers conformed, more or less congruently, to the events portrayed in the film *The Bridge* (*Die Brücke*) of 1959 (Welzer et al., 2002). The director of this film, Bernhard Wicki, belonged to the generation that had directly experienced World War II, and worked in both his personal experiences and the events that others had heard about and recorded. The result is a work of art that can be seen as a generally valid and aesthetic expression of the experiences of a whole generation in Germany. There is probably no other film of the postwar era that the last wave of combatants, the Hitler Youth, who only served in ground-based anti-aircraft crews or as the youngest Wehrmacht soldiers, has identified with to this extent.

Conversely, the film unwittingly served as a reservoir of experiences that many *could* have gone through and thus *must* have gone through, some time or other, when it came to retelling a generally plausible, that is, socially acceptable, story from the war. In other words, the history of any one individual's experiences was taken as a faithful rendering only if it conformed to the social expectations of the original participants and their intermediate audience of listeners: the rendering had to appear sensible and familiar enough to them. But, vice versa, many of the real victims of the Holocaust had difficulty in convincing others of what they had in fact experienced simply because their stories exceeded the limits of what their listeners could find plausible or even merely imaginable. It was too improbable, too unbelievably horrible, because it digressed too far from the socially expectable. Many of these survivors of the concentration camps remained isolated with their "unbelievable" accounts. Some had in fact experienced difficulty in integrating their experiences in their own personal histories (compare Welzer et al., 1997, pp. 130ff.).

All this shows how inextricably individual experiences are inter-mingled with social ones, or how deeply our own autobiographies, otherwise seen as absolutely individual and unique, in fact entail concrete or abstract elements from the biographies of others. Our own autobiographical memory does not distinguish between "true" and "false" remembrances: we need others to tell us then that we are erring.

Another case in point: In the United States, the "false memory debate" has been mainly concerned with the evaluation of true and false memories in cases of childhood abuse that were discovered a good number of years after the supposed events. Elisabeth Loftus, who has played a substantial role in that debate, traces the spontaneous life of false memories back to, among other things, the fact that a fictitious experience, if it is imagined intensely and repeatedly, becomes more and more familiar, and this increase in familiarity leads to associating false memories with "genuine" childhood experiences, so that the false ones are then actually imported into the ensemble of true memories, becoming indistinguishable from them. This could also explain why, in interviews we conducted with participants in wartime events, we were given detailed, "eyewitness" accounts of events that were identical with episodes from well-known feature films about the war (Welzer et al., 2002). The narrators elaborate their own autobiography with the help of spectacular and accepted story patterns and thus enliven the account of their own lives, but without ever noticing this. The film, it could be said, fits perfectly the facts of their own history "anyway". Indeed, much of what we consider our very own, most personal collection of experiences and past events did not actually happen to us. This phenomenon has been termed "source amnesia".

In the fields of memory and consciousness research, the natural sciences are now touching on central themes of the social and cultural sciences, and this has some decisive advantages. First, the social sciences have attracted less attention in these fields in recent years and may well profit from the findings in the natural sciences. Second, with their own particular methods, the social sciences may perhaps be in a better position to put the results into a fuller context, and thus evaluate them according to possible consequences, than the natural sciences could do on their own. Interestingly, this is the case when natural scientists believe they can discuss consciousness, the will, or memory and operate with a very circumscript concept of "information". Human brains do not only process information in the sense of reaction-inducing sensory stimuli, they also process stimuli which have meaning. The ability to confer meaning on a sensation is something very characteristic of humans. Something takes place between the direct sequence of a stimulus and the reaction or even between just an impulse and an action, a process of interpretation which then allows us to make the best use of the given options for reacting. Admittedly, even animals attribute certain meanings to certain signals; otherwise, Pavlov's dogs would not have secreted saliva when the bell rang. That is not a reflective meaning in the human sense, but rather the result of learning by conditioning. The dog has no conscious awareness that its appetite has been evoked because a bell rang; it has only learned to associate different stimuli.

Reflective "meaning" is not something that nature dispenses; instead, it is fashioned by social and cultural means. As we will show later while detailing results on the development of memory, meaning is fashioned from the day of birth onward in the interactions taking place between children and their social environment. In relation to the human brain and in particular to whatever has an effect on our consciousness and memory and whatever motivates our willpower, we are concerned with contents that have all been socially and culturally shaped and that select our very perception and thus our memories of the world according to criteria of meaning and significance.

For these reasons it is difficult to expect that we could understand what constitutes human consciousness and memory simply on the basis of the concept of information. Remembering, imagining, making judgments and planning rely not on data but on meaning. With this in mind, it is necessary to widen the neuroscientific perspective by including a social scientific one, and this means that as soon as we are interested in the contents of memory, we are dealing with a convergence zone between several disciplines.

Meaning is not developed or acquired by individuals on their own; it is rather mediated in processes of social interaction, in association with other persons. In a study now considered classic, Katherine Nelson (1986) demonstrated how a young girl gained access to the meaning of expressions in her language with the help of interactions with her parents (see also Welzer, 2002, pp. 83ff.). By now we have a large number of publications showing how the interaction between children and their parents has a major influence on what the children later remember, in the form of imprinting (Nelson, 1996, 2002; Nelson et al., 2002). Thus, if we want to understand how meaning is established and how distinctions are made between which information is relevant and which is irrelevant, and which behavior is functional or dysfunctional, we first have to understand the social, interactive process that produces and transmits meaning, a process that is also a kernel element in the ratchet effect of cultural transmission of knowledge and competence, described above.

One aspect of the interactive origin and acquisition of meaning is the fact that children learn at such an early stage that the same thing or circumstance can be seen in a different way the next time depending on the context. For example, it is not clear what a mother means precisely when she shows her 2-year-old child a rabbit running across the field and says, "rabbit". In such a situation, the word could signify an animal in general, a mammal of any kind, a special sort of mammal with the long ears, an animal with brown fur, something which is running, and so on. Referring to just this classic example, the philosopher Willard Quine (1969, p. 29) went on to show that the number of logically possible references for the word "rabbit" is in fact infinite. And today we still do not know how children actually learn to give an object its "correct" name, that is, its context-appropriate term, or, the other way around, how they learn to associate a name with the correct object. The same problem is seen when the same word can signify two completely different things (such as "court" or "wrench"). The possibility of looking at one single object in considerably different ways already shows that meaning is always formed and modified through social means. The capability for multi-perspective viewing also shows that we can very well recall completely different words and completely different dimensions for the same object when we are observing, talking about or thinking about something. Without any effort whatsoever, we can shift back and forth between substantially different levels of conceptualizing an object. This is true not only of seeing a number of aspects of the same object: We are also capable of experiencing an apparently simple, unequivocal situation and nonetheless occupying ourselves with absolutely different things, such as putting butter on a roll and at the same time reading the newspaper. We can answer somebody's questions and simultaneously still be completely aware that our train leaves at 9:31, while the subway connection for the train leaves at 9:16 and therefore we have just about enough time now, at 8:55, to pour ourselves a cup of coffee.

This simultaneousness of consciousness is connected to the ability of our working memory to keep from four to seven pieces of information, as it were, "online" at the same time, but it seems scarcely reconcilable with a central neuroscientific (as well as philosophical) postulate, namely, that consciousness is indivisible, unitary. This contradiction is in no way slight, in view of the fact that one of the most serious challenges at the moment for neuroscientific theorizing is the "binding problem", that is, how the brain succeeds in producing a congruent perception out of all the variable data of sensation that are processed in different systems within that brain. The debate on the yet unsolved problem of binding could take on critical dimensions if the possibility is maintained that consciousness is in fact not unitary, and that instead we process several objects, events or circumstances simultaneously. Surprisingly, although the neurosciences seem to attach considerable importance to radically rejecting everyday preconceptions of consciousness, in this controversy they refer to an introspective everyday experience that gives us the feeling that the present introspective aspect, the one we are focusing on at the moment, is in fact the only one that we are perceiving and processing. Whatever the debate brings in the future, the competence for multiperspective viewing and for simultaneousness of the contents of consciousness is definitely a product both of the multimodal experience that one has from the moment of birth onward and of the acquisition of representational language that enables one to work out abstract thoughts beyond the direct impinging immediateness of a given concrete object or a given situation. Both aspects, the multimodal experience and the acquisition of representational language, are constitutive factors in the genesis of the human's ability to give meaning to things, situations, acts of behavior, narrations, and so forth. The multiperspectivity and simultaneousness of perception and the processing of perception belong to the topics in which interdisciplinary perspectives are converging.

Meaning, furthermore, is not discovered anew by every generation; it is, rather, passed on intergenerationally, worked on further, negotiated, and modified. Communication is the essential element in this generational contribution (Welzer, 2002). One brain alone does not have the constitutive ability to decide on meaning. In the long run it would only persist with its preadjusted pattern of reactions, and at most it would merely modify and optimize these patterns through experiential learning and observation, and this is something animals do, too.

However, it must be taken into consideration that the epistemiological object of the neurosciences is the individual – in this case, the individual brain. Research based on imaging techniques, comparative studies of brain-damaged patients, and animal experimentation achieve results through studying individual brains. At present, we do not have the methods to measure the neuronal correlates of interactions, least of all *in actu*, directly while they are taking place. Neuroscientific theories are for that reason strictly individualistic and exhibit a strongly delimited definition as a discipline, as is now, however, generally recognized by prominent workers in the field. In the introduction to a study on the origin of consciousness, Gerald Edelman and Giulio Tononi stated "that the brain is not sufficient in itself to explain the origin of consciousness, and we are convinced that without exception the higher brain functions presuppose interactions not only with the physical world but also with other humans" (2002, p. 8). Similarly, Wolf Singer has repeatedly emphasized that human consciousness requires dialogue between brains, and that the self-perception of being a person with autonomous actions can be traced back to a cultural construct and thus is not directly accessible "for neurobiological explanation" (2002, p. 62). The *interactive genesis of the contents of both consciousness and memory* is therefore a further example of a convergence zone between the disciplines.

But neither Edelman and Tononi nor Singer have drawn the conclusion that they could develop concrete experimental designs on the interactive origin of consciousness or memory. Unfortunately, the present lack of technical ability to undertake such studies seems to rule out any theorizing from the very start. However, some of the other disciplines do have appropriate methods, so that we can in fact study such processes of interactive origins in memory or consciousness on the basis of experiments, observation, video material, etc., and this would allow at least a preliminary form of theorizing and description. These disciplines include developmental psychology, socialization research and neurolinguistics. With their experimental and phenomenological methodology and their analysis of dialogues, they can demonstrate how the process of social interaction in infants and children forms the ability to structure experiences according to meaning.

These disciplines are concerned with development, and one of the postulates accepted by all fields studying questions of consciousness, memory and the will, etc., can now be formulated. Since both for the present and for the near future, we cannot yet "decipher" from mature brains just which correlates are the relevant ones to associate a particular neuronal activity with the memory of a significant life event – the first kiss, passing an exam, a bad disappointment – we have to work on the developing brain. Brains still caught up in development can "reveal" when and where developmental prerequisites for feelings, reflections, autonoetic memories, etc., are functioning, and which joint activity in biological maturation and social experiences is responsible for how these developmental prerequisites work together.

By definition, development is a zone of convergence between the disciplines. Without neuroscientific findings, we cannot understand the conditions for the development of a system of episodic memory, and without social scientific findings we cannot realize how it structures itself and what it processes. For this reason we are convinced that progress to date in each of the disciplines relevant to memory itself has come to the point where the borders between these fields have to be opened and the fields perhaps fused with one another so that we can continue to make progress on methodological and theoretical issues. That is why we will propose a biopsychosocial approach for the study of human memory, with a developmental orientation, and we hope to show that this interdisciplinary approach is superior to that of any individual field of study, at least at the level of description.

3 Why other animals lack autobiographical memory

There are numerous though trivial aspects that distinguish animals from humans. Animals do not suffer from boredom, do not have the ability of imagination, and do not "plan ahead". They exist only in the here and now and cannot distinguish between the past, the present and the future. Their memory is not immediately concerned with the past at all but rather with helping to cope with demands placed on them in the present. Of course, they can rely on their memories to inform them where to find food they themselves have hidden, which places or animals pose particular dangers, which ones they should best avoid, and which techniques they need to get at termites or to open a nutshell. But when they do call up this information or these "memories", they are not aware that they themselves are remembering something. Recall is then only a direct reaction to a demand perceived in a situation, such as having to find food or a safe place, or to defend themselves against an opponent. This kind of memory is purely procedural and executes standard procedures or ones that have been learned. The mammals with the highest degree of development, even the nonhominid primates, basically have only an "experiential" memory at their disposal. As we will show later, this is also true of humans in their early developmental phases.[1]

This experiential memory is limited to a narrow world of immediate, direct experience which cannot be transcended by pausing for reflection, by having a moment's delay for planning. This automatically means that, once an experience has been had, it remains essentially private in a direct sense. It cannot be exchanged or shared with others because the ability of intersubjectivity, to assume the perspective of the other, is missing. For this reason the behavioral repertoire of the nonhominid primates is very limited when compared to that of humans. Even when anthropoid apes are raised by humans, this repertoire can only be extended within narrow limits. Although we share approximately

---

1 We have to add here that memory in humans is concerned with the past only in certain very restricted cases. Functionally, the work of our memory is most usually concerned with matters in the present and sometimes with those of the future as well. It is our growing overconcern with history that has given us the erroneous impression that we are truly involved with matters of the past when we are only talking about the past.

99 percent of our genetic code with our nearest evolutionary relatives, the chimpanzees, the organization of the brains of nonhominid primates is, as far as we can judge today, principally different from our own (see Box 3.1).

Box 3.1   Distinctions between the brains of humans and other primates

There are considerable differences in the shape and size of the brains of various animals (see Figure 3.1). Nonetheless, mammals in particular have a highly similar basic structure, as far as cortical areas and collections of cells (nuclei) are concerned. Strong differences appear when individual areas are studied in detail.

In spite of the high degree of genetic conformity and similarity in the evolutionary line (Figures 3.2 and 3.4), there are marked differences in the finer organization of the brain between nonhominid and human

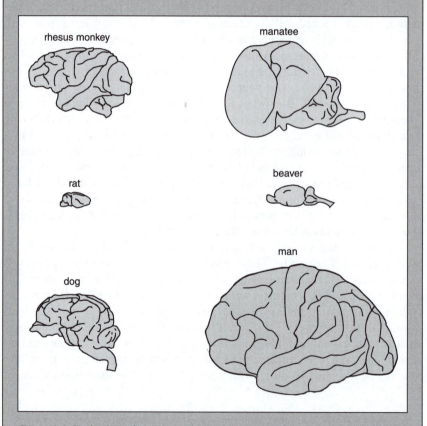

Figure 3.1 Sagittal sections through the brains of different mammals. Differences can be clearly seen in both size and the so-called degree of gyrification (the presence or lack of convolutions and grooves).

Kingdom: animals

    Phylum: chordates

        Class: mammals

            Order: primates

                Suborder: anthropoids

                    Superfamily: superhominids

                        Family: hominids

                            Genus: *Homo*

                                Species: *Homo sapiens*

Figure 3.2 Traditional evolutionary tree of the human species (see Figure 6.2 of Cartwright, 2000).

primates. This is the case not only for details of morphology but also for the connections between different areas of the cortex, as can be seen in the degree of lamination (whether an area has three or six layers) and the distribution of various neurochemical systems (compare Preuss, 1995).

The functional differentiation between the two hemispheres is one characterictic of the human brain (see Table 3.3, p. 45). In humans the right hemisphere is slightly more voluminous than the left. But if we look at various areas of these hemispheres in more detail, some distinctions become apparent. The pyramidal tract consists of approximately 100,000 nerve fibers and makes up the most important tract within the motor system, but in 87 percent of human fetuses the region between the cortex and the lower brainstem (the so-called medulla oblongata) is larger on the left side and crosses over to the other side in front of the right side of the tract (Nottebohm, 1981). The two cortical speech areas were named for the persons who discovered them, Broca's area (for expressive speech) and Wernicke's area (for speech reception), but they have salient "swellings" on, once again, the left hemisphere. Here we find a greater amount of tissue than on the right side as well as a different pattern of convolutions (Figure 3.3). Even in nonhuman primates, interestingly, the posterior region for speech reception (the planum temporale) is distinguishable in size from the same region in the right hemisphere (Gannon, Holloway, Broadfield, & Braun, 1998; LeMay, 1976), while on the right side it is far less functionally committed, possibly due to the fact that the structure of their larynx precludes differential speech production in anthropoid apes. Nonetheless, we find a larger percentage of right-handedness among chimpanzees (Hopkins, Wesley, Izard, & Hook, 2004).

In human fetuses, there is already an observable difference between the right and the left planum temporale as of the 29th week of pregnancy, and this is why the term "predetermined morphological capacity" has

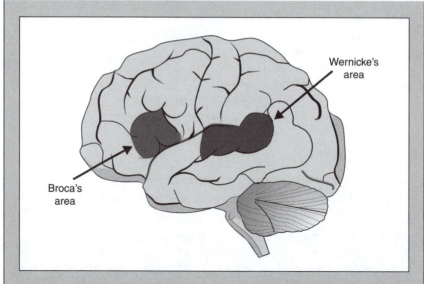

Figure 3.3 Asymmetry of the human cerebrum in speech processing structures.

been used to describe the development of speech functions in humans (Rubens, 1977). Differences between the left and the right hemispheres have been detected also for the sensory areas of the human cortex. If we look at the neuronal fine structure (that is, the cellular pattern of the layers) in the auditory region, the distribution of the various cell types, as well as the frequency of their occurrence (in percentages), shows clear differences between the left and right hemispheres. This is the case although the total area of auditory cortex is basically the same for both sides (Galaburda, LeMay, Kemper, & Geschwind, 1978).

Across phylogenetic development, the cortex as a whole displays more and more frequently six layers of cells in the neocortex the closer it approaches the human, and consequently less and less frequently the three- to five-layered cortex typical of phylogenetically older animals (Figure 3.4). An interesting sideline of this topic is the fact that dolphins have far larger and heavier brains than we do, but by far the largest part of their cortex consists of the phylogenetically older type of layers (Glezer, Jacobs, & Morgane, 1988).

Parts of the frontal lobes, especially, do not mature until well into adulthood, and during this time of growth, they change their patterns of connectivity, and that means their tracts for communication with other brain areas (Bourgeois et al., 2000). Here, changes also take place in the distribution of neurotransmitters and in the connections of their fibers, and are not completed until adulthood (Benes, 2001). This attains special relevance given the fact that the functions of the frontal lobes – empathy for other persons, understanding humor and irony, feeling sympathy with others – only develop very late, as well.

Even for the cerebellum, a phylogenetically old part of the brain, we find particular regions only in humans (within parts of the so-called nucleus dentatus; compare Hodos, 1988; Leiner et al., 1991; Matano et al., 1985). Leiner and coworkers particularly emphasized the differences in the nucleus dentatus between human and nonhuman primates as well as the fact that the human cerebellum here displays an area (the nucleus neodentatus) that is not differentiated in nonhuman primates (1991, p. 119) and may serve, as they propose, functions of consciousness.

Because the thalamus is situated "in between the brain" (thus accounting for its name "diencephalon") and due to its large number of fiber connections to other parts of the brain, it has been called a "gate to the cortex" and includes a series of nuclei that did not evolve until relatively late phylogenetically and that developed at the same time as the expansion of cortical structures in the frontal lobes and in particular in the prefrontal cortex and in the posterior association cortex. The thalamic mediodorsal nucleus and the pulvinar are particularly apt examples (see Figure 3.5). Thus, in the human brain, several dozen subnuclei can be distinguished in the mediodorsal nucleus alone, which are most probably related to the increasing differentiation in frontal lobe functions (processing special aspects of human personality, such as altruism, pity, humor, and "theory of mind" functions, all of which are concerned with empathy for others).

Another group of nuclei displaying a far greater degree of development in humans than in other primates, is found in the so-called limbic thalamic nuclei. The anterior nuclei here in particular, which send efferents to the cortical areas involved in processing emotion and memory (the gyrus cinguli, the hippocampal formation, the orbitofrontal cortex: Irle & Markowitsch, 1982), possess a substantially greater number of neurons than in other primates (Armstrong, 1982; Armstrong & Falk, 1982). In their relative sizes and their degree of complexity, they are more pronounced in humans than, for example, in the orangutan (Hopf, 1956).

Parts of the hippocampal formation (see Figure 3.6 for its position in the brain), which is the central brain structure for the processing of memory, demonstrate significant modifications even in adulthood. This is especially the case for a subdivision of the hippocampus, the gyrus dentatus (see Figure 3.7). Today we have reason to assume that this structure in fact gives rise to new neurons for many years postnatally (Serres, 2001; Tanapat, Hastings, & Gould, 2001) or even throughout the whole life span, as investigations in human brains have suggested (Tanapat et al., 2001). Even after the onset of Alzheimer's disease, an increase in the numbers of new neurons can be observed in the hippocampal formation in humans (Jin et al., 2004), although Pasko

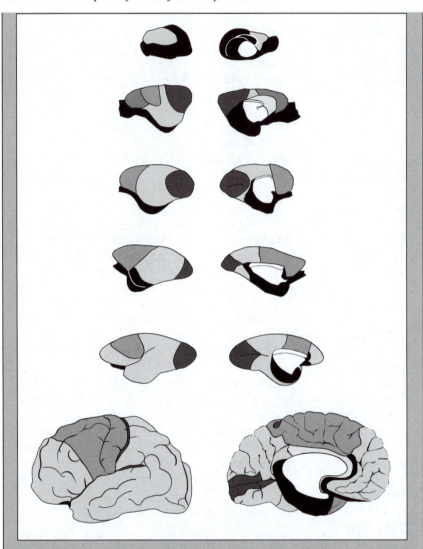

Figure 3.4 A quasi-phylogenetic developmental line within primates and
related species (from Bonin & Bailey, 1961). Shown from the top are
the brains of the elephant shrew, tree shrew (*Tupaia*), two prosim-
ians (tarsier and Senegal galago), a New World monkey (a marmo-
set), and the human. In black: the phylogenetically old olfactory
cortex.

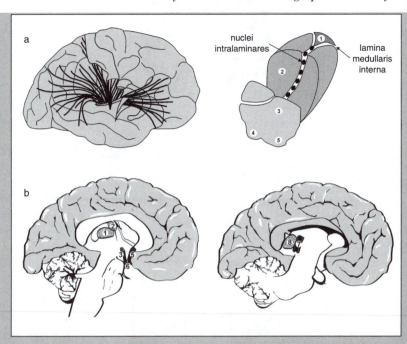

Figure 3.5 The thalamus as a gate to the cortex (panel a) and the thalamic
nuclei (pulvinar and the mediodorsal nucleus), which are particularly well differentiated in humans (panel b). On the left (panel a)
thalamic efferents ascending to the cortex, and on the right a three-
dimensional view of the thalamus. In panel a, 1 designates the position of the anterior thalamic nuclei, 2 that of the mediodorsal
nucleus, 3 the pulvinar, and 4 and 5 show the position of the medial
and the lateral geniculate bodies. Panel b gives two sagittal (longitudinal) views either through the middle of the brain (on the lower
left), showing the position of the mediodorsal nucleus, or (on the
lower right) somewhat more laterally on the right side (approximately 1 cm parallel to the middle line), showing the nucleus pulvinaris. Numbers designate: 1: the mediodorsal nucleus, 2: anterior
thalamic nuclei, 3: the mammillo-thalamic tract, 5: the fornix, 6:
mammillary bodies, 7: lamina medullaris interna, 8: the nucleus
pulvinaris.

Rakic, the authority on this topic, has warned that the significance of
this neurogenesis has not been clarified. Its extent is still only slight, and
even the death of neurons occasionally serves a normal biological purpose (Rakic, 2002a, 2002b; Rakic & Zecevic, 2000) such as decreasing
interference among the cells.

The hippocampal formation is now considered essential for the transfer of information from short-term to long-term memory. Many scientists think the hippocampus relays units of information in package
form, analogous to a drawer in a desk or a post-office box. It appears

hippocampal
formation

Figure 3.6 Frontal section through a human brain (approximately in the middle of the head). The hippocampal area is located within the temporal lobe, and resembles the spiral windings of a snail.

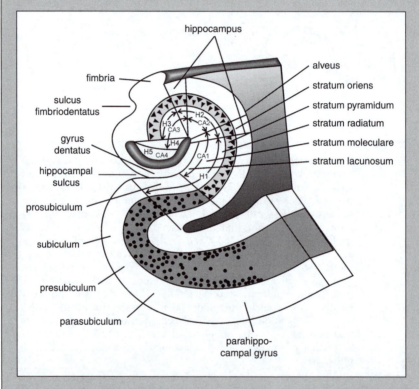

Figure 3.7 Schematic section through the hippocampus demonstrating the complexity of its inner structure with different types of nerve cells and clearly organized into distinct substructures (compare the early, "historical" drawing in Figure 3.8). The highly structured shape of the hippocampal area has repeatedly led researchers to speculations on a relationship between the geometrical anatomical differences and an exact functional role of the individual sections. H: hippocampus – numbers refer to subregions; CA: cornu ammonis – numbers refer to subregions.

to be particularly active in consolidating freshly stored information during sleep. It is also recognized today that subsequent to a lack of oxygen (as after a heart attack) the cells of individual sections in the hippocampus die rapidly. A similar form of neuronal necrosis occurs with repeated epileptic attacks when their origin is in the hippocampus itself.

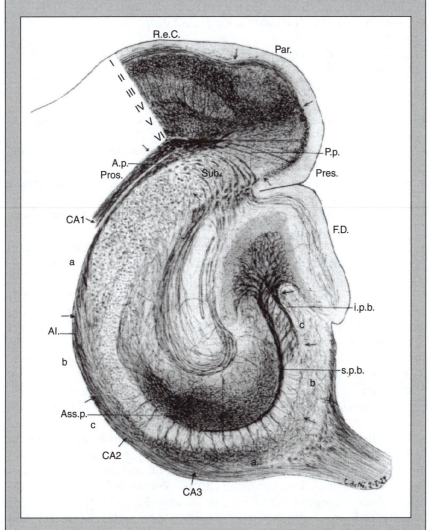

Figure 3.8 An early drawing of the "internal structure" of the hippocampal formation, from Lorente de No, one of the pioneers of neuroanatomy. Even at that early time, he emphasized – just as in the more modern schematic view in Figure 3.7 – the complicated organization in different sections and regions (CA: cornu ammonis, the term used for the hippocampus proper) (from Figure 3, Lorente de No, 1934).

In a review of the cognitive abilities of nonhuman primates, Tomasello (2002) concluded that they have the ability to:

- learn what is found and where in their environment
- realize the perceptible and the imperceptible movements of objects
- categorize objects according to perceptible similarities
- understand and compare the relevance of small amounts of objects
- solve problems with insight (Tomasello, 2002, p. 26).

In addition, Tomasello listed a series of sociocognitive abilities in nonhuman primates:

- recognizing individuals within their social groups
- basing direct contact with other individuals on whether they are relatives or friends and on their rank in the hierarchy of dominance
- predicting the behavior of individuals from their emotional state and their physical movements at the moment
- using different types of social and communicative strategies to deceive others for the purpose of obtaining important resources
- cooperating with conspecifics in problem-solving and in forming social coalitions and alliances
- engaging in different forms of social learning in which they can learn relevant things from their conspecifics (Tomasello, 2002, pp. 26ff.).

It is important to note that learning in nonhuman primates is mainly limited to learning from experience or "learning by emulating". This latter form of learning means that the animal can very well notice a change in a conspecific's state directly caused by that other animal, but fails to notice the strategy that this other animal has made use of that led up to that change in state, as when a young primate learns that insects might be lying under branches on the ground after seeing its mother lift these branches up. According to Tomasello, the young animal learns that it can find insects at such places, but it would do this just as well if the branch had been removed suddenly by any other cause, and not simply because of its first observing the mother's action (2002, p. 41). This last point is highly relevant to the topic of this book, as human children are capable of yet an additional form of learning: learning by imitation, meaning that they observe and try to imitate the behavior and strategy of others, in order to achieve a certain goal. Learning by imitation is essentially related to what other humans do, and we will show later that this is something infants already demonstrate at a very early age. Unlike these infants, however, nonhuman primates are generally not capable of learning through imitation. In fact, the only animals that demonstrate even its most rudimentary form are the ones that have been raised in a human environment.

Nonhuman primates have many capabilities, and some of these are indeed impressive when compared to those of the other mammals, but in spite of this, these primates show no aptitude for one central communicative ability: the ability to orientate themselves on the basis of the actions of others, that is, to imitate them and, by precisely this process of imitating, to acquire new abilities. In other words, they are not capable of decoding intentions. As we already said, they live in a solipsistic world. Of course, they can and do recognize and use social relationships, but without empathizing with their conspecifics. They cannot internalize others' perspectives of things, or share their own personal awareness of other things with them. In short, they lack the capacity for intersubjectivity (which is why, as Tomasello emphasized, they do not draw the attention of someone else to themselves through the use of signs or similar symbolic acts).

Later we will be concerned with the topics of how this ability develops in infants and then in small children and which prerequisites must first be fulfilled on the level of brain functioning, but for the present we will briefly touch on the question of how the social-cognitive abilities in humans may have developed across phylogenetic lines, though we admit at the very start that this treatment will remain highly speculative and tentative, without recourse to empirically verified data.

According to Merlin Donald (1991, 2001), our abilities to be conscious and possess an autonoetic memory are the product of a hybrid evolution. Donald shares Tomasello's view that characteristics of behavior typical of primates are still effective in human primates, but that they were amplified by three other evolutionary steps (which he calls mimetic, mythic and theoretic; for details, see below). Primates live, as Donald describes it, in the "episodic" world totally immersed in the present moment. The personal individual existence of nonhuman primates is centered on the satisfaction of needs. Their horizons for planning (for example, while hunting for food) are extremely short-term, their memory abilities are purely instrumental and do not show any form of reflective dimension (Nelson et al., 2002, p. 6). But two million years ago, *Homo erectus*, unlike these primates, developed a cognitive ability which Donald calls "mimetic" and which allowed humans to fashion stone tools and make use of fire. These achievements already required a good degree of planning ability and they also demonstrated an obvious competence in optimizing such techniques over time through practice and improvement. But, importantly, practice means that techniques, such as those for working on stone, must have been performed outside their immediate purpose (of making a weapon for use in the field) and that the same techniques, once improved on, could be transmitted to others. Nonhuman primates do not show any such capacity. According to Donald, this mimetic phase in development leads to a larger repertoire of gestures and ritual behavior, indicating a new level in social and cultural organization. In view of the considerable expansion in the kinds of activity available to humans once they have understood the far-reaching value of practice, imitation and improvement of techniques, Donald makes a particularly interesting point: These abilities translate models for coping with the external world into internal models. This represents a cognitive technique for delay; it opens up a space in time between a demand and then coping with that demand. Such a cognitive technique also has the potential for the uniquely human ability of representing one's own self in the form of thoughts.

This is then the origin of a key quality with decisive importance for cultural evolution: establishing the ability to recognize oneself and others as intentional beings, that is, to decide the goals of one's actions well in advance and, vice versa, to attribute such goals to other persons as well. And this in turn makes it possible to observe the actions of others and then to draw conclusions as to their ultimate goal, even when their actions have not yet been completed, as when someone else is forming a spear, but has not finished it.

Donald does not assume that these abilities, which developed in the mimetic phase, require an elaborate symbolic language to be already fully functional. Any number of simple gestures, sounds, expressions, or movements for just showing or acting out suffice to spread and accelerate processes of cultural transfer. Abilities which are acquired during the mimetic phase also supply the structural means for innovations in the following phase, which Donald calls "mythical" and which is characterized by the development of forms of symbolic communication. This is the stage at which *Homo sapiens* appeared, approximately only 200,000 years ago.

Box 3.2 points out some of the relationships between developments in evolution and intellectual abilities, from the points of view of modern anthropology and brain research.

The cultural innovations which are completed in this phase include not only the development of symbolic language but also the production of complex manual tools, the improvement of hunting techniques, and the use of better boats, dwellings, weapons, and musical instruments (Donald, 2001, p. 262). Funeral rites are introduced, clearly demonstrating an awareness of the past and the future and thus mark the end of the episodic world of timelessness and the immediate present of other mammals.

The cultural level associated with this stage is an oral culture. The potentials for cultural transmission that arise in this stage and show a dramatic course of growth are then radically improved upon by another development (approximately 40,000 years ago) already briefly touched on: writing and highly symbolic techniques, which make it possible to export the contents of memory and individual acts of remembering, experiences and knowledge away from any context of immediate social necessity, to give them a degree of constancy, and finally to communicate them over different limitations of space and time. This possibility of the externalization of memory is fundamental to the breath-taking acceleration of cultural transfer that we are in fact still experiencing today. We could rephrase it this way: In addition to the engram (the neuronal coding of an environmental experience of one individual person), we now have the exogram (Donald, 2001, p. 309), the

Box 3.2   Evolution and the brain: body weight and brain volume as indicators of intellectual maturity and abilities

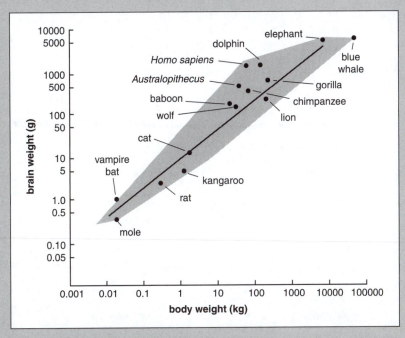

Figure 3.9 Relationship between the weight of the brain and of the body in different mammal species (on a so-called double logarithmic scale). While most mammals are positioned close to the line in the scatter plot, humans and dolphins are relatively further outside, meaning that they have an above-average brain weight compared to that of their bodies.

Researchers in the field of the brain have invested a large amount of effort to demonstrate the special status of humans in the course of evolution (Preuss & Kaas, 1999). One line of research aimed at measuring and then comparing intellectual abilities, using a variety of methods. Another line concentrated on comparisons of the brain itself. Figure 3.9, for example, shows that the human brain is well off to the left of a regression line comparing brain weight to full body weight, and thus has *relatively* the greatest amount of brain tissue, while in *absolute* terms of weight, the elephant and the blue whale have the largest brains (modified from Cartwright, 2000, and Young, 1981).

Similarly, a comparison of the brain weights of those animals used most frequently in neuroscientific studies still reveals an exceptional position for the human brain (Table 3.1). Within the evolution of

Table 3.1 Brain volume and encephalization quotient in selected mammals

Species	Brain volume (in ml)	Encephalization quotient (EQ)[1]
Rat	2	0.4
Cat	25	1.0
Rhesus monkey	106	2.1
Gorilla	506	1.6
Orangutan	413	2.4
Chimpanzee	440/410	2.5/3.0[2]
Human	1350	7.3

1 The EQ is defined as the actual brain volume divided by the predicted brain volume as calculated from the body weight times 0.12 to the power of two-thirds (see Jerison, 1973).
2 Differences due to variations in the results published.

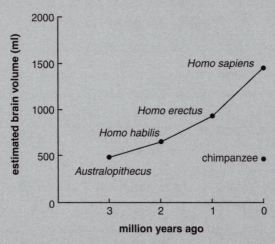

Figure 3.10 Increase in primate brain volume in different species during evolution (from Figure 3.3 in Grüsser, 1988).

hominids alone, there is but a slight increase in body weight throughout time, while brain weight increases far more strongly (see Figure 3.10).

These measures and the relationships derived from them are subject to controversy. For example, animals capable of flying, such as birds or bats, have by necessity a very slight body weight, while other animals require relatively more brain tissue merely for the purpose of three-dimensional orientation in space. Nonetheless, these data point to a preferential development in the direction of larger brains over time. And within the brain itself, there is once again a preference over time in favor of the so-called neocortical areas, showing that those brain areas increase in size that are involved in flexible, associative and interactive processing of information. This can be clearly seen in Figure 3.11.

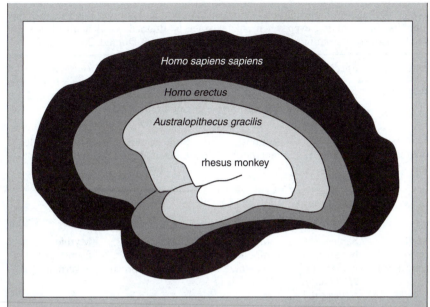

Figure 3.11 Outlines of different primates, in a lateral view. On the bottom, rhesus monkey, and then, successively, *Australopithecus gracilis*, *Homo erectus* and finally *Homo sapiens sapiens* (from Figure 3.7 in Grüsser, 1988).

symbolic coding of experience that is now available to others independently of the confines of time and place.

In summary, these three co-evolutionary transitions in cultural transfer make three uniquely human developmental steps possible: an improved, self-reflective control over behavior in the mimetic phase, an accelerated technique for cultural transfer and the ability for abstraction through the use of a symbolic language in the mythical phase, and finally another accelerated step in cultural transfer through the externalization of memory in a phase which Donald calls the "theoretical phase" and which is the phase we are still in. These phases do not in any way cease to be effective when the next phase begins; on the contrary, they expand rather symbiotically one with the other so that the uniquely human form of consciousness and memory still maintains all previous forms. The evolution of human cognition and culture can be schematically outlined as in Table 3.2.

When we view this whole process biologically, the final change on the level of the brain takes place in the transition from the mimetic to the mythical stage. *Homo sapiens* exhibits a morphologically well differentiated larynx and speech apparatus, unlike nonhuman primates. *H. sapiens* also possesses a degree of functional differentiation within the brain consisting of a largely unilateral speech representation and a series of further localizations within the two separate cortical hemispheres. For details, see Table 3.3.

Table 3.2 Stages in the evolution of human cognition and culture. Each stage maintains its own function even when a later stage is attained, so that all phases are simultaneously present in modern societies (modified from Donald, 2001, p. 260)

Stage	Species/period	Novel forms	Manifest change	Governance
Episodic	Primates	Episodic event perceptions	Self-awareness and event sensitivity	Episodic and reactive
Mimetic (first transition)	Early hominids, peaking in *Homo erectus*: 2 to 0.4 million years ago	Action metaphor	Skill, gesture, mime and imitation	Mimetic styles and archetypes
Mythic (second transition)	Sapient humans, peaking in *Homo sapiens sapiens*: 0.2 million years ago to the present	Language, symbolic representation	Oral traditions, mimetic rituals, narrative thought	Mythic framework of governance
Theoretic (third transition)	Modern cultures	External symbolic universe	Formalism, large-scale theoretic artifacts, massive external storage	Institutionalized paradigmatic thought and invention

After the transition we find no differences, neither biological nor anatomical, between the humans of the present and those of the prehistoric period. Although approximately 4000 generations separate us from these ancestors of ours, our brain is basically identical to theirs, and assumably achieves neither more nor less. This view is somewhat surprising, but reflects the dimension of co-evolutionary acceleration which is effected by human culture. At the same time, it means that (assuming a very imaginitive scenario) if, with the help of a time machine such as H. G. Wells wrote of, a modern person could be born back in that distant past with his present physical constitution, he would develop within the framework of the given cultural conditions of that time. On the other hand, this view also means that any child of *H. sapiens* from that day and period, 4000 generations ago, would have the same abilities as children today, if he were suddenly born in the modern world, and would have the same chance of becoming, for example, a jet pilot or a computer hacker. Everything that has happened during the last 200,000 years in the social life of humans – and that is certainly an impressive amount – is due to their self-changing ability to manipulate their own adaptive environment. And this means that, in biological terms, evolution

Table 3.3 Functional asymmetry of the two hemispheres (from Table 3.3 in Grüsser, 1988, and Figure 2.2 in Pritzel, Brand, & Markowitsch, 2003)

	Left hemisphere	*Right hemisphere*
Topographical planning	+	++
Elementary activity	++	+
Planning for tool making	+	++
Human averbal communication	+	++
Habits of clothing	–	+
Verbal language	+++	(+)
Musical rhythm	++	–
Sense of harmonies and musical tones	–	+
Painting, drawing	(+)	++
Modeling, sculpting	(+)	++
Mathematics	++	–
Poetic speech	++	+
Reading and writing	++	–
Temporal segmentation of information	+	–
Spatial segmentation of information	–	+
Intramodal concentration/vigilance	+	–
Intermodal concentration/vigilance	–	+
Global, holistic information processing	–	+
Detailed, serial information processing	+	–
Processing emotions	–	++

–: no engagement of this hemisphere; +: engagement of this hemisphere;
(+): engagement of this hemisphere in a minority of the population;
++: strong engagement of this hemisphere; +++: very strong engagement of this hemisphere; intramodal: involving only one sensory system; intermodal: involving different sensory systems.

denotes nothing other than the process of generating and delivering potentials for development (which, interestingly, is a decidedly classical definition of evolution; see Huxley, 1953). Evolution thus delivers developmental possibilities which can be evaluated one way or the other, as better or weaker, as optimal or suboptimal. The specifically human cultural evolution simply makes use of a developmental potential that the biological evolution of a particular species of primates opened up.

But when and where did the necessary critical developmental steps take place? Clarifying such questions is something for which neither evolutionary biologists nor evolutionary anthropologists have an adequate database. At different points in time, still unidentified, the primate evolutionary tree diverges into new branches (see Figure 3.12).

Whatever the cause may have been, one central principle of differentiation

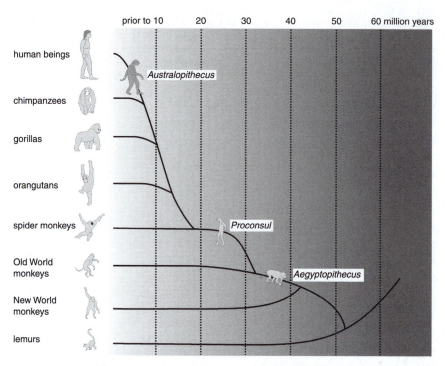

Figure 3.12 "Evolutionary tree" of humans.

between the human and the non-human primates at any rate lies in a fundamental difference in the social organization of their group for survival. While
nonhuman primates compete for food within their group and have developed
a social system that regulates the rights for food and mating within the group
according to a strict hierarchy and an incontestable social order, human
groups rely for survival on a different principle: that of cooperation. Cooperation magnifies the potentials of any one individual because it can focus,
combine, and accumulate abilities and strengths and thus unfold new abilities.
For just this reason, human groups survive by being principally communicative communities, because cooperation is naturally dependent upon communication. For this reason "readiness for communication" (Trevarthen,
1998) is a standard characteristic of infants. They are fully capable of communicating their survival needs through crying, their facial expressions and
body movements. From the very start of life, they are capable of communicative activity, which, however, does not mean that they in turn "understand"
communicative activity in others or that they could operate on an intersubjective level. Neonates and infants can very well give expression to a great many
things, which still does not mean that they "know" what they are doing when
they show clearly that they are hungry at the moment or are anxious or
happy. It only means that, viewed from their biological constitution, they

exist in a fundamental relation to their social environment and that the constant communication with just this environment supplies them through time with the ability of reflective communication, which in turn enables them, as of approximately the ninth month of life, to take part in an intersubjective world in which they can share their interest in something and their perspectives with others. The origin of this reflective ability is prepared for non-reflectively, through asymmetrical communication and through the development of a level of memory achievements that become better and better: from the implicit, unconscious experiential and body memory all the way up to explicit, episodic and autobiographical memory open to conscious awareness.

Section II

Development of autobiographical memory and the brain

4 Interdependent development of memory and other cognitive and emotional functions

The development of memory cannot be discussed in isolation, without mention of other cognitive functions. In fact, memory requires the formation and use of other functions for its own growth, and develops clearly interdependently of the differentiation and refined use of other abilities and skills. Primary among these are motor and sensory abilities, which are continuously activated and improved upon. Even at night, infants move and receive sensory input. By experiencing changes in external stimuli, the first forms of learning are initiated: *habituation*, which means becoming accustomed to essentially similar stimuli when they are repeated, and *sensitization*, which means becoming attentive after a change in external conditions.

Functions of the frontal lobes

Attention and concentration

Memory depends on other mental functions. The two simple forms of learning processes just mentioned show that the ability to pay attention to things is an essential and basic cognitive function. They already indicate that we only perceive things in a selective way and that we have to distinguish aspects of perception which are either conscious or unconscious. At the same time, these forms of learning, however simple they are, also show that we expect stimuli or actively construct our own patterns of expectation of the environment. We direct our attention to or avert it away from something. This means that we selectively make use of the resources at our disposal. A baby, for example, actively makes a selection, and he or she wants selectively. William James (1890) aptly described it in the words: "My experience is what I agree to attend to" (p. 402). Although as a baby and later as an adult, we do not first have to reflect consciously on what we would like to concentrate our attention on, we do frequently make decisions on significant questions that have a lasting influence on our feeling for life and our most personal picture of ourselves (Pritzel et al., 2003), all of which entails very conscious reflection.

The processes of paying attention occasionally give the impression of being rather simple mechanisms, because they are not completely subject to voluntary control, and then again they appear to be very complex ones, upheld by conscious thought. These mechanisms take place within the framework of alternating, mutual influence between the individual and the environment and are necessary prerequisites for the development of memory. Or, put simply, what we pay attention to is imprinted in memory; what we ignore is forgotten.

Processes of attention are nonetheless very diverse, spanning a continuum between simple and complex. The *orientation reaction*, for example, can be seen in animals as well as in humans and responds automatically to sudden or massive changes in the immediate environment. If one part of the room suddenly lights up, eyes automatically turn in that direction. If a sound becomes much louder, we either turn our heads in another direction or try to flee. *Selective attention* means actively, deliberately directing one's senses somewhere. *Sustained attention* means directing attention to a target over a longer period of time. And lastly, *shared attention* implies the ability to concentrate the senses on several different stimuli (almost) at the same time, to take them (and only them) into consideration. Babies and young children certainly have only a preliminary form of this ability, and only when they have had some practice. One prerequisite for shared attention is an adequately developed ability of *concentration*.

Attention can also be distinguished along other lines, such as structural versus energetic aspects. The structural aspects include selective attention ("What is important? And what is unimportant?") and shared attention (paying attention to several different stimuli at the same time). Energetic aspects emphasize the degree of activity (tonic-persevering versus phasic-fluctuating) and vigilance (degree of wakefulness and sustained attention). While attention can fluctuate and be distracted by changes in the environment, concentration designates a relatively active, voluntary ability under one's own control to compete with external stimuli or to concentrate on some to the exclusion of others.

These processes might seem to take place as if by themselves, and we may be able to subcategorize them rather easily according to the aspects of intensity and selectivity (van Zoemeren & Brouwer, 1994), but just how complex they are in reality is apparent as soon as we start working with brain-damaged patients who have lost the ability of attentiveness. There are in fact a large number of diseases and disorders, many of which are related to damage to the frontal lobes (Figure 4.1) and which make it impossible for the patients to direct their attention to something voluntarily or, vice versa, to stop concentrating on one thing and start on another. Anton and Zingerle (1902, p. 185) specifically called the "voluntary active fixation of attention, the concentration necessary for thought", a central function of the frontal lobes. Damage to these lobes may leave a patient incapable of turning his or her attention to something ("neglect phenomena") or, just the opposite, unable to dissociate mentally from something ("perseveration"). An interesting

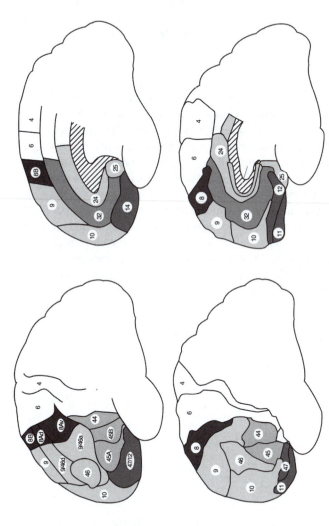

Figure 4.1 The frontal lobes in humans and their anatomical subdivisions, in two different views: a lateral view (on the left) and a medial one (from within the brain, on the right). The two upper views show the classical divisions according to Brodmann (1909) (numbers indicate Brodmann areas), and the lower ones show a recent suggestion from Petrides and Pandya (1994). The large size and extent of this area compared to the rest of the cortex can be easily recognized. The light gray regions in the front half are designated dorsolateral prefrontal cortex and are mainly involved in the control and planning of activity and in anticipatory thought. Dark gray regions in the lower frontal cortex (that is, both medial/from the inside and lateral/from the side) are involved mainly in the control and planning of emotional and social behavior (as in pity and altruism) and in the development of aspects of the personality. In this area, we find that correlates for the ability to put oneself in the situation of another person (see in this chapter the section on "The development of the brain", pp. 74ff., and in Chapter 7 the section on "Theory of mind: psychological understanding", pp. 175ff.).

example was given by Hans Berger[1] in 1923 in a description of a patient with
frontal damage who could not terminate activities once he had begun them,
as shown in Figure 4.2. Persevering and terminating (restraint, inhibition)
are thus two important aspects of attention that have to be learned from
childhood onward and that have an effect on how successful children are in
acquiring information in all other pursuits.

It is important to note that, as Figure 4.1 shows, the frontal lobes make up
the largest of the four lobes, and that they can be differentiated into a number
of subregions, most of which control or influence different functions.

Executive functions

Executive functions make up another group of behaviors primarily attributed
to the frontal lobes: the preparation, planning and performance of activities,
and then adhering to them or else terminating them. The intention, for
example, of following a moving stimulus, such as a mobile, with one's eyes, is
an example of an executive function. And one necessary prerequisite for such
an activity is adequate attention, and the executive function in this case is a
prerequisite for any successful processes of memory. Only when a person
plans and anticipates what might occur in the future, is he or she capable of
preparing for it on time, and then deciding on what to do first, second and
then third. It is not only patients with frontal lobe deficits who show problems
in accomplishing these things. Very young and very old persons do too
(Brand & Markowitsch, 2003; Kliegel, Ramuschkat, & Martin, 2003), the
young because their frontal lobe is not yet developed enough, and old persons

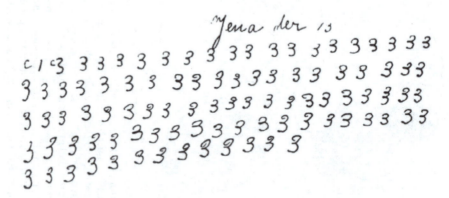

Figure 4.2 Perseveration in writing the date, in a patient with frontal lobe damage
(from Berger, 1923).

1 Hans Berger is best known for his discovery of the electroencephalogram (EEG) (Berger, H.
(1929). Über das Elektroencephalogramm des Menschen [On the electroencephalogram in
humans] 1. *Mitteilung: Archiv für Psychiatrie und Nervenkrankheiten, 87,* 527–570).

because their lobe has already lost considerable numbers of nerve cells and their connections.

Motivation and emotion: the limbic system

Our memory is modulated not only by processes of attentiveness and executive functions, but also by motivational and emotional factors. The will (the motive) to do something, or otherwise to avoid doing it, arouses our interest and perhaps invokes processes of learning. The will and one's interest are augmented by the fact that we are not neutral as far as our environment is concerned: on the contrary, we are moved emotionally. The expression "hungry for knowledge" clearly indicates a strong emotional-motivational element in gaining more knowledge, so that we react to the appropriate stimuli with an increase in blood pressure or in pulse, and our senses become all the more receptive and absorbed in learning. This also fits the inverted U-curve, a function we see again and again in studying psychological and physiological data (see Figure 4.3). A low level of stress, for example, is too undemanding for our nervous system and for our minds, while too much stress means an overload, possibly causing panic or, in some cases, leading to actual loss of connections between cells in the brain. Overmotivation decreases our mental flexibility, as does lack of interest. We need a form of stimulation in the middle of the range in order to function optimally. But, importantly, this "middle of the range" varies widely from person to person. Participants in extreme sports, such as hang-gliding or free rock climbing, need different stimulants of "adrenaline rush" from a knitter in her country home. This is also true of infants, though in this case the variation in stimulation is much more narrow.

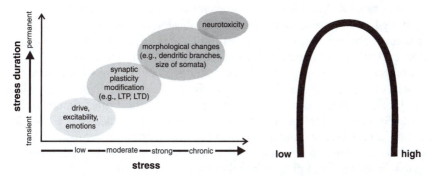

Figure 4.3 Stress as an example of an inverted U-function in biopsychology. The left part of the figure shows that stress, depending on its intensity and duration, has positive or negative effects on the nervous system. The right part of the figure demonstrates this graphically. When stress is too low, it "challenges" an individual inadequately, while a level of stress that is too high leads to an overload. LTD: long-term depression; LTP: long-term potentiation, that is, long-term changes in neuronal activity.

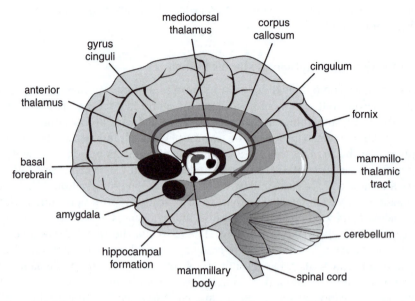

Figure 4.4 Main structures of the so-called limbic system. The corpus callosum, cerebellum and spinal cord have been added for orientation.

   But all such cases involve the limbic system (see Figure 4.4), a collection of nerve cells or nuclei (such as the amygdala, the "almond-shaped" nucleus) that are all phylogenetically very old or even belong to the first cortical structures to have developed (such as the hippocampus). With a high level of coordination between each other, they make the connection possible between the emotions that move us (sadness, fear, joy, etc.) and the cognitive contents or connotations, thus allowing some events to stick out in memory.
   In the limbic system, there is a distinct division of labor so that particular structures are responsible for processing the affective elements of information, and others are more involved in the cognitive-rational elements.
   For example, the amygdala is involved in the evaluation of stimuli (in a way which is often already established in early childhood; see Figure 4.5), while the hippocampus processes the novel aspects in the same stimuli and is generally responsible for integrating elements of time and space and for committing the recent contents in memory into long-term storage (see Boxes 4.1 and 4.2). The information involved in this integration is predominantly spatial in animals and predominantly temporal in humans.

World knowledge and consciousness

The still most perplexing problem for both the neurosciences and philosophy is explaining how consciousness came into existence – and "into" the human brain. Is consciousness an all-or-nothing process, in the concrete sense that

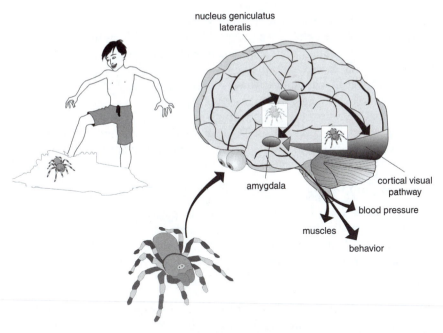

Figure 4.5 The amygdala as a central structure in the control of emotions, involved in evaluating the relevance of sensory information that has been preprocessed.

(most) humans have it, but animals generally do not, as maintained by the most famous living researcher on memory, Endel Tulving (2002)? Or is it, rather, a more gradual process that has developed across phylogeny and is typical in a rudimentary form in many mammals, but which, in the broader sense of the term and using stricter criteria, can only be attributed to a few species such as the great apes. In humans, then, it is present in varying degrees, so that children, and amnestic or demented patients are less conscious than adults with normal intelligence (Markowitsch, 2004a, 2004b, 2004c). Researchers who compare the ontogenetic development of human children with that of young apes argue along these lines (Tomasello et al., 2003a, 2003b).

Box 4.1   Urbach–Wiethe disease: the relevance of the amygdala to emotions

The role of the amygdala in the processing of emotions can be illustrated by a rare neurological disease, Urbach–Wiethe disease (a form of lipoid proteinosis). This genetic disease is characterized by the deposition of hyaline in the skin and in the area of the mouth and larynx. Over half of the patients present with a symmetrical mineralization in the amygdala of both hemispheres leading to a loss of function in this structure. As the destruction of the nerve cells probably occurs insidiously over a long period of time, the brain might well have the ability to adapt to this loss and recruit alternative neuronal pathways to process the original information. Nonetheless, a massive disturbance occurs in processing emotions, as we were able to demonstrate in a group of patients from South Africa (Siebert et al., 2003). Because of this loss in the amygdala, the patients also have difficulty in distinguishing between important and less important information and, as a result, acquire unnecessary or banal data as opposed to essential or meaningful ones. We demonstrated this in a male patient by telling him a story in which a woman, wearing a dress with yellow-black flower pattern entered a room in which, in the further course of the story, she is stabbed to death by a man who came in from behind without her noticing. When, half an hour later, the patient was asked to retell the story, he was able to relate surprising details of her dress but not the fact that she had been murdered (Cahill et al., 1995).

This case description demonstrates the important meaning of emotions for memory as well as the interaction between the various limbic structures in the processing of stimulus material. At the same time, it also shows what kinds of effects there are on the social competence of these patients as a result of the loss of emotionally founded interpretations. The interpretation that murder is eminently more important than the color of a dress is a socially important one. This patient would have major difficulty in getting along in his social environment and with the socially accepted, in fact expected, norms of interpreting everyday events.

In view of the fact that the contents of autobiographical memory are always coded along with emotional information, the adequate stimulation of the amygdala must play an outstanding role in further discussions of its role. On the one hand, it receives preprocessed information from all the sensory systems, and on the other hand, it has a specific function in the processing of the sense of smell. Since information about the mother is imprinted onto infants by means of smell (filial imprinting), and since a stable bond with the mother furthers the development of the child significantly, the amygdala can be seen as an essential organ in processing the emotional contents of memory – from the earliest phases of orientation, based on only olfactory stimuli (compare Box 4.3, pp. 62ff., and Box 4.4, pp. 64ff.), to much later memories called up by emotionally loaded smells.

Box 4.2 illustrates the importance of another limbic structure – the hippocampus – involved in the cognitive-rational aspects of memory processing.

Box 4.2   The hippocampus: an ancient cortex that made the phylogenetic journey from spatial analyzer to temporal analyzer of stimuli

The hippocampus is a so-called three-layered cortex, which is distinguishable from the "normal" neocortex with six layers found in over 90 percent of the brain's surface. Apparently, it represents a developmental link between subcortical nuclei and the more recent neocortex where, probably, the contents of our memory are largely laid down (as engrams in a network spread out over a large area). Birds already possess a hippocampus, which is mainly involved in navigation behavior. The human hippocampus, however, is thought to be primarily activated in the transfer of new information into neocortical nets, especially when this information has just been acquired and refers to emotional events. This view of the function of the hippocampus is mainly based on results from work starting in 1953 on a patient (H.M.) who suffered from otherwise intractable epilepsy and thus had to have both his left and his right hippocampus surgically removed.

More recent studies by a British research group (for example, Maguire et al., 2000) have demonstrated that the volume of the hippocampus in taxi drivers increased more, the longer they had been driving in London, and that asking taxi drivers to imagine driving through central London activated both the left and right hippocampus quite strongly. This points back to the original – phylogenetically old – role of the hippocampus in spatial integration, which apparently is still preserved even in the human.

However, the case of H.M. (see Corkin, 2002; Markowitsch, 1985) shows also that a person lacking the hippocampus is no longer capable of consciously retaining new information. For H.M., time stood still, as he described so poignantly in his own words: "Every day is alone, whatever enjoyment I've had, and whatever sorrow I've had". In spite of the damage to his brain, H.M. survived the surgery for more than 50 years, and so the function of the hippocampus for memory could be examined and analyzed extensively in his case and in a series of other patients.

The results show that while certain forms of information (those serving so-called procedural memory, important in the acquisition of motor skills) are successfully stored, others that make up one's personal, conscious memory (because they are fully identified according to specifics of time and emotional impact) cannot be stored, so that, as a result, they are no longer available for use in everyday life. This once again demonstrates the relevance of emotion to memory, and the close connections between various regions in the brain for cognitive-emotional information processing.

We find the same line of thought in discussions which argue in favor of different forms of consciousness, as listed in Table 4.1 (Markowitsch, 2004a, 2004b, 2004c): Here the first two forms are assumed to be typical of many species, while the others are reserved to but a few or even only to humans.

Consciousness cannot be separated from autobiographical memory. This form of memory is in fact defined almost by the presence of an "ego consciousness", an awareness of using the pronoun *I*. Katherine Nelson (2002, 2005; Nelson & Fivush, 2000; Nelson et al., 2002) has done original research in this field, showing that children first develop a very general, fact-oriented memory, and only after the third year of life do they develop conscious representational forms that subsequently make it possible for them both to integrate the events they have experienced into their own subjective world and to have a memory differentiated according to time, contents and emotions.

Before we go into some further determinants of the ontogenetic development of memory, we want to treat the more basic question of what memory is in principle.

What is memory?

From a broader neurobiological point of view, memory can be defined as a conditioned change in "the transmitter characteristics within the neural network", so that "under certain conditions both the neuromotor signals and behavior corresponding to the systematic modifications or engrams can be reproduced either partially or completely (Sinz, 1979, p. 19). We can adapt this definition to a specifically human perspective thus: Memory processes information that arises from the internal and external worlds of the organism and represents the meaningful emotional and cognitive contents of this memory that are formed socially.

How can we explain the development of higher forms of memory, especially those in mammals? The reason for the evolution of memory may well be found, as we already said, in the improved chances for survival of the individual and the species. An individual who was able to remember where

Table 4.1 Forms of consciousness

Being awake
Concentrating on something
Internal knowledge or conviction
Being aware of one's own thoughts
Body consciousness ("This body is my body")
Totality of thoughts of a person
Consciousness as a mental state (hoping, believing, fearing, expecting, wishing, suffering)
Self-reflection, feeling of time, proscopia (forethought)

good, tasty food could be found, which snakes had to be avoided, and which feeding place was the most fruitful, secured his survival and lived longer. Survival of the species as a whole is improved when its members remember who is most ready for mating under which conditions.

Each of these processes – the search for food and for a partner – is essentially supported in animals by the sense of smell, and that entails the brain structures that make up basic parts of an older section of the cerebrum, the limbic system. Box 4.3 reviews the special role of the sense of smell, explaining why smell is a uniquely social sense ("to smell a rat"). Watson (2001, pp. 210ff.) remarked that olfactory perception is directly processed in the limbic system and does not need any form of processing in conscious loops. It is no wonder that the memory for smell in humans, on the one hand, is hardly accessible to symbolization, but, on the other hand, under recognition conditions (as when the same smell comes up after many years), we can still have lively memories of the exact situation and the exact events associated with that smell. The "*petites madeleines*" of Marcel Proust (1953 [1913]) are a particularly good example: whatever reminded Proust's narrator of their taste caused a complete cascade of uncontrollable memories (*mémoire involontaire*). Vision and hearing are phylogenetically younger than the sense of smell and are processed in quite other parts of the brain. "The smell of something is neither organized according to spatial coordinates nor modulated according to temporal ones; it is an experience of the moment, free of the usual conditions of space and time" (Watson, 2001, p. 215). The modalities of encoding and recall can thus be involved in completely different ways depending on the senses which are evoked.

The differentiation of memory is likewise explicable along physiological lines. When the social behavior of a species becomes more complex, and the offspring become more dependent on their parents for longer periods of time, it is all the more essential to learn and maintain flexible structures in general activity and in recognizing the personally relevant stimuli for survival. Thus, for example, orangutans apparently need a period of care by their mothers of 8 years in order to learn the usefulness or the dangers of different tropical plants and the survival techniques for their particular territory.

Generalizations and concept formation are learned once recognition of external stimuli has successfully been made possible. Initial forms of imitation learning can be discerned in chimpanzees,[2] as well as emulation and experiential learning (learning by doing), and even initial forms of foresight (prospective memory) and learning by insight. All this performance in learning and memory appears to correlate directly with the size of the brain in the different species, including the human, and to increase in the degree of differentiation.

---

2 But apparently only in chimpanzees that have been raised and "socialized" by humans (Tomasello, 2002, p. 47).

Box 4.3   Sensory systems: the special sense of smell

The sense of smell is unique. With all the other senses (hearing and balance, vision, the somatosensory system including pain, and taste), processing of the peripheral sensory organs (the retina, for example) is first relayed to the thalamus – the "heart" of the brain, positioned in its center or middle – and only then reaches the cortex. In the case of sight, the route is a direct one from the eye to the lateral geniculate in the thalamus and then on to the visual cortex (see Figures 4.6 and 4.7).

For the sense of smell, on the other hand, the neural connections exit the nose and proceed to the cortex directly, in the phylogenetically old bulbus olfactorius (see Figure 4.7). From the bulbus, nerve fibers make up the tractus olfactorius and reach different areas, all of which are included in the extended limbic system. Due to having different

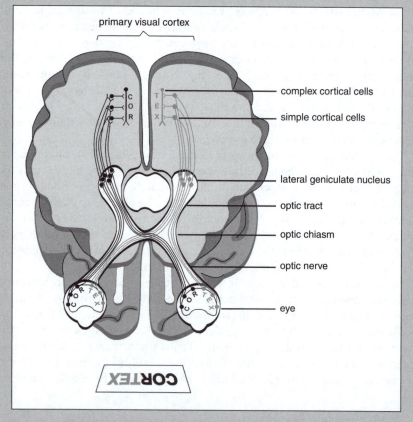

Figure 4.6 Pathway of an external stimulus (the word *CORTEX*) through the different main visual stations: retina (in the eye), thalamus (nucleus geniculatus lateralis) and cortex (primary visual cortex) in a horizontal section.

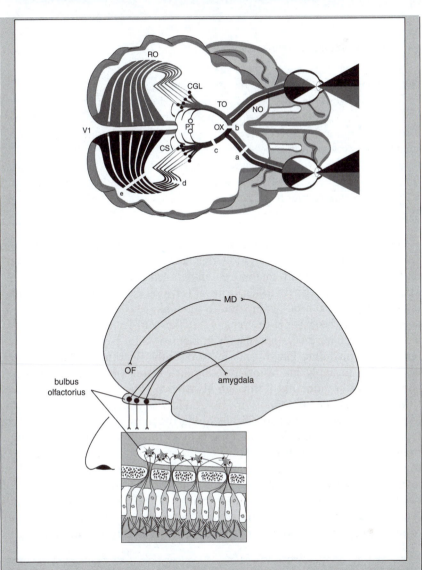

Figure 4.7 Comparison of two different sensory pathways from the peripheral organ to its respective brain center. On top: the visual pathway from the eyes, through the thalamus (lateral geniculate) to the cerebral cortex, seen in horizontal section. Below: lateral section through brain and nose, showing the sensory cells in the nose connecting directly with the olfactory cortex or bulbus olfactorius, which, just like the hippocampus, is a phylogenetically older form of cortical structure with but three layers of cells. From here, there are connections to both the amygdala (a major structure in the emotional evaluation of sensory stimuli; see Figure 4.5, p. 57) and (as of this level, just as in the other sensory systems) the thalamus (the MD or mediodorsal nucleus), and from there on to the orbitofrontal cortex (OF). Other abbreviations: CGL: corpus geniculatus lateralis; CS: colliculus superior; NO: nervus opticus; OX: optic chiasm; RO: radiatio optica; TO: tractus opticus; V1: primary visual cortex. a–e refer to possible points of brain lesions, which are irrelevant in this context.

pathways within the brain, the other sensory systems are involved at first in the sensory qualities of the perceived stimuli, whereas from the very beginning the sense of smell encodes for the emotional evaluation (the emotional loading) of perceptions. Interestingly, one of the next structures involved in processing the olfactory information is the amygdala, which is also primarily concerned with the evaluative, that is, emotional, processing of sensory stimulation, from the other modalities as well (compare Figure 4.5, p. 57).

One of the most influential methods in memory research has been work on animals, because of the conviction that learning in animals would reveal essentials of learning in humans, even in detailed questions. But because the majority of animals prefer other forms of learning (such as learning by training or being "broken in") compared to humans (who learn more by observing), there has been some discrepancy in the transfer of so-called laws of learning, which have been specifically implemented for psychology by animal researchers, including Pavlov and, more recently, Burrhus Frederic Skinner, who hoped to apply his results on animal learning (in particular through conditioning) to humans all through his working life. One of his books was titled *The Behavior of Organisms* (1938). He was convinced enough of this idea to raise his daughter specifically along the lines of his animal research. Other workers in the field of learning held to this hope even more strongly than Skinner did, such as C. L. Hull. They were convinced they could express the results on learning processes in general laws, mathematical terms and, in fact, equations that would then allow the formulation of "principles of behavior". Later, especially after the human-conditioning utopias in Skinner's sense of the word had proved unsuccessful, attention was directed rather more to the social conditions of learning (such as learning through imitation).

Box 4.4   Forms of learning

(1) Sensitization, habituation

This is the simplest form of adaptation in behavior. Sensitization means that individuals react more sensitively to similar stimulus patterns when they are repeated, whereas habituation means they reduce the level of their orientation reaction when identical patterns in the stimuli are repeated.

(2) Signal learning or classical conditioning

This form of learning is also known as Pavlovian conditioning. It is based on Pavlov's original experiment in which he first showed a piece of meat to a dog, which reacted with an increase in its saliva production. Then Pavlov rang a bell each time before he showed the meat again, pairing the idea of a bell with that of meat, so that with time the dog salivated strongly when it only heard the bell, which had become a signal for the meat (see Figure 4.8). A basic feature of classical conditioning is the fact that the unconditional stimulus appears independently of the behavior of the individual.

(3) Stimulus-reaction learning (instrumental conditioning)

Instrumental conditioning depends directly on the behavior of the individual, who now learns the association between a stimulus and a response. For example, in an experiment, a hummingbird receives a sweet liquid as reward when it flies to a yellow flower, but when it flies to a blue flower it receives none.

(4) Chaining (including verbal association)

"Chaining" refers to a series of reactions that either come automatically one after the other or each one is somehow dependent on the previous one, so that any one possible reaction determines the next one, and the reward is given only when the group of individual reactions is completed.

(5) Multiple discrimination

This designates learning to distinguish between stimuli which have one or more attributes in common.

(6) Concept learning

Concept learning means learning to react in the same way to a number of different objects or their attributes that in some way have an element in common.

(7) Learning by principles

This means acquiring knowledge on how to solve a series or set of problems that possess common attributes.

(8) Problem solving

This involves making appropriate use of the principles already learned or showing insights (being able to draw conclusions).

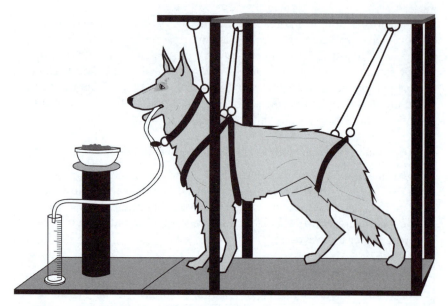

Figure 4.8 Ivan Pavlov's design for investigating classic conditioning (see Box 4.4 for details).

The development and meaning of these forms of learning can best be seen by asking to what extent animals are capable of acquiring information successfully with their help. Examples of such learning include simple conditioning events that have been demonstrated in the mere appendages of living organisms, as shown in Figure 4.9.

What kinds of memory are there?

Compared to the classification of learning and memory forms discussed up to now, Tulving (2002, 2005) offered an alternative taxonomy that distinguishes between one short-term memory system and five long-term systems. Short-term memory is seen as being effective in a time range of some seconds to a few minutes, while long-term memory accounts for all time periods lasting longer than that (see Figure 4.10).

As shown in Figure 4.11, long-term memory can be divided into five systems which function independently of one another and which have different organic areas of representation at the level of the brain:

1   Procedural memory is the memory system limited to motor performance, such as acquiring the skills of riding a bicycle, swimming, skiing, and playing the piano, all of which are largely performed unconsciously and in an automatic way. In infants, procedural memory begins to unfold when they grasp and handle objects. An interesting example of the

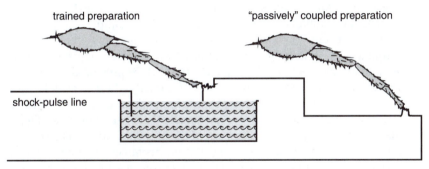

trained preparation

"passively" coupled preparation

shock-pulse line

Figure 4.9 An example of the probably simplest experimental design for demonstrating successful learning in an organism. It shows two legs surgically removed from the body of a cockroach. The left leg receives a shock impulse every time it bends and either just touches the water in the receptacle or submerges. At the moment of the shock in the left leg, the right one also receives a pulse through a wire joining it to the other leg. The leg which consistently receives shocks after contacting the water learns the unpleasant contingency and maintains an extended position for a longer time, whereas the right leg does not alter its pattern of flexor-extensor activity.

unconscious, quasi-automatic way that procedural memory functions in adults can be seen when trying to explain what we have to do first in order to change from second to third gear while driving a car. Most of us give the wrong answer, namely, "push the clutch down". In fact, the first movement is to take the right foot off the gas pedal. This shows to what degree procedural memory functions automatically.

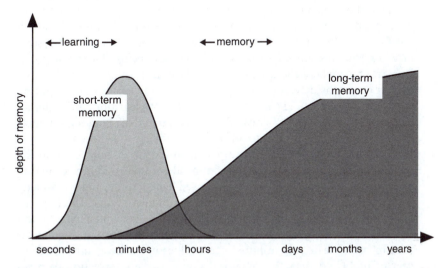

←learning→   ←memory→

depth of memory

short-term memory

long-term memory

seconds   minutes   hours   days   months   years

Figure 4.10 Classification of memory into a short-term memory component, covering a time period of seconds to minutes, and a long-term component that can store some information for a whole lifetime.

2   The priming form of memory is characterized by a greater probability of recognizing stimuli perceived unconsciously. For example, while we read the text of a stanza in a song, the melody of the song may come to mind automatically. When stimuli are perceived with the help of priming memory and are then presented again later, they can be processed more easily and are recognized more quickly and accurately. Radio and television commercials make use of this phenomenon when an advertisement is first given and then, after two or three others are shown, a slightly changed, perhaps shortened version of the first one is aired. The strategy behind this is the assumption that the first commercial functions as a "primer" and that before the second one is given, a kind of imprinting or preparation takes place so that the second one is raised to the level of consciousness and then develops a behavior-influencing effect.

3   Perceptual memory refers to the ability to recognize stimuli based on their degree of familiarity or their being generally well known. It is seen as a noetic (conscious) memory system, whereas procedural and priming systems are anoetic (unconscious). Perceptual memory involves knowing or identifying an object or individual although that object or individual does not necessarily have to be identical with any one actually previously seen. It is only necessary is that characteristic patterns of stimuli are present, such as knowing what the difference is between an apple and a peach or a pear. Because this memory system is based on experience and the individual has to complete a series of internal comparisons, it is more complex and thus appears later in the course of evolution than the anoetic memory systems.

4   The semantic memory is based on learning facts, which a person can repeat without recourse to their original context ("context-free"), that is, without specifically remembering the spatial-temporal context in which the fact was first learned. As the name implies, this memory system involves general knowledge that we learn without being able to remember later when or where the learning took place. But we do know that it is correct or is considered so. Examples can be found easily, as in acquiring a mathematical formula $((a + b)(a - b) = a^2 - b^2)$, learning rote material, or learning verbal expressions. The development of memory for facts goes hand in hand with the acquisition of language in children.

5   Episodic-autobiographical memory is involved in actively, consciously remembering episodes, usually biographical episodes that are colored in an emotional way and that can be followed back in time, and are directly associated with their contexts, in the manner of mental time traveling. On this point, Tulving refers to autonoetic consciousness and explicitly says that in the hierarchy of the five memory systems this form of memory is the highest, is seen only in humans, and does not appear until the third year of life. He defines this memory system as the intersection between subjective time, autonoetic consciousness (Markowitsch, 2003a), and one's personal self experiencing (Tulving, 2005).

Figure 4.11 Distinction of long-term memory into five systems. Procedural memory stands for skills (usually motor), priming stands for the higher probability of recognizing stimuli that were only perceived unconsciously, perceptual memory means familiarity or acquaintance with an object or person, the semantic memory contains (context-free) facts, and the episodic memory contains context-related memories that make mental time travels possible and that are linked with one's personal self-awareness and autonoetic consciousness (from Markowitsch, 2003a; Pritzel et al., 2003).

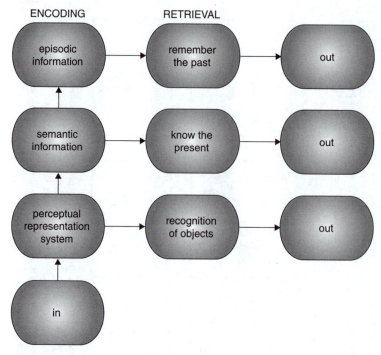

Figure 4.12 Tulving's SPI model (1995). Memory is arranged here hierarchically, showing that information must first "pass through" the more simple memory systems before reaching the more complex ones. The serial (S) (vertical arrows on the left) storage contrasts with a parallel (P) deposition and with an independent (I) recall. "Independent" here means that, even if information has been stored through higher-level memory system, it can still be recalled through a lower-level system.

One essential aspect for understanding these systems in Tulving's (1995) model (see Figure 4.12) is their manner of storage and then recall. Storage takes place in a serial direction (which, importantly, is also the case during acquisition of these systems in childhood development), but the storage itself is parallel and recall ensues independently of the manner of original storage.

As far as recall is concerned, it is important to note that we usually know far more than we think we do. A large amount of information is regularly suppressed and concealed under other material, though it is rarely deleted from the brain completely. Figure 4.13 shows an extract of a letter from a woman who, at a very advanced age, remembered poems that she had not recalled for over half a century.

In everyday life, the difference between actively knowing some piece of knowledge and merely knowing that it was successfully stored at least some time or other can be demonstrated in the different recall modalities, which psychologists have classified in three basic types (Table 4.2).

Dear Professors,

I was very glad to see a program on TV about health which finally said something about the brain. I am puzzled about the abilities of the brain, for the following reason.

I used to think I was terribly forgetful, at least for things of the recent past. But on Bismarck's birthday I turned 93. For the last two years poems have come back into my mind that I learned 75 or 80 years ago, and in fact I remembered them word for word, and some of them were long poems, like Schiller's "The Hostage" ["Die Bürgschaft] or Uhland's "The Singer's Curse" ["Des Sängers Fluch"]. In all the time since leaving school I hadn't once thought of what we had read then.

I admit I've led a rather exciting, demanding life, which isn't quite so surprising considering how old I am: going to school, dances, visits to the theater, travel, practical job experience, marriage, two children, moving several times, two wars and times of hunger, my husband off to the war for four years, birth of our second child during that time, surviving terrible air raids with my daughter and the baby, loss of our apartment, 11 years in refugee camps, then moving into our own house with a large garden, helping out in schools at the age of 60, the death of my husband, then moving into a small apartment, an operation, old-age ailments and pain, losing the ability to walk, needing a wheelchair, giving interesting lectures on my travels with my husband.

And now, without any direct reason, all these poems come to mind for the first time in 75 or 80 years. Is it possible for a brain to keep something that long, unconsciously? The people I know are amazed, too, that I can still see the old apartment and our neighborhood in my mind's eye, from the time when I was so young, two places where we lived before I was six. Have you seen other cases like this one in your psychological work? It would interest me very much to hear from you.

Figure 4.13 Letter from an older woman, astonished to find out she could recite poems from school, some of them with several stanzas, 80 years later.

Table 4.2 Forms of information reproduction

Free recall	Recall without help, the information must be generated fully on one's own Example: *What is the name of the Queen of England?*
Assisted recall	Recall with external help, such as the first letters of the answer Example: *What is the name of the Queen of England? The name starts with an E.*
Recognition	The correct answer can be seen directly in the material presented Example: *What is the name of the Queen of England?* Shown are the names, *Camilla, Diana, Elizabeth, Maria, Victoria.*

Which areas of the brain are involved in information processing?

On the one hand, the whole nervous system is involved in processing memory, starting with the peripheral nerves and the spinal cord, and on up to the cerebral cortex. But on the other hand, certain specific regions are more directly concerned with encoding, storage and recall of information.

Figure 4.14 gives a general view, which looks somewhat confusing at first, on how information is processed at the level of the brain. It shows that encoding takes place through the sensory systems, but is then differentially processed depending on which memory system is involved.

The simplest way to explain the way the brain activates the different memory systems is to take those systems which first develop and function in animals as well as humans, and which operate automatically for the most part: the procedural, priming and perceptual memory systems. These systems cannot be divided into a short-term and a long-term component. As far as we know, there seems to be no distinction between specific areas for storage or for recall. Instead, the information for storage and recall appears to be processed in discrete, homogeneous areas combining both functions. For procedural memory, these are primarily the basal ganglia (large nuclei in the anterior areas of the brain, below the cortex, which were considered earlier as mainly important in the control of motor acts) and parts of the cerebellum and the premotor cortex. For priming as well as for perceptual memory, cortical areas in the posterior brain are most probably mainly activated; they are responsible for the information of only one modality (for example, sight) or have polysensory or associative functions.

 Areas involved in the knowledge system and episodic memory are different, in that separate areas of the brain are activated for encoding, storage and recall. In addition, this information is first subject to storage in short-term memory and only then does it receive further processing in long-term memory. As soon as this information has been received by the sensory systems, it is held in a short-term storage that contains only limited amounts of information. Then it is transferred to structures of the limbic system and analyzed

---

Figure 4.14 Schematic representation of information processing in the brain. Numbers 1 to 4 give the sequence of processing: (1) Information gains access to areas within the skull through the sensory systems, where at least part of this information is given short-term storage at (2), lasting from some seconds to at most a few minutes. Then, information of general knowledge and for episodic memory that successfully reached short-term storage is transferred into – somewhat simplified – the structures of the limbic system situated in the middle of the brain, where it is evaluated for its biological and social relevance, associated with similar information already stored ("binding processes"), and whence it is then transferred to areas involved in long-term storage. These are, most particularly, structures in the cerebral cortex that represent their contents in widespread networks (3). Recall then results when regions in the frontal lobes and the anterior temporal lobes become activated and synchronize (4) the networks for the recall of specific contents. Processing takes place in a somewhat different way for the contents linked to systems of procedural, perceptual and priming memory. It is presently assumed that the areas for storage, representation and recall are fundamentally identical. For priming and perceptual memory these are the unimodal (limited to one sensory system) regions in the cortex, and for procedural memory the subcortical structures, the so-called basal ganglia, and, presumably, in other (even cortical) parts of the motor system (see Markowitsch, 1999a, 2002a).

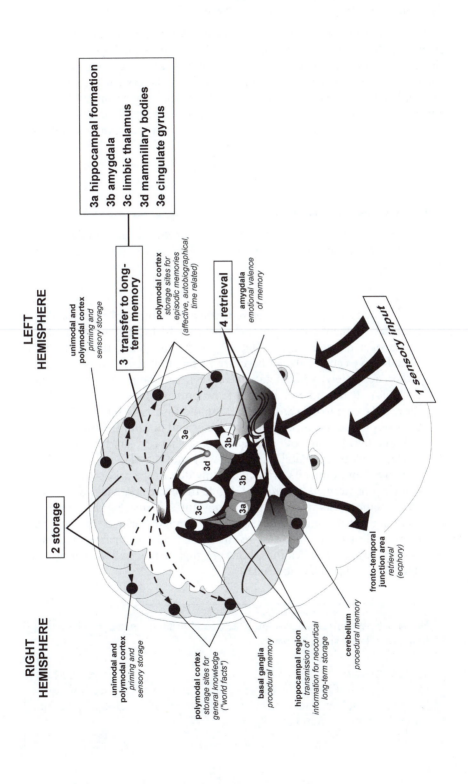

LEFT HEMISPHERE

RIGHT HEMISPHERE

2 storage

3 transfer to long-term memory

3a hippocampal formation
3b amygdala
3c limbic thalamus
3d mammillary bodies
3e cingulate gyrus

unimodal and polymodal cortex
priming and sensory storage

polymodal cortex
storage sites for episodic memories (affective, autobiographical, time related)

4 retrieval

amygdala
emotional valence of memory

unimodal and polymodal cortex
priming and sensory storage

polymodal cortex
storage sites for general knowledge ("world facts")

basal ganglia
procedural memory

hippocampal region
transmission of information for neocortical long-term storage

cerebellum
procedural memory

fronto-temporal junction area
retrieval (ecphory)

1 sensory input

3e
3b
3d
3c
3b
3a

further, associated, and linked with similar information already stored and evaluated (Markowitsch, 2002a). The final storage of the information classified as "worth keeping" takes place over extensive cortical networks, whereby the left hemisphere is more involved in the system of knowledge, and the right in episodic information. It is generally thought that such episodic material evokes not only neocortical networks (see Box 4.2) but also limbic areas that are primarily involved in processing emotional information.

The development of the brain

Several basic mechanisms participate in the protracted maturation of the brain, as described in Box 4.5. The following factors are fundamental in this maturation:

1   The exponential increase in nerve tissue in the course of embryonal and fetal development (with "embryo" being used to refer to the first few weeks of a pregnancy, and "fetus" for the time after that). The individual nerve cells of the embryo are so few that they can be estimated rather accurately, while fetal nerve cells can range between 12 and 20 billion at the time of birth. At the present state of our knowledge these cells seem to decrease, rather than increase, after birth.

2   An overproduction of nerve cell tissue at and around the time of birth, followed by a pruning out (see pp. 9–10 in Chapter 1, and Box 4.5).

3   The continuous postnatal increase in weight of the whole nervous system to more than double its original, mainly due to the arborization of cell connections (termed "neuropil"). While the nerve cells themselves basically remain constant in number, a substantial increase in number takes place in dendritic and axonal tissue and in supporting and trophic (nourishing) cells (that is, glia cells; *glia* meaning "glue" or "paste" in Greek). (There are recent indications, however, that glia as well as neurons can develop postnatally; Götz, 2003.)

Box 4.5   Myelinization, synaptogenesis and pruning: mechanisms of functional development in neurons

The processes of *myelinization, synaptogenesis* and *pruning* are referred to repeatedly in this book. They all serve to optimize connections between nerve cells, and are of primary, though not exclusive, importance in the early phases of brain development.

Myelinization

Myelinization denotes the formation of insulating myelin sheaths (see Figure 4.15 for sheaths stemming from oligodendroglia cells), which envelop the axons (the fibers extending from the cell body that transfer information to other cells) so as to insulate them, thus greatly increasing the speed of conductivity between the different nerve cells (by a factor of up to 100). There are two kinds of insulating myelin sheaths originating from either Schwann's cells in the peripheral nervous system, or the oligodendroglia in the central nervous system. These two kinds of cells are not proper nerve cells but rather somatic cells that can be found in the nervous system. A relatively high number of such cells collect around one axon in a series, leaving a minute space that is not insulated (termed "Ranvier's node") between the individual sheaths. Bioelectric potentials are conducted from one node to the next, "leaping" forward far more precisely and at a far greater speed than in nerve cells that are not equipped with such sheaths. When myelinization is reversed, as in multiple sclerosis, a disease of the nervous system, defective connections and circuits and deficient information processing result. That can go so far as to seriously limit any motor activity or cognitive processes.

During early ontogenesis, the majority of nerve cells are not myelinized at all or not yet sufficiently so, resulting in an incomplete integration of information that originates in other areas of the brain. For example, when a young child tries to chase an adult who suddenly turns to one side, the child usually tends to keep running in the original direction before finally turning the same way the adult is now running. In this case, the sensory systems are functioning adequately: The younger child sees perfectly well that the adult has changed direction. But the cognitive-interpretive processing of what has been seen correctly and the ability to inhibit the motor acts once they have begun, are not yet sufficiently coordinated and are thus delayed. But, interestingly, the process of myelinization progresses largely under the influence of precisely such external stimuli. Axons are coated with insulating sheaths when there are external demands (the recruiting situation) for the appropriate connections in the brain and when cognitive processes take place, such as forming associations and synchronization. And because some regions in the brain are not activated to any appreciable extent by external demands until relatively late in ontogenesis, myelinization is not completed for a long period of time, and in some cases not until after 20 years (compare Figure 4.18).

How important rapid transfer of information is for normal functioning can be seen when the insulation layer is gradually damaged, as in multiple sclerosis. The more the axons lose their insulation layer, the less the patients can perform everyday activities, leading in extreme cases to inability to walk or to stand up. But, in contrast, in the course of its development, the improvement in the amount of cellular insulation increases the ability of the brain to assume more and more functions. The nerve tracts that connect the brainstem with other regions or with muscles and the organs are almost completely myelinated, while other regions subserving "higher" cognitive functions, such as planning, self-reflection or speech, have scarcely any myelin at all at the time of birth (Klingberg et al., 1999; Yakovlev & Lecours, 1967).

Synaptogenesis

A second mechanism that has an extraordinary relevance especially during ontogenesis is that of synaptogenesis. Synapses form the contact sites between one nerve cell and the next. At the synaptic endpoints of one cell, chemical substances (neurotransmitters) are released, which are absorbed at the so-called postsynaptic site by receptors from the following cell (see Figures 4.15 and 4.16). Synapses are thus the fundamental elements of communication between nerve cells. Synaptogenesis,

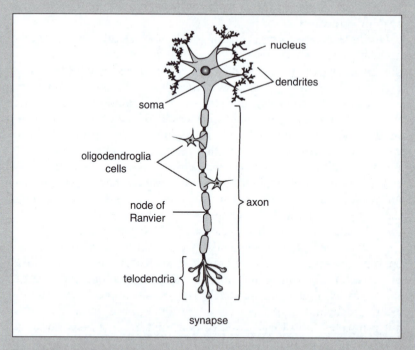

Figure 4.15 Schematic view of a typical cell in the central nervous system. Ranvier's nodes are the narrow spaces between the oligodendroglia, which function as a kind of insulation for the axon. Information arrives mainly through the dendrites, passes to the nerve cell, and is then transmitted to other nerves via the synaptic endings.

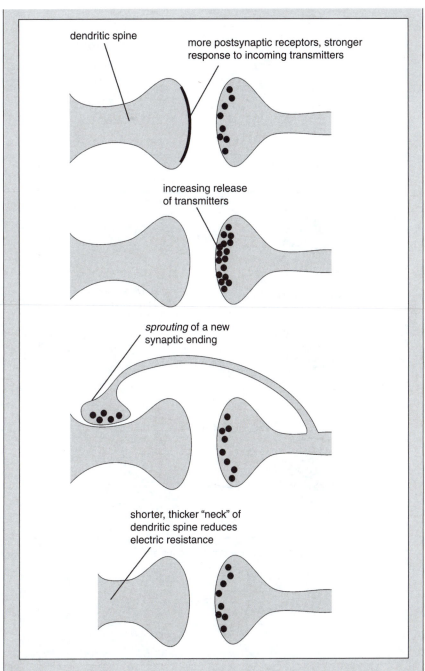

Figure 4.16 Different patterns of and changes in the connectivity between two nerve cells as a result of appropriate environmental stimulation. On the right, the synapse from the "information-donating" nerve cell, on the left the dendritic spine of the "information recipient". Changes such as those shown here are probable, for example, in learning processes and occur particularly during early childhood.

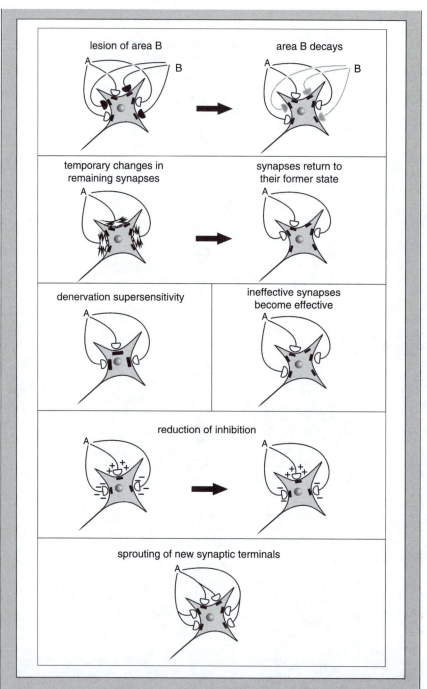

Figure 4.17 Examples of possible adaptations between nerve cells in a region in the brain after regional atrophy or damage.

then, signifies the process leading to the formation of these synapses. This starts in the mother's uterus and continues for up to 2 years after birth, whereby a remarkable peak of up to 15,000 synapses per second can be reached in each neuron (Huttenlocher, 1990). As in the case of myelinization, there is a direct relationship between the synaptogenesis in one region of the brain and demands on its "use" at a particular phase in time. The earlier a region is actually needed, the earlier synaptogenesis takes place there. In infants and small children, we find a unique development in that far more synapses are established than will be needed later. They are identified in the brain as superfluous by not being used at all or by being underachievers, and are consequently eliminated. Also, there are changes in the constellations between neurons that occur when a whole region atrophies or is damaged (Figure 4.17). Thus, synaptogenesis is dependent on environmental influences to a major extent.

Synaptogenesis also plays an essential role in *critical* or *sensitive* phases. Only if the appropriate environmental stimuli are available during a critical period in the development of a newborn infant or a child, can synaptogenesis occur at the level of the brain, with a corresponding development in functioning or in behavior. This has been demonstrated, for example, in young cats, whose nerve cells in the visual cortex require environmental stimulation in order to be conditioned for seeing. A similar condition is found in children with the Kaspar Hauser syndrome, who were insufficiently exposed to linguistic stimuli before reaching adolescence. (In 1828, Kaspar Hauser was found wandering in Nuremberg, Germany; aged about 10–14 years, he had apparently lived "in the forest" without having learned any language.)

In any region of the brain, a critical density of synapses has to be attained before its particular function can develop. Synaptic density is thus a measure of the developmental status of a region of the brain.

Synapses are too small to be counted even in a discrete region, and thus an indirect measure is used to evaluate synaptic density: the energy requirements as seen in the use of oxygen or glucose, which is quantified with the help of positron emission tomography.

Figure 4.17 shows which variants are possible when changes occur in the afferent connections among brain cells. The cell in the center receives afferent connections from regions A and B within the brain. After destruction of area B, axons exiting the area for the cell atrophy, resulting in (a) a temporary reinforcement of the afferents from area A, (b) an increase in the sensitivity of the cell to these connections from area A ("denervation supersensitivity"; an increase in the effectiveness or relevance of synapses which were up to now ineffective), and finally (c) a decrease in inhibition or the sprouting of new synapses.

Pruning

The reverse process is termed "pruning" in which the sites of connectivity at the level of neurons are re-established, although the expression originally means cutting back some of the branches of a tree in order to graft others on. Pruning is another example of a process that takes place in interaction with environmental factors. Only those dendrites which are sufficiently often "addressed" by other nerve cells will survive; all the others are superfluous and thus decompose. This gives the brain the possibility of creating complex networks with functional associations that can be similarly complex. Most pruning is complete by the third year of life; after that the majority of the connections attain a lifelong stable linkage.

In a series of studies, Katharina Braun found that pruning phenomena are effective even when they are not expected at all in this form. When young animals were removed from their mothers, more dendritic spines were formed than in those which lived together with their mothers, and these unexpected spines disappeared when the young and the mothers were joined together again (see Braun & Bock, 2003; Ovtscaroff & Braun, 2001; Poeggel et al., 2003).

4   The selective maturation of individual brain regions, at different rates, whereby precisely those regions most important for higher mental functions – and thus for autobiographical memory – are those requiring the longest time to reach their final stage of maturation (but they also lose their cells rapidly under certain conditions). This selective process in maturation was already described in the nineteenth century by a well-known neurologist (Flechsig, 1896a, 1896b; see Figure 4.18).

5   The relative increase in the size and volume of individual structures within the class of mammals. In mammals, it is less surprising that the cerebral cortex and especially the frontal and temporal lobes have increased in size so massively. But it is all the more interesting that some structures have increased enormously in size that are phylogenetically quite old but that have apparently assumed at least a partial change in or extension of their function in the evolution of mammals. Examples include the mammillary bodies (a pair of rather small nuclei in the lower diencephalon at the base of the brain near the hypothalamus) and the anterior thalamic nuclei, which receive afferents from the mammillary bodies (see Figure 3.5, p. 35, and Figure 4.4, p. 56) (Armstrong, 1986; Rapoport, 1990; Stephan, 1975). Both structures constitute components of the Papez circuit (Figure 4.19), which is of central importance in the processing of memory (evaluation and transfer into long-term memory). This is similarly the case for the septum or, more appropriately, the septal nuclei (Andy & Stephan, 1976; Cramon & Markowitsch, 2000; Stephan,

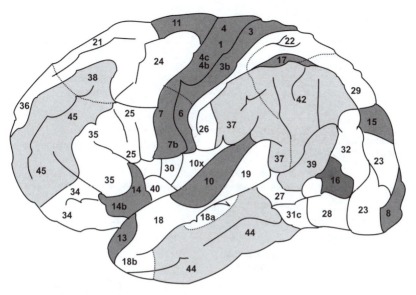

Figure 4.18 Flechsig's map of the brain (in a lateral view of the cerebral cortex; his numbering of brain areas), showing the different rates of maturation in individual areas. White areas require the longest period until full maturity is complete, light gray areas need less time, and dark gray areas are practically mature already at the time of birth. White regions are mostly the so-called association cortex, responsible for higher cognitive functions and are concentrated in the frontal, temporal and parietal lobes. Flechsig reached these conclusions by studying prenatal and postnatal brain tissue (Flechsig, 1896a, 1896b).

1975), which have expanded in size from a rather subordinate structure in the limbic system and which are incorporated in a second circuit (also relevant to memory processing and in particular to integration of emotion and memory): the basolateral limbic circuit (see Figure 4.19). The septal nuclei are part of the basal forebrain and contain nerve cells that release the neurotransmitter acetylcholine, which itself plays an important role in learning and memory, and project fibers throughout large areas of the cerebral cortex.

6   The extraordinary relevance of adequate environmental stimulation in the development and the further growth of nerve tissue (such as in the "critical" or "sensitive" periods for the maturation of the sense of smell or the power of speech). On this point, it has long been recognized that, for example, normal language and speech ability cannot be learned by humans who have had no contact with the sounds of speech (as in the Kaspar Hauser syndrome). On the other hand, we know from everyday experience how much more quickly children learn a foreign language, and even speak without an accent. However, the older they get, the more they lose this gift. Experiments with animals have confirmed this

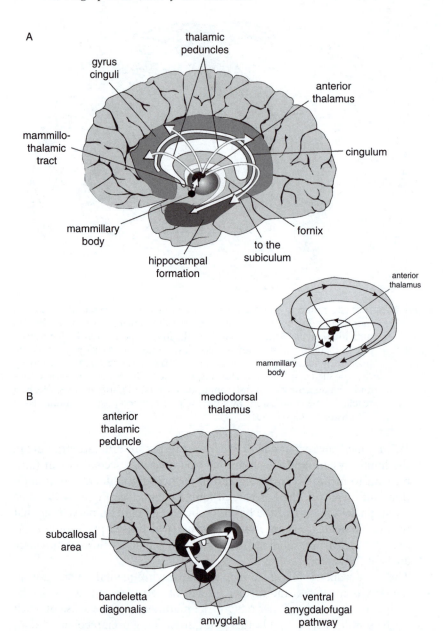

Figure 4.19 The Papez circuit (A) and the basolateral limbic circuit (B). Both subserve
in particular the storage of episodic-autobiographical events, but also less
emotional factual information. The basolateral-limbic circuit is probably
more involved in the emotional evaluation of experiences than is the
Papez circuit.

Figure 4.20 Example of Kaspar Hauser experiments. A kitten is kept in an environment of restricted visual stimulation, with the result that its nerve cells in the retina are imprinted for only the one kind of stimulus, namely vertical black-and-white stripes.

tendency. Young cats, for instance, who just after the first weeks of life were exposed to a constantly simple, homogeneous visual environment, were later no longer able to "see" normally and thus had difficulty in orienting themselves in their environment (Figure 4.20).

The course of development in the nervous system: phylogenesis and ontogenesis

Our brain could be described as going through its development almost "from back to front" or "from bottom to top". Starting from the rather more amorphous form of the neural tube, the first area to originate is the spinal cord; only after that do the more anterior regions arise: first the metencephalon, followed by the mesencephalon and the diencephalon and finally the telencephalon (Figures 4.21 and 4.22).

Up to a certain point in development, ontogeny and phylogeny develop in parallel. The human fetus thus goes through a number of differentiations similar to those the vertebrate brain went through while developing from lower to higher animals in phylogeny (for example, from fish to monkeys).

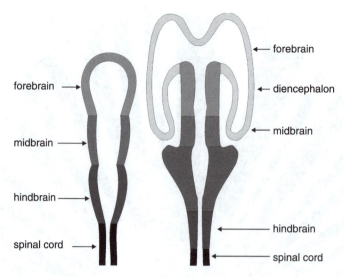

Figure 4.21 Development of the nervous system from the phase of a neural tube to that of the neonate (and thus of the adult as well).

But this development only represents the basic framework, the skeleton, as it were. On the one hand, the cerebral cortex becomes substantially larger and heavier in the course of postnatal development, growing mushroom-like to envelop most of the other structures; on the other hand, many small grooves or sulci form in this cortex (Figure 4.18, p. 81) and so greatly increase its total surface area. In addition, the human brain has a high number of areas as well as fiber structures (or tracts that join different areas together) that continue to grow partially even years after birth (for up to 20–30 years later in one extreme case). In the case of the tracts, the axons (the "cables") of nerve cells extend their insulation layers, and so improve the quality of both their communication and their storage abilities. The areas which are particularly dependent on external influences for proper development include regions within the limbic system (see Figure 4.4, p. 56) and the so-called association regions in the cerebral cortex (see Figure 4.18, p. 81).

Maturation of the limbic system

Compared with the neocortex, a six-layered cortex (see Figure 4.23), the cortical structures of the limbic system usually have fewer than six layers, and occasionally only three, as in the case of the olfactory bulb (the bulbus olfactorius) and the hippocampus. This argues for a rather early maturation process, since phylogenetically old structures generally conclude their immature phase in development and reach full adult functioning much before the phylogenetically newer ones. Paul MacLean (1970) – well known for his research on the limbic system around the middle of the last century – spoke of the

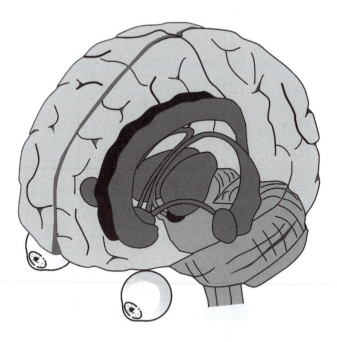

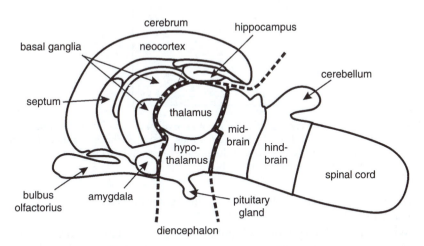

Figure 4.22 Typical view of the human brain (above) and, for comparison, a sagittal view of a prototypical mammal brain (below), showing the larger sections of the brain and the conventional terminology. The cerebral cortex arches around basically all structures with the exception of the spinal cord, which extends down the vertebral column and the back.

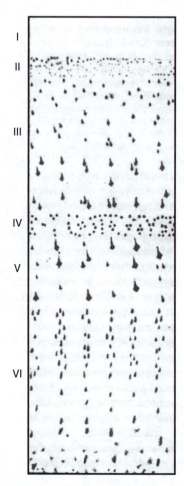

Figure 4.23 The six cell layers typical of the mammalian cortex. The first, uppermost, layer is almost totally free of neurons. The other layers contain different types of nerve cells. Small dots represent granular cells. The largest cells portrayed are pyramidal cells.

"triune brain" and called the structures in the middle part the limbic system (see Figure 4.24).

Within the limbic system, the majority of the structures mature relatively early, while a few only reach full functionality rather late, including the area of the hippocampus and the fornix, which is the largest fiber tract leaving (and partially re-entering) the hippocampus (compare Figure 4.4, p. 56). And within the hippocampus area, there are individual sections which appear to be organized very tightly, so that reference is frequently made to a specialized architecture (Figure 3.7, p. 36, and Figure 3.8, p. 37). One of the neuronal sections of the hippocampus, known as the gyrus dentatus,

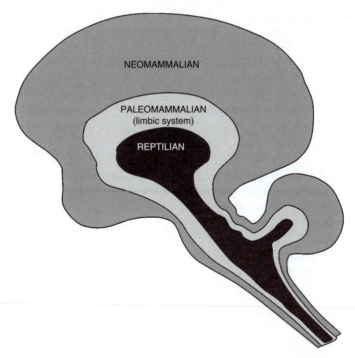

NEOMAMMALIAN

PALEOMAMMALIAN
(limbic system)

REPTILIAN

Figure 4.24 MacLean's (1970) schematic view of the mammal brain made up of shells (similar to onion skins). The limbic system is situated in the middle between the lower-lying brainstem, which controls functions vital to life, and the neocortex on the upper surface (consisting of more recent, six-layered cortex; compare Figure 4.23), which subserves both the fine-graded processing of sensation and motor behavior and higher mental functions.

generates neurons for almost as much as a year postnatally. The formation of dendrites and synapses continues for years after birth (Serres, 2001). Recent research is finding increasing support for the new formation or replacement of old, dead nerve cells over the whole life span in the gyrus dentatus.

Nerve fibers making up the fornix do not start to insulate themselves with myelin sheaths until after the second year of life, and the process of insulation continues well into late childhood (Brody et al., 1987; Diamond, 1990; Yakovlev & Lecours, 1967). This means that certainly the most important circuit in the human brain for evaluating incoming information and then transferring it into long-term storage, the so-called Papez circuit (Figure 4.19, p. 82), does not function adequately until late childhood.

As of the third year, the brain concludes the essential "pruning processes" (compare Box 4.5, pp. 74ff.). In this way, it acquires a network character during this time that remains stable for the rest of life. This will include the integration of the different levels in the brain. The phylogenetically old brainstem, responsible for basal, vital functions essential for survival of the individual,

Table 4.3 Total surface of the frontal region (regio frontalis) (in mm²) and its relation to the total surface area of the cerebral cortex (in %) for selected mammals (taken from Brodmann, 1912)

Order	Species	Total surface of cortex of one hemisphere (in mm²)	Percentage of regio frontalis within total surface area of the cerebral cortex	
			in mm²	in %
Primates	Human, *Homo sapiens*	135,470	39,287	29.0
	Chimpanzee, *Pan troglodytes*	39,572	6719	16.9
	Siamang, *Symphalangus syndactylus*	16,302	1839	11.3
	Mandrill, *Papio sphinx*	21,321	168	10.1
	Hamadryas baboon, *Papio hamadryas*	20,594	967	9.5
	Yellow baboon, *Papio cynocephalus*	20,376	2111	10.3
	Moor macaque, *Macaca maurus*	15,308	1733	11.3
	Guenon, *Cercopithecus* sp.	14,641	1625	11.1
	White-headed capuchin monkey, *Cebus capucinus*	13,682	1260	9.2
	Black-tufted marmoset, *Callithrix penicillata*	1649	148	8.9
(Family: Prosimians)	Red-bellied lemur, *Lemur rubriventer*	4054	337	8.3
	Greater dwarf lemur, *Cheirogaleus major*	921	70	7.2
Chiroptera (bat-like)	Flying fox, *Pteropus edwarsi geoffroy*	1097	26	2.3
Carnivores	Dog, *Canis familiaris*	9527	657	6.9
	Cat, *Felis domestica*	4474	152	3.4
Lagomorphs (rabbit-like)	European rabbit, *Oryctolagus cuniculus*	1627	36	2.2
Insectivora	West European hedgehog, *Erinaceus europaeus*	575	–	–
Edentata	Big hairy armadillo, *Chaetophractus villosus*	2010	–	–
Marsupalia	White-eared opossum, *Didelphis albiventris azarae*	804	–	–

unites functionally with the structures of the limbic system that regulate our emotional functions. These limbic structures then communicate with the cognitive-neocortical ones so that an integrated, mature personality can develop by the age of 9 or 10 years, in middle school. If, however, at this time there are major emotional problems – such as the loss of one of the parents or violence in the form of sexual abuse – the integration between limbic and cognitive functions is incomplete, resulting in so-called dissociative personality disorder or, in the extreme case, "double" or "multiple personality", in which the symbiotic unity of a person's rational-cognitive and affective-emotional levels fails to take place. Emotional elements force their way through into the foreground and suppress the reflective-cognitive abilities, thereby making it impossible to find an internal expression (the ability of verbalization) for feelings and thoughts. Such patients are caught up in stereotyped, uncontrollably recurring mental images or, in extreme cases, in delusions (Fujiwara & Markowitsch, 2003).

These examples suffice to show that an integrating association between the levels of the brainstem, the limbic system and the neocortex is a necessary prerequisite for what MacLean called the triune brain (compare Figure 4.24).

Maturation of the neocortex

As we have already mentioned, the phylogenetic evolution in the cortex is particularly evident in association areas, especially in the frontal lobes, which are most notably differentiated in the orbitofrontal and the dorsolateral parts (see Figure 4.1, p. 53). But the development of the frontal lobes is described somewhat differently by various authors depending on the criteria they used for defining the extent of these lobes. The classical definition put emphasis on the cytoarchitecture, that is, the presence and distribution of particular nerve cell types. This method was particularly promoted by Korbinian Brodmann for describing the boundaries of particular areas in the cortex (and thus measuring its size) (Brodmann, 1909); he concluded that the mammal prefrontal cortex attains by far its greatest size in humans (see Table 4.3; Brodmann, 1912). And thus his evaluation of this region, relying on purely anatomical data for definition, conformed to a very early assessment made by Huschke in 1854 – one that has been repeated many times since then (Markowitsch, 1988) – namely that the frontal lobe area is the "seat of intelligence". Other authors have criticized Brodmann's cytoarchitectural criteria and have instead suggested using only the thalamo-cortical projections as a means of defining the regio frontalis, in which case the mediodorsal nucleus in the thalamus would be the pivotal source for delineating the frontal area (Rose & Woolsey, 1948), but this method has been called into question by others as well (Markowitsch & Pritzel, 1979).

Whatever the outcome of these disputes on the various methods for defining the area, it is apparent not only that the frontal lobe area in humans constitutes a large portion of the entire cerebral cortex but also that the mass of tissue is potentiated through the functional asymmetry of the hemispheres (Geschwind & Galaburda, 1982; Springer & Deutsch, 1989). This "duplication" is seen not only in the speech center or Broca's area, which is morphologically measurable (see Figure 4.28, p. 100), but also in the results obtained by modern functional imagery techniques on the different ways the two frontal hemispheres process memory functions. In line with these results, Tulving and coworkers (1994) proposed the HERA model (the hemispheric-encoding-retrieval-asymmetry model) to show (among other things) that the left frontal lobe is essentially involved in the storage, and the right frontal lobe in the retrieval of episodic information.

The phenomenon of hemispheric dominance can be seen in the frontal lobes in another field, in the differential processing of world knowledge (semantic memory) in the left hemisphere versus that of autobiographical memory in the right (Kroll, Markowitsch, Knight, & von Cramon, 1997; Markowitsch, 1999b). In view of these differences in hemispheric processing, considerable importance has to be attributed to the effect of the environment and thus of cultural influences in developing preferential engagements of the hemispheres for different functions. We see this in the processing of memory but even more so in that of speech. A large number of studies have been published on people in the Far East who make use of whole symbols for words or even word groups, showing that in these people processing of words is performed more strongly by both hemispheres together than in people of Western cultures (see, for example: Dong et al., 2000; Hellige & Yamauchi, 1999; Kamada et al., 1998; Matuso et al., 2000). Interestingly, Zilles and coworkers (2001) were able to show that not only ethnic factors but also characteristics of gender have an effect on the morphology of the brain. Gender, of course, represents a major variable in the differential functional engagement of the hemispheres (Pritzel & Markowitsch, 1997). Even in the fully healthy subject, differences can be found in the processing of speech, emotions and cognitions (Canli, Desmond, Zhao, & Gabrieli, 2002; Davatzikos & Resnick, 1998; Gur et al., 1999), in the volume of the frontal lobes as opposed to the limbic temporal lobe area (Gur, Gunning-Dixon, Bilker, & Gur, 2002), in the brain's biochemistry (Kaasinen, Nagren, Hietala, Farde, & Rinne, 2001), and in processes of brain maturation dependent on environmental influences (De Bellis & Keshavan, 2003).

As to brain maturation, the older parts of the brainstem (the "reptilian brain" in Figure 4.24, p. 87) remain, as could be expected, the most constant. But limbic areas, which also belong to phylogenetically old areas (some limbic structures can be seen as far back as in salamanders), go through considerable changes in ontogenetical development, which at least partially go hand in hand with an alteration in their functions. The newer areas of the neocortex, finally, experience both structurally and functionally the largest expansions and changes. Within the neocortex, the peak in developmental change can be seen in the temporal lobe and, to an even greater extent, in the (dorsolateral) frontal lobe (compare Figure 4.1, p. 53).

On this topic we would like to refer to one of the "most human" cognitive abilities, the ability to "feel with" another person. The origin of this ability in childhood and its relevance will be treated in Chapter 7 (in the section "Theory of mind: psychological understanding") (see also Perner, 2000; Perner & Dienes, 2003; Perner, Lang, & Kloo, 2002), but, for now, we will go into the functional-anatomical aspects. Psychological understanding, a highly social behavior, seems to be intimately coupled with orbitofrontal, but also to a certain extent with dorsolateral, parts of the frontal lobe (compare Figure 4.1, p. 53) (Abu-Akel, 2003; Bird, Castelli, Malik, Frith, & Husain, 2004; Calarge, Andreasen, & O'Leary, 2003; Channon & Crawford, 2000; Gregory, Lough, Stone, Erzinclioglu, & Martin, 2002; Rowe, Bullock, Polkey, & Morris, 2001; Shallice, 2001; Siegal & Varley, 2002; Stone, Baron-Cohen, & Knight, 1998; Stuss, Gallup, & Alexander, 2001). Interestingly, one structure plays a significant role in this respect and has gone through a strong differentiation and extension of its subnuclei in primates and thus humans too (Stephan, 1975): the amygdala (compare Figure 4.4, p. 56) (Fine, Lumsden, & Blair, 2001; Shaw et al., 2004; Siegal & Varley, 2002; Stone, Baron-Cohen, Calder, Keane, & Young, 2003).

A series of very informative studies on this point was conducted by Julian Keenen and coworkers of Harvard University. Their subjects were shown faces of strangers as well as their own face (Keenan et al., 1999; Keenan, Wheeler, Gallup, & Pascual-Leone, 2000). In the most interesting study of this series, functional imaging techniques were applied while pictures of prominent people (such as Bill Clinton) were shown that gradually (in altogether 20 steps) changed into the face of the subject. As soon as the subject recognized his or her own face, the imagery techniques registered a selective activation in the lateral-inferior frontal lobe on the right side, which was thus a correlate for self-recognition. Another group (S. C. Johnson et al., 2002) studied the neural correlates of processes accompanying self-reflective behavior. Their subjects were asked to decide whether statements such as "I have a quick temper" or "I am always friendly to others" were true. Statements which were true led to an activation of medial frontal lobe areas. This result points to the importance of the frontal lobes for one's own personality and confirms similar studies that found an association between changes in frontal lobe characteristics (such as a reduction in metabolism and changes in the tissue) and antisocial and criminal behavior (Blair, 2004; Pontius & Yudowitz, 1980; Raine, Lencz, Bihrle, LaCasse, & Colletti, 2000; Raine et al., 1998a, 2003; Raine, Stodard, Bihrleb, & Buchsbaum, 1998b). It also highlights the conclusion reached by Eslinger, Flaherty-Craig, and Benton (2004) that early influences on the frontal lobes can especially impair the integration and the cooperation of cognitive, emotional, self-regulating and executive/metacognitive processes significantly.

To what extent processes of maturation influence the frontal lobes was the subject of a series of studies performed by Patricia Goldman-Rakic and coworkers. Working on the so-called Kennard principle, which was highly controversial at the time (Kennard, 1938, 1940, 1942), Goldman-Rakic and her coworker Galkin performed intrauterine removal of the frontal lobes in monkey fetuses (Figure 4.25). The Kennard principle (see Box 4.6, p. 94) maintains that the brains of young individuals react to brain damage in a far more adaptive way than do those of adults. The results showed that the animals in the study, after lesioning and after birth by cesarean section, differed in various ways from the animals who did not sustain similar lesions until after attaining adulthood. In adult monkeys, such damage leads to degeneration in the corresponding mediodorsal nerve cells in the thalamus. But these cells were preserved in the brains of the fetuses with intrauterine damage. There are different explanations of this result, as seen in Figure 4.25. Even more surprising, however, was the finding that the young monkeys were not impaired when later given tasks that adult animals without the frontal lobe usually fail. The results seemed to confirm the Kennard principle. Brain damage can be compensated for, at least partially, although there is no change in learning behavior. However, later studies showed that the young monkeys later did have a massive disturbance in adolescence, especially when looking for a partner and in maintaining the contact over time (Goldman-Rakic, 1987).

We had similar experiences with a female student who had had two epileptic attacks at night and was admitted to a hospital. Computer tomography and magnetic resonance tomography both revealed that she was suffering from neuronal heterotopia, a rare developmental disease of the cerebral cortex in which the cortex fails to migrate outwardly during the embryonal phase and instead remains in a subcortical position, in isolated portions or as connected tissue. This congenital malformation is usually found in both hemispheres and involves a severe deficit in intelligence. But in the patient we examined, the damage was restricted to her left hemisphere and she had no problems, for example, in studying for a university degree. In such cases with congenital disease, the Kennard principle holds that the brain should demonstrate an impressive compensation ability in the further course of development. And in fact, the patient had had problems as a young child in acquiring speech that necessitated speech therapy, and a neurological examination by positron emission tomography revealed that her speech centers were now localized on the right side of her brain. Neuropsychological and personality tests showed that, as would be expected from the results of Goldman and Galkin (1978), the student's social and emotional developmental status was more like that of a child than that of an adult. Thus, it is apparent that the brain of a child also has limits to its capacity for compensation. We assume that in the case of our patient the greater demands during early childhood were on acquiring speech and that as a result her speech "shifted" to the right hemisphere. This in turn reduced the fine-caliber coordination of emotional and social abilities that would otherwise have been the task of the right hemisphere, and thus impaired the 21-year-old student in these abilities.

The full range of social and emotional abilities that should be available to a

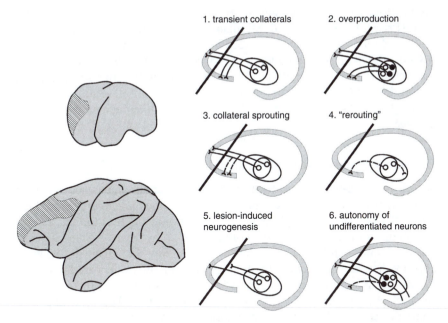

Figure 4.25 Left top: fetal brain of a rhesus monkey, and left bottom: brain of the adult. Shaded portions are the areas removed from the dorsolateral frontal lobe that in the normal brain are essential for solving learning tasks which require remembering a change in direction. On the right: schematic longitudinal sections ("parasagittal sections") through the brain of a monkey; the cerebral cortex is on the outer surface, and the large oval represents the thalamus, and the small oval, the mediodorsal nucleus, which projects axons to the lesioned area. The survival of cells in the nucleus despite the lesion in the frontal lobe is surprising and needs explanation. Possible changes in the routing of fiber connections from the mediodorsal nucleus to the frontal lobe, depending on the lesion, are given in nos. 1–5; the possibility of a neogenesis of nerve cells is likewise given, in no. 6. No. 1 assumes that axons can redirect themselves and reach the undamaged, lower part of the lobe; 2 assumes an overproduction in the cells such that sufficient numbers of "active" cells are preserved; 3 describes a damage-induced change in the routing of the axons; 4 shows the completely new development of axons in another direction; 5 represents the development of whole new nerve cells; and 6 shows the survival of cells that do not have any specific targets or functions.

person appears to depend essentially on unimpaired maturation of the frontal lobes. This is clearly the conclusion from the studies cited above as well as from a large number of others (e.g., Case, 1992; Dawson, Panagiotides, Klinger, & Hill, 1992; Dennis, 1991; Eslinger, Grattan, Damasio, & Damasio, 1992; Grattan & Eslinger, 1991; Eslinger et al., 1992; Marlowe, 1992; Williams & Mateer, 1992). The frontal lobes probably show, better than any other region of the brain, that damage sustained in childhood leads to extensive deficits in adulthood, especially in the realm of social abilities, including insight, foresight, social judgment, empathy and drawing complex conclusions (Price, Daffner, Stowe, & Mesulam, 1990). There are interesting results on this relationship from comparisons between the behavior of patients with frontal lobe damage and children. Kolb, Wilson, and Taylor (1992) found that before the age of 14 children do not show ability to recognize, distinguish and understand facial expressions on a level with that of adults, while children between the ages of 8 and 13 years perform like patients with frontal damage.

Development and localization of speech

Speech is an ability unique to humans, and symbolic languages are what make the whole universe of culture and tradition possible, a universe which forms our coevolutionary developmental environment. It is for this reason that studies which purport to find communication by means of sign language (the deaf-mute sign language, such as American Sign Language) in the great apes are viewed with skepticism, and this is all the more the case for studies by, for example, Kaminski, Call, and Fischer (2004), who, as their title suggests, claimed to find that dogs could learn words ("Word learning in a domestic dog: Evidence for 'fast mapping' "). Attempts to reproduce the results noted that the dog in question, who identified 200 objects when their names were called out, did this only by "holophrastic" association (purely according to the sounds of the phrases), whereas children learn words in completely different contexts and with reference to the objects (Markman & Abelev, 2004; compare Bloom, 2000).

Box 4.6   Plasticity: environmental influence on neuronal maturation

"Neuronal plasticity" has become almost a modish term; in fact, this led to a journal taking it as its title (*Neural Plasticity*). The term designates the quality of neuronal tissue for being reshaped or for changing in the face of maturation processes or, even more, environmental influences. Just as a muscle can become larger or smaller either through training or through the opposite, lack of use, nerve cells can change the degree of branching or arborization (its *neuropil*; compare p. 74).

A number of studies have documented the fascination that the concept continues to exert (Bateson et al., 2004; Buonomano & Merzenich, 1998; Finger & Almli, 1984; Finger & Stein, 1982; Kolb, 1989; Kolb & Whishaw, 1998; Röder et al., 1999; Rosenzweig & Bennett, 1996; Stein, Rosen, & Butters, 1974). The research goes back to studies beginning in the 1930s and 1940s. Margaret Kennard (1938, 1940, 1942) used monkeys of different ages, ranging from very young to adult, induced lesions particularly to the motor cortex, and identified a clear gradient.

The younger the animal, the quicker it was able to recover from the consequences of the lesion and, also, the more delimited the remaining deficits were. Young animals were able to recover their sense of balance rather quickly after the surgical treatment. They could run, reach out for food, and so on. On the other hand, adult animals with similar-sized lesions in the same position (motor cortex) frequently remained paralyzed for months or were incapable of moving the muscles of the contralateral side of the body when the lesion was performed in only one hemisphere. The Kennard principle thus proved to be robust; it was later extended to sensory abilities as well, and attained a good degree of generalizability. Case descriptions of individual patients emphasize again and again how clinical experience demonstrates that children recuperate better from head injury than do adults (Zuccarello, Facco, Zampieri, Zanardi, & Andrioli, 1985, p. 161).

Later, work by Rosenzweig and coworkers (1972) became particularly well known, showing that the neuronal connectivity in brains of adult rats is clearly different depending on whether the animals are reared in "solitary confinement" and merely vegetate in this state, live in partnership with another animal, or interact in a larger social group with a good deal of variety in their environment (Figure 4.26).

The surprising effectiveness of plasticity was seen in studies with highly differing designs. In patients who have lost one sensory modality, the cortex assigns an appropriate region to the remaining senses as compensation. In other studies, it became apparent that motor training in fact increases the extent of motor and somatosensory areas on the surface of the cortex (De Volder et al., 1997; Knecht et al., 1998; Liotti, Ryder, & Woldorff, 1998; Musso et al., 1999; Pantev & Lütkenhöner, 2000; Papathanasiou, 2003). Functional imagery furthermore yielded evidence on which brain areas take over sensory and motor functions if limited brain damage or even removal of a whole hemisphere has occurred (see, for example, Bernasconi et al., 2000).

Nonetheless, when we compare the brains of rats and rhesus monkeys to that of humans, it has to be remembered that the much more complex brain of humans is subject to age-related processes such as gender-dependent maturation. The brains of boys and girls mature at markedly different rates (Heller, 1993), and the behavior induced by steroid hormones appears at different times during the respective ontogenesis. Considering the differences between the genders, the distinction between one's prenatal predisposition and its later realization always has to be kept in mind, as well as the differences in personal development stretching across at least 10–12 years. During this course of development, certain behaviors are acquired, such as cognitive strategies, which in their specific cellular substrate interact with various morphological "standard settings", that is, they make different use of the plasticity of the brain. A case in point can be seen in the gender-specific

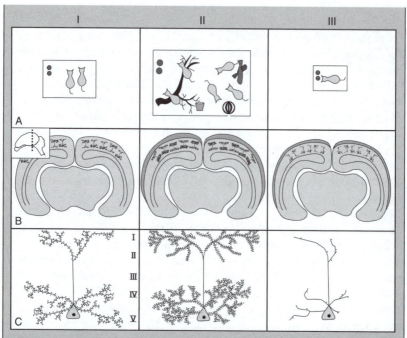

Figure 4.26 Schematic representation of adult rats who live in different environments (row A) and the corresponding neuroanatomical changes (rows B and C) that apparently ensue as a result of the influence of such environments on the structures of the nervous system. A: The size of the cell is basically similar for each rat in all conditions: the standard condition I (two rats, water and food basins), the enriched environment II (five rats, water and food basins, additional objects), and the "deprived" environment III (solitary cell for one rat). The different conditions of rearing influence the resultant thickness of the cortex and the differentiation of pyramidal cells (which have their cell bodies in cortex layer V), but not that of astrocytes (for a description of these layers, see Figure 4.23, p. 86). B shows frontal sections of the rat brains, cut at the level shown in the inset. Left: astrocytes; right: pyramidal cells in the cortex. Compared to the standard condition (I), the cortex and the dendritic arborization of the pyramidal cells of rats reared under condition II increase in size, while under condition III there is a decrease in size. How extensive the differences (or the similarities) can be is shown in row C for a pyramidal cell: condition II apparently induces a larger arborization of distal dendritic endings and thus an enormous increase in communication possibilities with other neurons. Under condition III, the basic appearance of the pyramidal cells may remain fairly the same (one apical and four basal dendrites), but, importantly, the arborization and the number of spines (represented by dots) to which the synapses of other cells are connected are considerably decreased; also, the apical dendrite does not extend the whole way to layer I (cortical layers I–V are shown in the lower left quadrant). This figure summarizes the results of Rosenzweig, Bennett, and Diamond (1972) as well as of other studies that concur in demonstrating the influence of the environment on the formation (or reduction) of neuronal tissue.

differences in memory that originate in early childhood. From this early phase in life, girls remember more emotional elements, and boys more activity-related ones (Friedman & Pines, 1991).

As to the close association between brain development and behavioral qualities, it has been shown that persons with special gifts (which they may have trained and perfected even further) also show exceptional developments within the brain corresponding to their particular abilities. Having a good ear for music and the corresponding abilities necessary to perform music are associated with having a larger than average corpus callosum (the largest connection between the hemispheres), which is important for the coordination of certain musical abilities such as rhythm and tonal appreciation (Schlaug, Jäncke, Huang, Staiger, & Steinmetz, 1995). It has even been proposed to take the corpus callosum as a measure of the differentiation of cognitive abilities in children with learning disabilities (Njiokikjien, de Sonnevill, & Vaal, 1994; Zaidel, 1989). Recent work has shown that environmentally induced plasticity and adaptivity are universal processes that can be seen equally well in sensory, motor and cognitive behavior. They are important not just in individuals growing up but also in the adult and the aged population, and to that extent they offer an explanation of the individuality and unique characteristics that are so typical of various talented persons – we only have to think of chess geniuses, artists, philosophers and acrobats. Our present knowledge of the relevance of plasticity and adaptivity highlights once again the intertwining of nature and culture, or of biology and psychology (Li, 2003; Neville & Bavelier, 2000).

However, at the same time, we have to mention the reverse side, the disadvantage of functional plasticity, which can mean that children, as opposed to adults, are more subject to negative experiences in the environment such as being separated from their mother (Cirulli, Berry, & Alleva, 2003) or being deprived of proper sleep (Frank, Issa, & Stryker, 2001). Here there are some rather intriguing case descriptions of patients who suffered a so-called mnestic block syndrome, usually in early adulthood. We were able to examine a number of these patients with extensive neuropsychological tests and functional imagery, and in almost all cases there was evidence of massive problems in childhood or adolescent development. As in a similar theory on the origin of depression (Aldenhoff, 1997), we came to the conclusion that if negative childhood experiences take place before the child is able to build up adequate protection, they lead to a form of "biological injury" involving a change in the way neurotransmitters function. Processing in the brain then becomes defective and subsequently leads to mnestic disturbances in the recall of autobiographical memories (dissociative amnesia; see Markowitsch, 1999b, 2001a; Markowitsch, Fink, Thöne,

Kessler, & Heiss, 1997b; Markowitsch, Kessler, Van der Ven, Weber-Luxenburger, & Heiss, 1998; Markowitsch et al., 1997a). Persons with the mnestic block syndrome appear otherwise normal, and they do not seem to have emotional problems or to suffer in any way. They are perfectly capable of acquiring new long-term information (which, however, may be for neutral, factual knowledge rather than for emotionally coded, episodic information), and remember very well general knowledge (such as who the president is; how to do basic arithmetic, writing, and reading; and social manners). The part of their autobiography which has been blocked and is thus lacking may be compensated for by knowledge of dry facts, but it never attains the affective valency that is typical of autbiographical memories otherwise.

Plasticity therefore shares something of the two-faced head of Janus. On the one hand, it can reduce the effects of damaging influences, or, on the other hand, even magnify them. Important for the consequences of these events are such factors as the nature of the event and the state of the organism at the time when it takes place. A number of studies, including those by Goldman-Rakic (1987) and Calabrese and coworkers (1994), have referred to this aspect, from different points of view (see also Corkin, Rosen, Sullivan, & Clegg, 1989; Isaacson, 1975, 1988). One publication by G. E. Schneider (1979), entitled "Is it really better to have your brain lesion early? A revision of the Kennard principle", had a good deal of influence on further research. Schneider warned of possible belated damage after all, in spite of the child's having seemingly recovered in an impressive way from whatever happened.

Broca's area and Wernicke's area, responsible for speech processing (compare Figure 3.3, p. 32), are found in their specific forms only in the human brain (although there is apparently a precursor for Wernicke's area in the great apes (see Box 3.1, pp. 30ff.). The two areas were discovered in the nineteenth century by Paul Broca and Carl Wernicke, and have since then been seen as the central brain areas for motor speech ability (Broca's area) and speech reception (Wernicke's area). According to a rather simple "philosophy of life" current at the time, it was assumed that both areas were to be found in over 95 percent of humans in the left hemisphere and also functioned relatively independently of each other. These views found basic support at the time in the simplistic belief that anterior parts of the brain served only direct motor functions or those closely related to motor performance, and posterior parts served sensation or its closely related functions (see Figure 4.27).

Modern research has, however, shown that the relationships between speech processing and speech areas or "centers" are far more complicated: gender differences, tracts connecting the different areas, and other variables all "dilute" simple theories on the direct relationships between localization

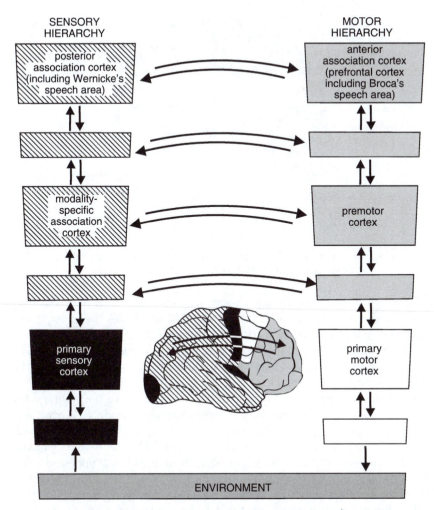

Figure 4.27 General diagram of the brain distinguishing between the posterior sensory and the anterior motor cortical areas (from Fuster, 1997a, 1997b). It shows, in outline form, that there is a division of labor in the cortex. In the front (anterior) part are regions controlling all aspects of motor behavior (body movements, purposeful activity, and planning), and in the back parts (posterior) are receptive regions that process whatever we have perceived through our senses.

and function. It is still valid, nonetheless, that language ability in general and speech develop postnatally dependent on the variable of time. Children at the age of 2 months already direct their attention within a quarter of a second to words they already know (priming: compare Figure 4.11, p. 69) (Thierry, Vihman, & Roberts, 2003). Newborn infants can distinguish a series of tones according to their frequency characteristics (Winkler et al., 2003). These

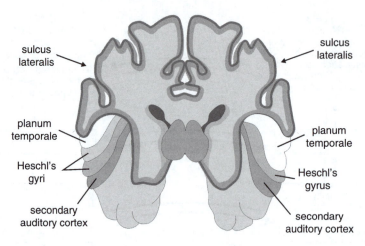

Figure 4.28 Position of Wernicke's motor speech area (planum temporale) in the left hemisphere (left side of picture = left hemisphere).

abilities, which are basically innate, identify humans as essentially comparable to each other and as different from animals, which lack the prerequisites for language and speech acquisition, even though there are exceptions, such as the ability to imitate human sounds in some bird species. This, however, has nothing to do with understanding speech and the meaningful use of the different sounds of real speech.

The Broca hypothesis predicts that in this one speech area the programs for the formation of speech sounds are stored. Speech is produced when these programs activate the adjacent convolution, the gyrus praecentralis, which controls the muscles of the face and the oral cavity. The ability to understand speech is the work of Wernicke's area which is situated in the uppermost and hindmost part of the left temporal lobe, directly behind the auditory cortex, which is generally involved in processing acoustic signals (Ojemann, 1998).

The innate predisposition of the left hemisphere for speech is most clearly found in the planum temporale, which is the essential area for understanding speech. It forms a broad triangle of tissue on the border between the temporal and parietal lobes, and it includes Wernicke's area (see Figure 4.28). In almost all humans at the time of birth, the planum temporale is more strongly developed on the left side of the brain than on the right. The right side, on the other hand, appears to be more involved in the perception and production of speech melody. It is also assumed that it is, above all, the right hemisphere that is activated when emotions are recognized in the verbal expressions of another person (Ojemann, 1998), inasmuch as it is far more involved on the whole in the processing of emotions than the left.

Early, "classical" neuropsychology was strongly interested in making statements on the functions of brain areas in healthy individuals by studying patients with discrete damage in those areas. But when drawing such conclusions in that way, Chow's warnings (1967) still hold. First, if a lesion in some brain region has no particular effect on a task or function, it cannot be concluded that this region is irrelevant to the task or function in undamaged, healthy persons. Second, if a lesion in some brain region does influence the performance of a task, this does not mean that that region is the only neuronal structure involved in the task. Finally – and this is perhaps the most important argument – ablation as a method (meaning in animals destroying or removing the brain tissue) cannot clarify the search for the function of a brain area because it destroys what it has set out to study, namely that area of brain.

But we can still maintain that damage to Broca's area leads to a syndrome called "motor aphasia" or "Broca's aphasia". Patients with this aphasia understand both written and spoken speech, and while their own speech preserves meaning for the most part, it is noticeably slow, effortful, replete with short phrases, and poorly articulated. Such patients make extensive use of nouns and avoid more complex grammatical expressions. If only Broca's area is damaged, the deficits are frequently only temporary, so that patients can reacquire their previous speech capacities. Larger damage, however, extending beyond Broca's immediate area, often leads to chronic speech disturbance.

Discrete lesions to Broca's area cause deficits that are less serious than when Wernicke's area has been affected. Aphasia in this case is primarily receptive in nature: The patients seem to be incapable of understanding either the spoken or the written language. Interestingly, they have no difficulty in producing speech, but what they say usually has no comprehensible meaning. They use incorrect words that may only resemble real words based superficially on similarities of sound, or they produce a series of their own word creations. At the same time, their speech can still demonstrate the structure, rhythm and intonation of real speech (Ojemann, 1998).

The classic description of aphasia, which we just outlined above, attributes motor speech production to Broca's area, and speech reception to Wernicke's area. But as we have already alluded to, this classification has now been called into question. Apparently, the two areas distinguish language according to semantics on the one hand and according to syntax on the other hand. Broca's area is particularly active in grammatical processing, and Wernicke's area is active "when it is important to understand the meaning of words. For example, Broca's area is activated when a person taking part in an experiment has to compare two different sentences each with the exact same meaning, but differing in word order, that is, differing in their syntactical structure" (Eliot, 2001, p. 512). Patients with damage to Broca's area are not impaired in the production of speech per se, which Broca had assumed, but rather in their sense of grammar. Their effortful speech and their short bursts of real speech are then the result of their difficulty in conjugating verbs and using articles or adjectives such as "the", "a" and "any" or prepositions such as "from" and "to" in the correct context. "Persons with these deficits are nonetheless fully capable of understanding speech, because verbs as carriers of the meaning are in fact less necessary. As an example, every inhabitant in the Western world can fully understand the following, 'verb-less' series of words: I . . . lunch . . . McDonald's . . . Big Mac . . . French fries . . . Cola. Aphasic patients whose Wernicke's area has been damaged have far greater difficulties. They have preserved their knowledge of the rules for joining words one after the other, that is, the conjugation of verbs, the use of prepositions and conjunctions, but in their impaired mental dictionary there are simply not enough words left over for them to say (or understand) something meaningful" (Eliot, 2001, p. 513).

Development of the speech areas in the brain

The specialization of the left hemisphere for language is already established well before birth (Eliot, 2001).[3] Genetically determined speech deficits can have their origin in the embryonic stage although they do not appear until long after birth (Trevarthen, 1998). Events that occur during the early development of the brain also have a strong effect on later speech acquisition.

Unexpectedly, however, speech is not localized in the child before the sixth year of life in the same brain areas as in the adult; the neuroanatomical speech regions in infants are thus not just an immature form of the speech areas in adults, but something basically different. They have to go through several developmental stages before reaching this adult level (Nobre & Plunkett, 1997; Trevarthen, 1998). Although the planum temporale, the neural correlate of speech lateralization, already demonstrates a distinct asymmetry in favor of the left hemisphere at birth, the brain of the infant and young child, up to the age of 2 years, does not show a left hemispheric dominancy in processing and producing language (Nobre & Plunkett, 1997). At first, the right hemisphere is more strongly developed than the left, and electrophysiological studies on the brain have consistently shown stronger activity during speech processing in the right hemisphere than in the left up to about the age of 2 years (Chiron et al., 1997). One possible explanation for this stronger right hemispheric activation persisting to the age of 2 was given by Trevarthen (1998): The right hemisphere is more involved in processing prosodic characteristics (such as speech melody, intonation, rhythm) and the emotional elements that play a larger role for children at that age than the meaning does.

This lack of lateralization in speech up to the age of 2 can be seen in a number of studies on children who were examined after suffering lesions in the left hemisphere (e.g., Hertz-Pannier et al., 2002; Vargha-Khadem et al.,

---

3 This corresponds to the phylogenetic development as well, as could be demonstrated in the brains of the great apes (Hopkins, Marino, Rilling, & McGregor, 1998; Marshall, 2000; compare Box 3.1).

1991). The majority of children who have sustained damage to the left hemisphere at a very early age or whose left hemisphere had to be surgically removed for medical reasons in fact show normal speech development. But the later the damage or surgical intervention occurs, the greater are the speech defects that ensue. Children with damage to their left hemisphere before their second year of life usually show a relatively good recovery in speech abilities (Liégeois et al., 2004; Vargha-Khadem et al., 1991, 2003). However, under more detailed study, they frequently show subtle deficits of grammar in active speech (Aram, Ekelman, Rose, & Whitaker, 1985; Trevarthen, 1998). These results may have to be relativized, as they were usually published after studying patients with serious cases of epilepsy or with congenital unilateral brain damage (Bernasconi et al., 2000; Duchowny, 2004; Empelen, Jennekens-Schinkel, Buskens, Helders, & van Nieuwenhuizen, 2004; Kossoff, Buck, & Freeman, 2002; Leonhardt et al., 2001). Because of the very early age at which the brain damage occurred, the other, healthy, hemisphere developed compensatory functions very early as well.

Phenomena of plasticity (see Box 4.6, pp. 94ff.), such as those naturally occurring during maturing, and environmental influences play a particularly important role in the development of speech and language abilities. After early damage to the left side, the brain regions involved in speech processing and active speech develop in the right hemisphere (Ojemann, 1998; Vargha-Khadem et al., 1991). The capacity of the brain to recover certain functions after damage is dependent on its neuronal plasticity, that is, on its ability to change itself, adapt itself, in interaction with the environment. An essential prerequisite for neuronal plasticity is the degree of density of direct neural contacts – that is, the synapses – during the first years of life. In the frontal lobe, which is intrinsically involved in speech production, synaptic density is very high up to the seventh year of life and only decreases gradually after that time. By the time of adolescence, the number of synapses has been reduced to a level that remains relatively constant into old age (Huttenlocher, 1994; Huttenlocher & Dabholkar, 1997).

The high degree of plasticity of the brain during the first 7 years of life is one prerequisite for learning language in normal, healthy development, and this holds true for the mother tongue as well as any foreign language learned later (Newport, 1990). The number of synaptic connections has decisive influence on how changeable our brain is. Until the age of 6 or 7 years, the number of such sites is very high and the brain is thus in the best position to acquire language, especially the rules of grammar. As of adolescence, the ability to learn basic rules of grammar decreases successively, and by early adulthood the number of synapses has decreased so that learning a new language, especially one with a completely new kind of grammar, is possible only with difficulty (Eliot, 2001, p. 518). As in the development of visual abilities, there is a time window in which external stimuli can have strong effects on the brain and so form it, but if the stimulation is lacking during this time, the brain ceases to be capable of normal development, and deficits result that are lasting, from then onward, as the case of "wild children" shows (Eliot, 2001, p. 516). "The connectivity necessary for normal speech to occur develops regularly and remains functional only if the child is confronted with the consistent combination of the sounds, meaning and the grammar of a particular language during the sensitive period" (Eliot, 2001, p. 515).

As speech acquisition progresses through early childhood, areas in the left hemisphere assume the speech-relevant functions (Nobre & Plunkett, 1997; Trevarthen, 1998). An increase in dendritic sprouting occurs in Broca's area between 18 and 36 months, at the same time when the first combinations of syllables and words appear (Trevarthen, 1998). It is generally assumed that Wernicke's area and the other, more posterior speech regions have developed before that. The number of synapses in the border region of the left-sided temporal and parietal lobes (the site of Wernicke's area) reaches the maximum between the eighth and the 20th month of life, whereas Broca's area does not reach this expansion until between the 15th and the 24th. Similarly, Broca's area is not completely myelinated until well after Wernicke's area. At the age of 2 years, myelin can already be demonstrated in all the cortical layers of Wernicke's area, whereas Broca's area does not reach this status until 4 or 6 years (Gibson, 1991). Measuring brain activity with the EEG, Mills and coworkers (1991) found that a switch occurs in the localization of areas relevant to comprehension of speech in children 20 months old from the right to the left hemisphere.

While the rules of syntax are gradually being learned, axonal connections increase at the age of 2–5 years between the left-sided frontal lobe (site of Broca's area) and the border region of the left-sided temporal and parietal lobes (the site of Wernicke's area) (Eliot, 2001, p. 515; Trevarthen, 1998). At the age of 5 years, when the basic elements of speech have been successfully acquired, we find only a few additional changes in the brain. As of this age, speech production and comprehension in by far the majority of cases are controlled by areas in the left hemisphere (Trevarthen, 1998).

In summary, we can conclude that the brain experiences considerable changes during early childhood as far as speech development is concerned. At first, it is the right hemisphere which is more active than the left in both speech production and comprehension. In the course of further development of speech abilities, increasingly more speech-relevant areas evolve in the left hemisphere, until speech is almost exclusively localized there, and the right hemisphere is only concerned with the processing of prosody and the emotional characteristics of language. Yet, in spite of this early work showing that the right hemisphere has a predominant and more active role in speech, at least initially, most research today concludes that the left hemisphere nonetheless has a genetic predisposition to speech, as indicated by the congenital asymmetry of the planum temporale as well as the subtle speech deficits found after left-hemispheric damage in early childhood.

Processes of maturation in the brain: prerequisites for the origin and consolidation of memory

The development of speech can be viewed as one of the most important prerequisites for higher forms of memory to evolve at all and then to become consolidated (compare Figure 4.11, p. 69). Inasmuch as we are accustomed to giving names to the whole world of living and nonliving objects around us and to communicating from birth onward by means of different kinds of sounds (including crying and laughing), preserving or "anchoring" our environment with the help of verbal expressions is a standard characteristic of our intellect. Tulving (1995, 2002, 2005; Tulving & Markowitsch, 1998), relying on the earlier work of others, especially Katherine Nelson (Nelson, 1973, 1974, 1989, 1993, 1996, 2002; Nelson, Monk, Lin, & Carver, 2000; Nelson & Fivush, 2004; Nelson et al., 2002), assumes that the development and differentiation of memory systems take place in a hierarchical manner. Initially, motor acts that are subject to voluntary control (such as grasping and holding objects) are imprinted into procedural memory, which develops early. Subsequently, priming memory develops, which encompasses the quicker, longer-lasting and more reliable recognition of stimuli. Following this stage, percepts (such as the faces of one's mother, father, brothers or sisters) are learned on a presemantic level. The semantically organized memory (the system of knowledge) requires still more time to develop and is only possible when the acquisition of words is functioning. Because the main speech centers develop only very slowly over long periods of time (due to the processes discussed above such as myelinization), functional determination, the ability to anchor words in memory, or generate and acquire them remains in an instable condition for a considerable time, well into late childhood. It is no wonder, then, that we usually do not retain any episodes which we experienced at that early age (compare Chapter 7, "Theory of mind: psychological understanding", pp. 175ff.).

It cannot be emphasized too often how important our inner state, our momentary as well as our longer-lasting condition, is for our ability to remember. This is not only apparent in the mnestic blocks described in Box 4.6, but it is also clearly at work in all situations. Although we are not conscious of it in everyday life, we are subject to false memories, memory distortions, and other factors with detrimental influence on our memory. Conscious, reliable remembering is no longer possible (1) when considerable time has elapsed between the moment a childhood experience took place and the moment we remember it (as is the case not just with some, but with all memories from our childhood), and (2) when the physical state of the brain at the two different times differs substantially. But, interestingly, just the opposite can be the case, too. When the present state of the brain and memory approximates that of an earlier, more immature, condition, episodes that have never been recalled until a much later phase in life can well be remembered again (see Figure 4.13, p. 71).

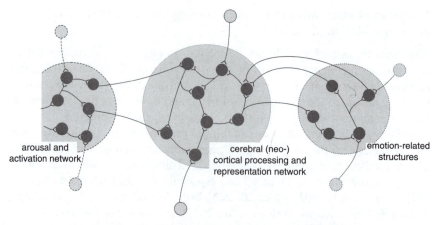

arousal and activation network

cerebral (neo-) cortical processing and representation network

emotion-related structures

Figure 4.29 To obtain an integrated representation and an integrated recall of the autobiographical contents of our memory, it is necessary for several different networks in the brain to interact simultaneously. One network, responsible for general alertness and the disposition for reacting, is mainly under control of the brainstem; another one, containing the cognitive attributes of memory, is localized in the neocortex; and one network of structures is responsible for emotional evaluation.

The important prerequisite for autobiographical memories is the simultaneous confluence of cognition and emotion. The child has to go through the steps of collecting new impressions, learning to control motor abilities, evaluating the newly acquired information, and, importantly, relating that information to his or her own person and comparing it over time. The intersection between subjective time, autonoetic consciousness, and the individual self experiencing itself are basic elements, according to Tulving (2005), for a definition of episodic-autobiographical memory. The child has to be capable of experiencing its own self with a past and a limited future; it has to realize that it is independent of a mother or any other persons in its own world, and it has to be capable, furthermore, of observing itself, so as to understand the meaning of "sun returns after the rain". Children can store memories so as to *basically* recall them as their own experiences, but only after they have learned to reflect on emotions, to fit them into a temporal pattern ("I won't always be sad"), and to distinguish acts with a primarily emotional background from those motivated by rational-cognitive reasons. These will make up memories that are *basically* recallable for the simple reason that there is no guarantee of any kind of identical and reliable recall the next time it occurs. This is weakened by both the dependency of memory on its state at any one moment and the experience parents have when recalling the development of their own child: A 4-year-old can recall experiences of the previous year while at the more advanced age of 6 years, the same child will have forgotten what occurred at the age of 3. Memories fade because we ourselves change. And precisely because children change so much more rapidly than adults, their autobiographical memories fade more rapidly as well, unless they are stored and recalled again and again, and are thus reintroduced to the cycle of remembering, with all the new connotations of time, place and persons.

We rarely experience a discrepancy between cognitive and affective characteristics in our memories. But this can be the case, and in a very dramatic way, in patients suffering from so-called dissociative amnesia (compare Box 4.6). These patients preserve their memory of general knowledge rather well while memory of their own personal past is extinguished. This is assumed to be due to a dissociation, a separation of the emotional and the cognitive-rational elements in the contents of autobiographical memories (compare Box 4.1 and Box 4.2), which makes an integrative and simultaneous recall of the two different kinds of elements impossible. This can advance so far as to cause a total breakdown of the personality structure in many cases, so that a person's own identity is in fact "forgotten" (Markowitsch, 2000a) (Figure 4.29).

The various reports on patients with dissociative amnesia (Markowitsch et al., 1997a, 1997b, 1998, 1999b; Markowitsch et al., 2000) clearly demonstrate how important it is that processes of maturation be successfully completed for the development of autobiographical memory. Problems in childhood in the form of psychic stress and traumatic experiences induce a "biological wound" at the level of the brain, making it all the more susceptible to stress as a consequence. The injury disrupts the normal transfer functions for autobiographical content, possibly blocks these functions completely, and shifts the balance of transmitter substances so as to become pathological (Fujiwara & Markowitsch, 2003; Markowitsch, 2001a). Recent research in animals and humans emphasizes the essential role of a qualitative mother–child interaction in early childhood for adequate development of emotional and cognitive aspects of behavior, and shows that stressful experiences in early life can result in lifelong problems (De Bellis & Keshavan, 2003; De Bellis & Thomas, 2003). In fact, such negative experiences lead to a reduction in structural plasticity (compare Box 4.6) in such brain regions as the hippocampus, which consequently is no longer capable of reacting adequately to stress in later life (Mirescu, Peters, & Gould, 2004).

Work on another group of neurological patients has offered some corroboration of this line of argumentation, that is, patients with Urbach–Wiethe disease, who have a direct, genetic defect in the area of the amygdala and, as a result, cannot synchronize affect and cognition (see the detailed account of the disease in Box 4.1). These two groups of patients, one with neurological brain damage and the other with dissociative memory disturbance, both highlight the relevance of adequate brain development in childhood and adolescence for molding and stabilizing autobiographical memory. They furthermore emphasize the importance of coordinating influences from the external environment with those of the internal environment of the brain (the neuronal processes of maturation) for learning and then maintaining certain abilities. Recent results have indicated that processes of maturation within the brain establish the basic prerequisites for a person to be able to relate to his or her environment, and that such a qualitative communication

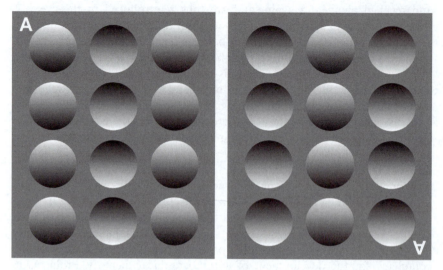

Figure 4.30 Illusion: rotating the figure 180° makes the convex rows look concave, and the concave rows look convex. This is due to the fact that we are accustomed to thinking of light as coming from above us and thus interpret shadows on rounded surfaces as being below our viewpoint.

between a person and the environment itself helps to form and maintain connections in the brain ("commuication tracks") (M. H. Johnson, 2001, 2003; S. P. Johnson, 2003). During times of practice or the very first experiences with a completely new behavior, an "epicenter" of activity can arise within the brain, which may change to another area once the activity has become routine work (compare Figure 1 in M. H. Johnson, 2003). This can be shown for rather simple tasks such as solving the easier algebraic equations (Qin et al., 2004) as well as for complex behaviors such as empathy or psychological understanding (Saxe, Carey, & Kanwisher, 2004). On the other hand, however, negative experience leaves an equally long-lasting trace on the body and mind: it constitutes a "memory of the body" (Bauer, 2002).

Priming versus consciousness: how modifiable are we?

The fact that autobiographical memory is encased within a context ("context encasement") is not in any way identical to the context-related acquisition of information. In context-encasement, the person has conscious thoughts about his or her own existence, relationship to the environment, and well-being, while the acquisition of information is much less concerned with self-reflection or making something fully conscious and can occur, in extreme cases, completely unconsciously. Only recently have systematic investigations taken place on the influence that our knowledge, our memories, our preconceptions, and the context of external stimuli have on our perceptions. Convincing somebody that the letter X is in reality a U might seem like an exceptional case, but examples that were previously known only to a few

17

P 13 E

12

Figure 4.31 The symbol in the middle is read either as *B* or as *13*, depending on
whether it is first read horizontally (together with *P* and *E*), or vertically
(with *17* and *12*).

experts in the field of perceptual psychology are now regularly commented
on in the science sections of daily and weekly newspapers (see Figures 4.30
and 4.31).

Even a glance at the history of literature shows an awareness of our ability
to be fooled by the context of things. Shakespeare (in Act V of *A Midsummer
Night's Dream*), says, "in the night, imagining some fear, / How easy is a bush
suppos'd a bear!" Advertisements make use of the lasting effects of emotional associations by showing, for example, automobile tires together with
women in erotic clothing. And scientific investigations have shown, on a
somewhat abstract level, that we can make quite different decisions or have
very different opinions depending on the context of the situations we are in.
A good example is the "Labov illusion": Depending on the context, the same
object can be taken first as a bowl and then as a vase. If potatoes make up the
contents, even a long, narrow container can be interpreted as a bowl, whereas
if flowers are the contents, even the flatter, shorter container can be seen as a
vase (Figure 4.32).

Brain research and the cognitive sciences both concur with the observation
that humans are most easily manipulated when they are already motivated and
committed to a specific goal (when, for example, they are already in search of
something, or have built up an expectation). If the final result fails to fit the
goal, then the "next best fit" can become an alternative ("the desire has to be
crowned with some deed or other, there has to be a satisfactory result somewhere"). Psychologists refer to the "Zeigarnik effect" in this respect: A person
wants to conclude things he or she has already begun, and has the tendency to
forget rather quickly what has in fact been successfully completed.

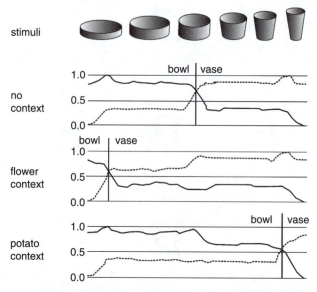

Figure 4.32 The so-called Labov illusion. Depending on the context (in this case, whether flowers or potatoes make up the contents), the stimuli on top (different-sized containers) will be interpreted as either a bowl or a vase.

Referring back to the brain, it is primarily the frontal lobes (or some of their parts) that motivate such behavior (see Figure 4.1, p. 53). These lobes belong to the most recent developments in the mammal brain and only attained their full size and level of performance in humans (see Figure 3.11, p. 43), and for these reasons their relevance to our cognitive, social, and emotional behavior is of a high order and will also be formed and re-formed by suitable stimulation from the environment throughout the whole course of life. Every "normal human" will have temporary phases of reduced insight and self-control, or, vice versa, of increased suggestibility. Simple lack of sleep or an increase in distractibility – through, for example, problems at work or in the home – can raise the susceptibility to external stimuli and thus influence further behavior. But even in situations in which we believe that we are free of such influences, we are still subject to a variety of external influences or contextual encasements, but because we experience this process gradually and continuously we fail to notice it, as a rule (Markowitsch, 2004a, 2004b, 2004c).

However, this means that much of what we learn is only partially conscious to us at all and as a consequence is largely unavailable to episodic memory. It is processed instead in priming memory, which, though it developed much earlier in life, is still functioning in advanced age. In the long run, in the house of the brain and memory, we are still only partially the master.

Section III

Autobiographical memory: a lifelong developmental task

5 Development of learning and memory: the prenatal period and the first months of life

Prenatal and transnatal development of memory: earliest forms of learning

The moment of birth (Boksa & El-Khodor, 2003) and some few years afterwards are not the only periods that are important for a healthy cognitive-emotional development – even before the moment of birth there are forms of imprinting through the environment that set the stage for a child's developing a greater or lesser degree of sensitivity. The mother–child symbiosis, extending as it does from the early fetal period through the first years of life, is the most decisive determinant for stable development of the child and has an extraordinary importance, on the one hand, for avoiding developmental disorders as well as psychopathological conditions and, on the other hand, for the nervous system to mature successfully (Cirulli et al., 2003).

The simplest forms of learning can already be demonstrated in planarian flatworms and are well developed in earthworms (Dahl, 1922), as well as in preparations of the spinal cord in mammals, all of which show habituation and sensitization (compare Box 4.4). And these forms of learning also function in a human fetus within the womb. Habituation (similar to familiarization or acclimation) means the gradual adaptation to a repetitive stimulus. The first reaction to a particular stimulus, such as a sound, a touch or an odor, is slowly decreased after several repetitions. Apparently, the stimulus leaves a representation of itself in memory, which is then compared to the stimulus each time it is presented again. If the internal representation and the stimulus are congruent, as is the case with a direct repetition, then the stimulus is recognized as something known, and the reaction to it this time is reduced or even fully extinguished.

Habituation occurs completely without involving consciousness. Recognition of a particular stimulus configuration only expresses itself in a change in the physical reaction to the stimulus, without the individual person becoming aware of this process at all. As mature organisms we only realize that we are accustomed to the stimulus when it suddenly fails to occur or when its physical characteristics up to now, such as loudness, pitch or duration, suddenly become markedly different, and in that case we become "dishabituated".

From the viewpoint of biological evolution, habituation has an adaptive character in that it enables the organism to differentiate between new, and thus potentially dangerous stimuli, and older ones that have already been experienced, and then to adopt the appropriate reaction. This differentiating takes place within the space of a few seconds, without any cognitive evaluation of the stimuli having to occur first. Thus, through habituation, an organism can move about in the environment without necessarily deciding explicitly for every event whether it is a threat and how to react to it. Moreover, habituation makes it possible to ignore repetitive and non-threatening stimuli – such as the heartbeat of the mother. Habituation is therefore an instrument of survival, and constitutes the first form of memory. Long before consciousness develops, this form of learning and memory puts an organism in the position to distinguish important stimuli from the unimportant ones.

Habitual learning does not require an advanced brain. Much of what we know today about the neuronal mechanisms involved in habituation was discovered by working on the simple sea slug (*Aplysia*), which is only 40 cm long and weighs approximately 500 g (see, for example, Kandel et al., 2000, pp. 1248ff.). Even simple organisms and sections of a nervous system (such as the spinal cord) of higher animals are capable of demonstrating habituation behavior, and this fits the finding that habitual learning is regulated by those parts of the neural tube which are the first to develop ontogenetically, the spinal cord and the brainstem (compare Figures 4.21 and 4.24, pp. 84 and 87; in the bottom of Figure 4.24 the brainstem encompasses all brain parts behind the lower end of the diencephalon: the midbrain or mesencephalon, rhombencephalon (with the pons, cerebellum) and the medulla oblongata). The brainstem is particularly important for regulating and controlling such vital functions as breathing and heartbeat.

The considerable improvement in habitual learning during the last weeks of pregnancy is probably the result of an accelerated maturation of the brainstem, which can be seen in, first, the rapid increase in the number of synaptic contacts toward the end of pregnancy, and, second, in the continued progress in isolating more and more axons that have myelin sheaths, making a more rapid transfer of information possible. Studies on fetuses have shown how important an intact nervous system is for habitual learning. Fetal brains that have been damaged as a result of a lack of oxygen, genetic anomalies, or other prenatal disturbances, need essentially more repetitions of the same stimulus in order to show an effect of habituation. This effect can be applied clinically to determine whether a newborn child is neurologically healthy.

The developmental processes with particular relevance to memory include those which improve information transfer in the brain, such as insulating nerve cells with myelin, which develops early, but which is not concluded in individual brain regions until the third decade of life. Two additional processes are the formation of points of contact between nerve cells (synapses; see Figure 4.16, p. 77) and the following activity-dependent task of eliminating these synapses (pruning; see Box 4.5). The formation of synapses (synaptogenesis; see Box 4.5) has already begun before birth and continues up to 2 years postnatally, peaking at 15,000 synapses per second for each neuron (Huttenlocher, 1990). Synapses rapidly develop in different regions of the brain. Those regions which are already functional at a very early age are also the first to exhibit a high number of synaptic terminals. For this reason, it is assumed that there is a close association between the density of synapses and the time at which particular abilities, such as memory or language, first function (Webb, Monk, & Nelson, 2001, p. 155). Interestingly, during infancy and early childhood, the cortex produces almost twice as many synapses as will actually be needed later. Excess synapses are reduced in the course of development, so that only those terminals that are in fact required for use remain and become consolidated. We will return to this topic later when treating sensitive phases in development.

Infants can retain "memories" of sensual experiences which they had pre-natally. A number of studies have shown that, because hearing is almost fully developed as of the 27th week of gestation, it is particularly the voice of a child's mother that is remembered after birth. But tastes, rhythms, etc., are also remembered transnatally. Transnatal memory therefore already locates elements which have a degree of familiarity in the totally unknown extrauter-ine situation, thus making it possible for emotional bonds to be established at a very early time. Newborn children, for example, can distinguish the voice of their own mothers from those of other women (DeCasper & Fifer, 1980), and sounds such as the beat of the heart or other bodily sounds that a child experienced during gestation can have a relaxing effect on the baby postnatally (e.g., Salk, 1962).

Newborns recognize more than sounds: they are capable of remembering prosodic elements, the rhythm and intonation of their mother's language, as has been demonstrated in studies in which women repeatedly read a story or a poem out loud during the last weeks of pregnancy. When the babies then heard the same or different material later after birth, they reacted to the "familiar" story or poem, with its admittedly very complex stimuli, in ways clearly distinguishable from their reaction to the "unfamiliar" material (DeCasper & Spence, 1986). It can be assumed that a form of early connecti-vity plays a role here, which will be important for the later development of speech ability.

At any rate, the experiential world of the neonate is strongly influenced by the abilities to hear, taste and smell, and experiences of smell and taste are in addition strongly associated with emotions. An unpleasant odor or taste arouses reactions of aversion and disgust, while smelling or tasting something pleasant can arouse a feeling of well-being. One difference between sounds or pictures, on the one hand, and odors, on the other, is that smells are mainly processed in the emotional centers of the brain, and the specific emotional connotation associated with odors is given by the amygdala, among other areas (see Box 4.1, p. 57, and Figure 4.4, p. 56). The amygdala is closely con-nected with the autonomic nervous system, that is, with that part of the

Box 5.1   Brain structures of unconscious learning: basal ganglia and unimodal cortex

The brain of an infant contains subcortical regions which, already firmly interconnected and developed, are traditionally classified with the extrapyramidal motor system, and which have sensory processing structures as well as extensions into the cortex (see Figure 4.21). Within the extrapyramidal motor system, there are nuclei, from the medulla oblongata and up to the largest nuclei in the telencephalon (the basal ganglia), which control large portions of our voluntary motor activity. Earlier, these structures were considered relevant to the precise coordination of movements, while today they are increasingly associated with the control of behavior within the procedural memory system. Controlling movements in their correct sequence and synchronizing those which involve different parts of the body (from single fingers to arms, legs and trunk as a unit) are the work of the basal ganglia, parts of the cerebellum, and specific areas of the cortex that are situated at the transition between the motor cortex (which develops very early) and the adjacent premotor-prefrontal areas. This is the area in which the so-called frontal eye field is found, an area which plays a decisive role in the motor control of eye movements and which, in concert with a number of small nuclei in the brainstem, enables us to observe the environment even when we are strongly confined in our movements otherwise, as when a baby is so cramped in bed that it can hardly move at all. In view of the facts that infants already demonstrate the ability to imitate other persons and that movement gives them obvious pleasure, coordination by means of the various synchronous activities of the extrapyramidal system can be seen as a basic requirement for procedural memory.

Relevant to this topic is the observation that, both phylogenetically and ontogenetically, the maturation of sensory systems proceeds "from multimodality to unimodality". For the frog and the human infant, it is not so important which sense is mainly being activated as that a sensory stimulation of any kind at all is being given. This is why we have two visual systems: one that develops only rather late and is responsible for object recognition (and is thus called the "what system") – the retino-geniculo-striatal system (which extends from the eyes, through the thalamic lateral geniculate nucleus to the primary visual cortex or area striata; compare Figure 4.6, p. 62, and Figure 4.7, p. 63), and another one, the more primitive extra-geniculo-striatal system (which extends from the eyes into the colliculus superior in the mesencephalon), which could be called the "where system". The colliculi process information from different sensory systems, but in a somewhat general or cursory manner, so that rapid movements are coordinated. Thus, a chameleon protrudes its tongue if a small object appears, such as a fly, but ducks if something much larger flies into view, such as an eagle.

An infant reacts analogously. Small stimuli in the environment are attractive, while large ones are frightening. The first cases of conditioning in a person's life succeed due to this system, as well as the first attempts at coping with these demands. Events take place, and reactions are performed, but without any relevance being attached to the specific details. In fact, the details cannot even be identified. The meaning of this extra-geniculo-striatal system is referred to again and again to explain cases of "blindsight". Patients who are blind due to damage to their visual cortex in both hemispheres, as a result of, say, an infarct, are still capable of associating some simple stimuli in the environment within three-dimensional space, without their being aware where this ability or "revelation" comes from. When such patients are placed in front of a screen and are shown spots of light every so often, with the instruction to point at the position of these spots, many patients succeed at the task astonishingly well, although they cannot explain the ability. In fact, they are not even aware that they have such an ability. It is assumed that the visual system in the mesencephalon functions subconsciously and accurately takes in stimuli and processes them; but because this system, as opposed to the cortex, only fashions subconscious connections and associations with the stimuli, the patients never become aware of their knowledge and think they are merely guessing at the answers. Infants perform in the same way, without any conscious realization of their performance or their environmental associations.

nervous system which controls the internal processes of the body. Strong emotions lead to strong changes in the autonomic system: for example, the heart might beat faster, the hands might tremble, or sweating can become profuse (see Figure 4.5, p. 57). Such physiological reactions to an external stimulus are then evaluated and interpreted by the centers processing emotions, and in this way the feeling of fear can arise. At the time of birth, the emotions of the infant are still completely under the control of the amygdala (Schore, 2001, p. 24). Higher centers, which are involved in the evaluation and control of emotions, have a slower course of development and do not become functional until the seventh month of life. In the early stage of development, odors are particularly processed by nuclei within the amygdala, and specifically by those in the right hemisphere (Schore, 2001, p. 24). The right half of the brain controls a large proportion of functions in the first 3 years of life, while the left side of the brain goes through a somewhat retarded course of development and only assumes its – as of then lifelong – dominant role as of the third year of life (Chiron et al., 1997; Markowitsch, 1998/99). It is not only in the perception of odors but also in the memory of prenatal experiences of odors that nuclei in the amygdala play the relevant role.

Memory during the first months of life

In a way, transnatal memory permits a moderate transition from fetal existence to extrauterine life, and, in addition, it seems essential for establishing a successful early bond with the mother. It constitutes the matrix in which postnatal experiences can be arranged. This concerns mainly the functioning of implicit memory. Nothing we experience at this early age is available to us later; it just cannot be remembered. This is the result of the fact that the phylogenetically older brain regions exert control over memory during the first months of life, while conscious active remembering is a function of cortical areas. In view of this background, a number of obscure techniques appear to be but wishful thinking when, as with "rebirthing" in the Church of Scientology, they purport to make a person's "experience of birth" relivable again. At the start of life, human memory is comparable to that of simple mammals: its contents cannot be verbalized and express themselves exclusively on the level of activity, and thus we can talk of "experiential memory" (Nelson, 1996, p. 154).

Figure 4.10 (in Chapter 4, p. 67) shows the differentiation of memory into a short-term and a long-term component, and Figure 4.11 (p. 69) shows how long-term memory can be further divided into five subsystems. These memory systems can be distinguished partly by the kind of information that they process, and partly by the particular brain structures capable of such processing. As we already indicated at the end of Chapter 4, procedural memory is initially the predominant form of memory: An infant learns new information mainly through motor patterns of activity and simple associations of stimuli. Priming and presemantic perceptual memory develop almost in parallel to procedural memory. At this time, infants find it increasingly easy to recognize persons, places and objects they already know, even though they still cannot place them into a space-time context and thus do not know where and when they first experienced the people or objects. The knowledge system and episodic memory are the last forms to arise, whereby episodic memory goes through a notably slow development, well after all the other forms are functioning.

Procedural memory

The essence of procedural memory has been aptly captured in a Swahili saying: "Mautie moset kolany ketit" (a monkey never unlearns how to climb a tree). A basal form of learning within procedural memory is seen when two stimuli are associated with one another instead of together; this is termed "classical conditioning" (see Box 4.4 and Figures 4.8 and 4.9, pp. 66 and 67).

Somewhat simplified, classical conditioning can be viewed as experiential learning. Memory preserves pleasant and unpleasant experiences with a particular stimulus, and this stimulus is in future associated with the experience (Lipsitt, 1990).

In the tradition of Pavlov's work (see Box 4.4), the first studies on classical conditioning in infants were undertaken in Russia. They supported the rather pessimistic suppositions of Russian brain research that the cerebrum of a neonate is too undeveloped to permit any form of learning and that neonates are consequently not conditionable. Not until the middle of the twentieth century did researchers gradually withdraw from this position, when it became apparent that the process of conditioning was under the control of mainly subcortical structures and thus did not require a highly advanced cerebrum (compare Lipsitt, 1990). In addition, a series of studies clearly demonstrated experiential learning in neonates with the help of the eyelid reflex. This reflex can be evoked by directing a slight stream of air at the eyeball. This is an unconditional stimulus that always evokes the same reaction: closing the eye. The conditional stimulus, such as a sound, is then presented immediately prior to the unconditional one again and again so that an association is established between the sound and the reflex and, as a result, the infant closes his or her eye as soon as the sound is heard.

As with most forms of memory, experiential learning improves over the course of development of an infant. As the child gets older, fewer and fewer numbers of trials are needed to learn a new stimulus association and it remains longer in memory (Lipsitt, 1990). Some studies have demonstrated that conditioning of the eyelid reflex is mostly dependent on the cerebellum, a brain structure that is functional at a very early stage (Kim & Thompson, 1997) and that it, in fact, can be evoked even in amnesic and demented patients (Gabrieli et al., 1995; Schugens & Daum, 1999; Woodruff-Pak, Romano, & Papka, 1996), while other studies have reported finding deficits in learning the eyelid reflex in these patients, especially when conditioning took place over longer periods of delay (McGlinchey-Berroth, Brawn, & Disterhoft, 1999; McGlinchey-Berroth et al., 1995; McGlinchey-Berroth, Carrillo, Gabrieli, Brawn, & Distehoft, 1997).

Another form of early learning is learning through reward or punishment, or operant conditioning (see Box 4.4). This form of learning has considerable relevance to the ability to adapt to the environment because learning which consequences follow which actions allows the child to gradually build up an adequate repertoire of behavior. Actions that, for example, better serve adapting to the environment are rewarded (sucking reduces the feeling of hunger; smiling is rewarded with a positive reaction from caregivers) and dangerous behaviors are punished (touching a hotplate causes pain). In this way, children will repeat and also improve on adaptive behaviors, while avoiding unsuited ones, as soon as they learn that such actions lead to negative consequences.

The most frequently used method for studying operant conditioning in

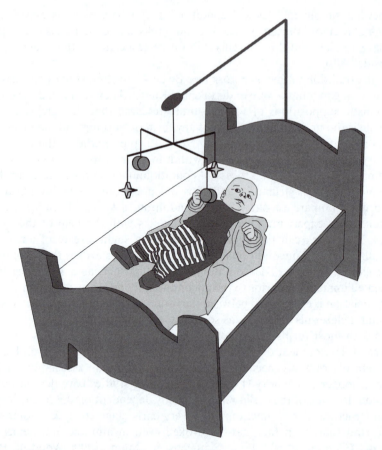

Figure 5.1 Example of "mobile conditioning", a frequent and widespread form of
        learning.

infants is conditioning with the help of a mobile. Such studies usually consist
of a learning phase and then a test phase (see Figure 5.1). For the learning
phase, a mobile with different colored objects is hung up over the infant's
bed, and then a cord is affixed to the child's ankle and the cross-bar of the
mobile, so that any movement of the leg can make the mobile move, too.
Infants at the age of 3 months learn the association between leg and mobile
movements very quickly. After some time they start kicking their leg
intensely, more so than up to that moment. By then, they have learned that
they can influence the movement of the mobile with their own movements
(Rovee-Collier, 1997; Rovee-Collier & Hayne, 1987, 2001).

The sudden appearance of such intense, deliberate leg movements provokes
an old question that has yet to be answered unequivocally, that is, whether or
not (or under which circumstances) learning conforms to a gradual process or
an all-or-nothing process (see Figure 5.2). It is frequently assumed that we
learn information piece by piece and that would mean we do it slowly and

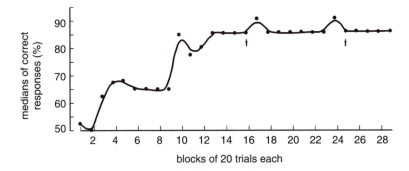

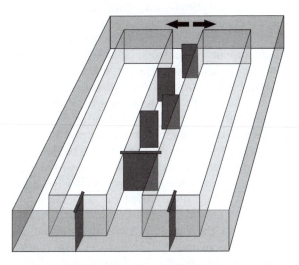

Figure 5.2 Example of a typical learning curve, which shows success in doing a task, given as the average or (as in the figure) the median values for several different animals (guinea pigs) in a longer course of training day by day. By averaging the success for each day, the strong impression is gained that the animals improve their learning rate slowly and continuously. The task here was to learn that, after leaving the starting area at the front and going toward the back in the labyrinth (a so-called T-labyrinth), the animal was to choose just the opposite side of the T into which it had gone at the last trial. In the figure, the animals first stay in the starting area, being prevented from leaving by barriers. As soon as the "guillotine" door in the middle of the passageway is lifted, the animals can enter the corridor and, if they then choose the correct side of the T, and circle back to the front, they receive a food pellet as reward. The middle passageway has several half-barriers to avoid kinesthetic strategies ("body or gut memory") helping the animal in learning (from Kessler et al., 1980).

gradually. The alternative view is that of "eureka learning", whereby a flash of insight, the ingenious solution, just suddenly pops into our mind, and we now understand "everything", whereas a moment before we were completely ignorant of the truth. This kind of learning does occur, for example in solving mathematical problems, where a person can suddenly see the solution needed or understands the meaning of a rule or law of mathematics. Inasmuch as the majority of studies on operant conditioning require a large number of trials and the success in learning is averaged over several different individuals, it is quite possible that learning in such cases appears to be but a gradual progression in information acquisition whereas, in reality, each individual realizes the correct solution in a sudden flash of insight, and only makes a few accidental mistakes as of then. As far as infants are concerned, it would of course be quite exciting to find out whether in such an experimental design they arrive at their understanding spontaneously, or whether they learn more by just trying, like animals, that is, whether, in mobile conditioning, they simply move around and then by accident discover that there is a connection between their activity and that of the mobile.

How long, then, can a 3-month-old infant remember the association between leg and mobile movements, once it has been learned? In the test phase, the mobile is kept out of sight for a certain delay and is then reintroduced, but this time without the cord so that any leg movements fail to have an effect on the mobile and rewards are completely absent. Typically, when, after a successful learning phase, infants see the mobile after a pause of a week's time, they start kicking their legs intensely. A 6-month-old infant can remember how to get the mobile moving after a pause of 2 weeks. The older the infants get, the longer they can remember how to manipulate the mobile, but, what is more, they get better and better at transferring what they learned to new situations. A 6-month-old infant will start kicking its legs even when the mobile has been altered in the meantime, that is, even if it does not correspond exactly to the one seen while the association was first being learned. Three-month-old infants fail to react even one day after the first training if more than one element has been exchanged for another (Rovee-Collier, Hayne, & Colombo, 2000). Older infants react less sensitively when their bed is placed in a different room for doing the memory test. While 3-month-olds react to the sight of the mobile with kicking only when they are in the same room as during the learning phase, changing the environment scarcely has any effect on the memory performance in older infants. We can easily hypothesize that the younger ones have integrated more details from both the mobile and the environment in the memory trace and thus react so sensitively after any alterations.

Again and again it has been shown that younger infants are rather more context-dependent and perform less generalizingly than the older ones. Analogous behavior – the high relevancy of the particular setup of stimuli in the spatial environment of the labyrinth – can be seen in rats learning tasks in complex six-armed or even eight-armed labyrinths. In this respect, it is interesting to note that it is precisely that structure which seems so essential for episodic memory – the hippocampus – that originally coded for spatial information (Gilbert, Kesner, & DeCoteau, 1998), and this can be seen in the existence of dedicated place cells (Hollup, Molden, Donnett, Moser, &

Moser, 2001; Olton, Branch, & Best, 1978) as well as in the deficits in performing spatial tasks in patients with hippocampal damage (Kessels, de Haan, Kappelle, & Potsma, 2001; Luzzi, Di Bella, & Piccirilli, 2000). These findings have induced some researchers to try to unite spatial and episodic memory under one common category (Rolls, Stringer, & Trappenberg, 2002). Phylogenetically, memory of olfactory stimuli played a significant role in the development of memory at all in mammals, whereas insects such as bees, with their dance as a form of bodily speech, show the great importance of having a good memory for places in social communication (Menzel, Brandt, Gumbert, Komischke, & Kunze, 2000; Menzel & Giurfa, 2001).

There are good arguments for thinking that older infants also store spatial information, but that they actively overlook it. If they are presented with a new mobile, as long as their memory of the older one is still fresh, they react as if it were the original one. But when the time between learning phase and memory test becomes longer and longer, their performance becomes all the weaker if, instead of the original mobile, a new one is shown to them. When their memory of the original learning situation becomes weaker, they need more memory aids in the form of visual details (color and shape of the mobile, the look of the immediate environment) to reactivate the memory (Rovee-Collier, 1997; Rovee-Collier et al., 2000).

As mentioned above in relation to the eyelid reflex (Kim & Thompson, 1997), classic and operant conditioning are mainly controlled by a phylogenetically old brain region, which, very much different from the cerebrum, is already relatively well developed in even primitive mammals: the cerebellum (see Figure 5.3); this makes up only 10 percent of the whole brain mass but

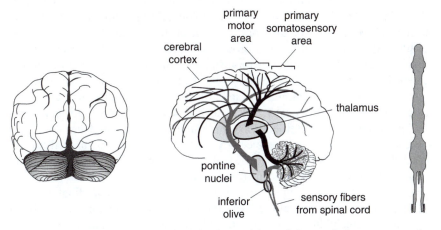

Figure 5.3 The cerebellum. On the left, the position of the cerebellum seen on the back of the brain. In the middle, schematic representation of the main connections from and to the cerebellum. On the right, view of the total surface of the cerebellum; unfolded, it would stretch to about 1.5 meters in length.

contains more than half of all the nerve cells. The cerebellum plays a role particularly in the precise control of movement. It integrates information (coming from motor areas in the cerebrum) on movements which have been planned with information (originating in the spinal cord and organs of balance) about movements already being conducted. Patients with damage to their cerebellum are no longer capable of precisely balancing the strength, speed and amplitude of their individual movements or adapting them all to changing conditions. They have difficulty in preserving a constant position (such as standing straight), and attempts to do so often bring on bouts of strong tremors. In addition, the ability is lost to associate several stimuli with each other, already indicating that patients with such damage are not conditionable at all or only in a rudimentary way.

A significant portion of all learning processes that take place in the first months of life concerns motor abilities and thus almost always involves the cerebellum. And this region plays a special role in the fine control of movements. Without an adequately functioning cerebellum, the infant would be unable to pick up and hold objects so precisely with the thumb and index finger. The gradual improvement in controlling movements that, up to then, were very uncoordinated depends largely on the cerebellum, which functions as a command center for all movements taking place at any moment and which, when necessary, can introduce corrections in performance. Because this region is so essential for the motor development of infants, it is already relatively advanced at a very early age. At birth, it already belongs to those regions with the highest energy requirements in the brain, an indication that here new synapses to other regions are being formed at a remarkable rate. In addition, its axons start developing their insulating myelin sheaths even before birth, and this process is fully completed by the third month of life (Chugani & Phelps, 1986; Gibson, 1991). The improvement in memory performance, both in classical and operant conditioning, in the course of the first months of life is the result of this rapid process of development, which establishes a much better path of communication between the neuronal structures in the cerebellum. And precisely because of its strict architectonic uniformity, this part of the brain more resembles the hard disk of a computer than any other single region. In 1967, Eccles, Ito, and Szentagothai realized this similarity and published a book entitled *The Cerebellum as a Neuronal Machine*.

Operant conditioning is subject to control, however, not only from the cerebellum, but also from a series of subcortical nuclei called the basal ganglia, which play a significant role in initiating movements. Their damage leads to strong deficits in voluntary motor abilities. A coordinated chain of motions such as speaking, walking or shaking someone else's hand become extremely difficult for persons whose basal ganglia, as in the case of Parkinson's disease, do not function normally. Their movements are frequently disturbed by an uncontrollable trembling, by sudden jerking movements, or by just the opposite, a rigidity that is extremely difficult to overcome voluntarily. The basal ganglia are just as important for learning a whole series of coordinated movements as the cerebellum is, and they are likewise developed at a similarly early age. Insulation of their axons with myelin begins in the fifth month of pregnancy and is almost completed by the eighth month after birth (Gibson, 1991; Hasegawa et al., 1992). In addition, a sudden increase in the number of synaptic connections can be seen between the third and the fifth postnatal months of life.

At the start of life, memory is closely linked to body experiences, and thus the contents of procedural memory are often called "bodily" or proprioceptive memories. Learning takes place mainly through movements and through pleasant and unpleasant sensations. The experiential world of the infant is, as we have already pointed out, especially influenced by odors, sounds and tactile sensations. A considerable number of early sensations are made through the skin: children sense things very intensely when they are being touched, rubbed or tickled. Skin contact in infants evokes pleasant sensations, and, as a rule, they try to maintain as much contact with the mother as possible (Harlow & Zimmermann, 1959). Odors as well as sounds and tactile sensations are stimuli from the external world and give essential information to the infant about that world. At the same time, the brain is processing a series of interoceptive stimuli, that is, stimuli which give information about the infant's own body.

The neonate already has a well-developed depth sensitivity, meaning the ability to perceive motions and position of the different parts of the body, a perception which is made possible by sensory receptors in both the muscles and the joints. Most persons know very well where their right hand is in three-dimensional space even when they keep their eyes closed while they continuously move their arms around. The basis of this knowledge is information which comes from within one's own body. Importantly, without such interoception, motor learning would be impossible. Depth sensitivity is a basic requirement for all forms of procedural learning, and there are several indications that neonates are already capable of effectively processing signals from within their bodies. The nerves that conduct information to the cortex as to movement in and position of the different body parts initiate myelinization prenatally, and at the time of birth, they are completely insulated with myelin (Yakovlev & Lecours, 1967). The cerebrum processes this information in a specific area, designated as the somatosensory cortex. It is only in this area that a well-developed metabolic activity can be demonstrated already at the time of birth, although the rest of the cortex is still underdeveloped (Chugani, 1994; Chugani et al., 1987).

Priming as a form of memory

Priming is a subconscious form of memory in which stimuli are recognized more quickly, better or sooner because they resemble or are identical to ones presented earlier. Priming permits the reactivation of subconscious, hidden material from memory, or maintains it in memory over long periods of time.

In this way, babies can retain the association between kicking movements and the movements of a mobile for an astonishingly long time, as long as their memory is "refreshed" every so often in the meantime. To reactivate this material from their memory, some aspect of the original learning situation has to be presented to the infants again for 2 or 3 minutes, but at a time when they have basically already "forgotten" the association. For example, the person conducting such an investigation could move the mobile while the children are watching, or for a short time they are placed in a bed in which the sides are covered with the same material that the original bed had in the training phase. After 24 hours the infants are tested. Two-month-old infants usually no longer kick intensely when they have not seen the mobile for only 1 or 2 days after training, but even after a pause of 5½ months they do remember the association if in the meantime their memories were refreshed once every 3 weeks (Rovee-Collier, 1999; Rovee-Collier & Hartshorn, 1999; Rovee-Collier & Hayne, 2001). However, the content of these memories can only be refreshed if and when the original stimuli of the learning experience are reused. If the mobile is changed somehow or even if the material on the sides of the bed only has a different color, the infant fails to show any kicking reaction to the mobile.

The priming form of memory has proven to be very robust in the face of brain damage. Amnesic patients who have considerable difficulty in freely recalling a list of words they have once learned show a quite unexpected good performance when they are shown parts of the same words, of only three letters, and are then asked to reproduce the word from the list they learned beforehand, such as remembering "balcony" after seeing just "bal" (Cramon, Markowitsch, & Schuri, 1993; Markowitsch, Cramon, & Schuri, 1993). They have no conscious remembrance of the words they learned, and are hardly capable of naming even just one word from the list, when asked to do so. Still, the words are stored somewhere in memory and the memory is successfully reactivated as soon as only a part of the word is given to them. Interestingly, if they were asked whether the words they have just completed appear familiar to them for any particular reason, they would definitely deny this. The infant, too, has no conscious remembrance of the mobile, but the picture and the associated learning experience are stored and are activated as soon as only some aspect of the learning situation (the so-called "prime") is presented again.

Almost all forms of learning in early infancy, both classical and operant conditioning and priming, have one thing in common: they belong to implicit memory. Implicit memory processes all abilities, habits and learned reactions that we gain through experience but that are for the most part subconscious. Implicit memory, in addition, is relatively stable when the brain is damaged. First, the contents are maintained over long periods of time and, second, even massive brain damage rarely causes a complete loss in this form of memory. Patients who have had an accident causing serious deficits in memory can generally form simple stimulus associations; they also preserve motor abilities such as swimming or bicycle riding, and learn through trial and error. The reason for this lies in the brain structures that participate in implicit memory. They are all situated outside the limbic system (see Figure 4.4, p. 56), the region which is essentially responsible for conscious memory. If this region is damaged, the memory deficits which ensue are those we see in amnesics.

Perceptual memory

For a considerably long time, researchers in this field assumed that during the first months of life infants are capable of only those forms of learning classified as belonging to implicit memory (Nadel & Zola-Morgan, 1984; Schacter & Moscovitch, 1984). It was assumed that the brain, little developed as it was at that age, could only permit such "primitive" memory activity as is seen in patients who are incapable of forming any kind of conscious memories, including both classical and operant conditioning and priming. The successful coordination between structures of the limbic system and the neocortex is essential for the development of conscious memories.

In relation to the limbic system, there is a form of division of labor or specialization in the sense that individual structures within the system process more the affective aspects of information, and others are more involved in the cognitive-rational aspects. The amygdala, for example, is involved in the evaluation of stimuli (this, interestingly, is frequently already established at a very early age) (see Figure 4.5, p. 57), and the hippocampus is involved in novel aspects of the stimuli and generally in the integration of space-time information as well as in transmission of newly learned material into long-term memory (see Boxes 4.1 and 4.2). In animals, the hippocampus is particularly involved in integrating the spatial aspects of stimuli, whereas in humans the emphasis is on the chronological aspects. The concept of a quasi-phylogenetic "functional shift" in the region of the hippocampus has arisen due to this slight change in functions.

Persons who, as a result of an accident have damage to parts of the limbic system in both hemispheres, can remember new information for only a very short period of time. Everything that takes place after the accident is lost to memory. In the case of severe amnesia, events and the persons involved in them are forgotten within a few minutes. Even personally known people and places are not recognized, or cannot be placed into properly situative context or a frame of reference. On the other hand, however, memories of life before the accident are generally intact. It is not unusual for an amnesic patient to fail to remember a conversation he or she has taken part in just a few minutes before but to give a detailed account of experiences from school days (Markowitsch et al., 1993; Markowitsch, 2002a).

Investigations on amnesic patients have thus shown that the limbic system is mainly responsible when new memories are formed. It would be reasonable to assume that the inability to remember events from the earliest months and years of life is the result of the limbic system not being sufficiently developed at that period (Nadel & Zola-Morgan, 1984; Schacter & Moscovitch, 1984). Experiences at that time, it could be assumed, fail to be remembered because the limbic system is not yet sufficiently developed to enable a lasting storage of memories to take place. However, the main problem with this assumption is the fact that infants at a very early age already show good performance in memory tests that apparently require an intact limbic system (see particularly the discussion on "Processes of maturation in the brain: prerequisites for the origin and consolidation of memory", in Chapter 4).

With advancing age, an infant needs less and less time in order to remember a new, unfamiliar stimulus and, further, to recognize it for longer periods of time. At the age of 3 days, an infant has to view a new stimulus over a period of many seconds or even minutes in order to establish a memory of it, and even then, after a pause of but a few minutes, the memory has been lost and the infant cannot recognize it (Pascalis & de Schonen, 1994). But at the age of 6 months, babies need only a few seconds to remember a new stimulus and in some cases they can remember it even after a pause of 2 weeks. In comparison, amnesic patients with damage to the limbic system show poorer performance in these tests than the 3-day-old infants. The adult patients usually have already forgotten the stimulus after only 2 minutes, and show no signs of recognition whatsoever (McKee & Squire, 1993).

As the term already implies, perceptual memory is dependent on perception. Tests of recognition most frequently involve the visual system, because sight plays such a dominant role in humans. When an infant has to observe stimuli for a longer length of time in order to remember them, and then seems to have forgotten them a short time later, this is definitely related to the fact that the sense of sight itself is hardly well developed yet at that age. The development of perceptual memory and that of vision go hand in hand. In the first few months of life, infants' perceptions of their environment are only very indistinct. Then, as of the sixth month, all the different qualities of primary vision (such as depth perception, color vision, acuity and fixation) are fully developed, meaning that infants are now perceiving the environment in basically the same way as adults who need glasses but are not wearing them at the moment.

To a considerable extent, improvement in acuity during the first months depends on changes in the optical characteristics of the eye and of the photo-receptors in the retina. Compared to later, the eye of an infant is shorter and the pupil is smaller, and thus any image covers a much smaller area on the retina (see Figure 5.4, p. 129; compare also Figures 4.6 and 4.7, pp. 62 and 63) (Daw, 1996). In addition, photoreceptors in the fovea (the area with the sharpest vision) are larger than in adults (6 µm, compared with the 1.9 µm in adults), and are positioned farther apart, meaning that infants are not capable of resolving an image sufficiently that is projected onto their retina. Until the fourth month of life, the photoreceptors continually change their shape (Yuodelis & Hendrickson, 1986).

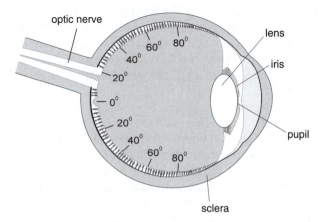

Figure 5.4 A section through the human eye showing the pupil, which, in infants, is relatively smaller in comparison to total eye size in adults. The diameter in the eye of children is also relatively smaller compared to that of adults. The photoreceptors are all located together with the other nerve cells as a lining along the inner surface of the back of the eye. The fovea (an indentation of the optic nerve at 0°) forms the area of sharpest sight, containing color-sensitive photoreceptors (cones) without any of the color-insensitive rods.

If visual perception were only dependent on the morphological characteristics of the eye, then, at the age of 4 months an infant would see, at least theoretically, as well as an adult. But the eye only takes in visual information, whereas the actual "image" is a function of other structures within the brain. There, the relevant developmental processes take place that allow us to see the environment three-dimensionally and in color. During the first 6 months of life, the number of synaptic contacts in the visual cortex increases 10-fold, although this in fact entails more than will later be preserved (Huttenlocher & deCourten, 1987). The brain, it could be said, is equipped with a surplus of neuronal hardware, and requires experience to discard the excess synapses, which in the long run is a far more economic way of eliminating the cells than if a genetic code had to be set up by natural processes to determine beforehand the exact form of connectivity between literally millions of nerve cells. Thus, in the visual system, as well as others, we can observe an experience-dependent selection of surplus synapses. In the early 1960s, two neurobiologists (and later Nobel Prize laureates), David Hubel and Torsten Wiese, prevented cats and monkeys from having any visual sensations whatsoever from birth by surgically stitching their eyelids. This total stimulus withdrawal led to profound changes not only in the structure of the visual cortex but also in its function. The brain needs stimulation so as to form and consolidate synaptic contacts, with the consequence that if stimulation fails to occur, faulty connections occur, and this can lead to serious deficits in function. Thus, phases in which the numbers of synapses increase rapidly or, vice versa, in which they are discarded, make the brain particularly sensitive to environ-mental influences. If the brain is not sufficiently stimulated during such "time windows", certain functions such as vision and speech cannot develop along normal lines. For this reason, we talk about "sensitive phases" (compare Box 4.5), and for the sense of sight this phase in humans extends from the fourth month up to the sixth year.

The experience-dependent selection of synaptic connections and the con-comitant stabilization and differentiation of neuronal circuits in the visual system bring about a gradual improvement in visual performance. The most significant jump in visual development, however, takes place during the first 6 months of life, and the most significant progress in perceptual memory takes place at this same time, as well. The experiential world of the infant becomes more and more dominated by visual information the more the visual capacity improves. It becomes essential for the infant to organize all these impressions of the outside world, meaning that he or she must recognize them when they reappear. Recognition presupposes that information on the object in question has been stored for a certain amount of time in memory and can then be recalled. The limbic system plays the main role here; however, in humans, no other sensory system has so many different areas of represen-tation in the cortex and so many different and large nerve pathways for visual information to reach central areas within the brain and from there the cere-bral cortex. A characteristic of these pathways is the combination of both parallel and sequential connectivity (Pritzel et al., 2003; see Figure 5.5).

Among the structures in the limbic system there are some which develop relatively early while others develop only much later. One of these is the hippo-campus, which makes considerable developmental progress within the first 9 months of life but which nonetheless does not attain its final state until much later. It grows very quickly within these first 9 months after birth, with the individual nerve cells increasing both in size and in the numbers of connec-tions to other cells, so that a more and more effective level of communication between them is made possible. In addition, the insulation of the axon sheaths improves steadily up to the age of 9 months, so that information transfer between the cells becomes all the more rapid (Arnold & Trojanowski, 1996).

It is this developmental process in the hippocampus which most probably accounts for the fact that perceptual memory improves so markedly as of the sixth month of life and that infants can recognize visual stimuli even after several weeks. Once the visual system becomes this far advanced, an infant experiences a veritable flood of new visual impressions which are stored more or less permanently in the limbic system. This means that the hippocampus is now being highly stimulated and such stimulation effects a further, rapid growth in the neural network. But, still, we cannot refer to a fully matured hippocampus until the age of 3–4 years. In one particular segment of the hippocampus, the gyrus dentatus, new neurons still develop throughout the first year, and the final synaptic density is only complete between the third and fourth years (Nelson, 1998, p. 62).

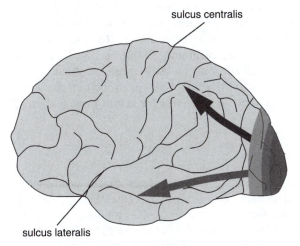

sulcus centralis

sulcus lateralis

Figure 5.5 Lateral view of the human brain, showing the two main projections within the visual system from the primary visual cortex at the occipital pole to the anterior regions. The so-called ventral projection extends to the anterior areas of the temporal lobe and is "responsible" for all activity connected with object recognition, including recognition of faces (the projection for "what" something is). The dorsal projection is involved in all activity subserving spatial information and localizing objects (the projection for "where" something is).

Interestingly, the hippocampus requires a relatively long period for development, not only to attain the final state of maturity of its individual cells, but also to reach an effective degree of communication with other areas of the limbic system. The axons of the fornix, the largest tract in the limbic system, which connects the hippocampus with the other limbic structures, are still very poorly myelinated at birth. Adequate insulation only starts as of the sixth month and continues well into late childhood (Brody et al., 1987; Yakovlev & Lecours, 1967).

It must be emphasized, however, that no single brain structure functions alone and independent of others (compare the remarks of Chow, 1967, in our Chapter 4, under "Development and localization of speech"). For this important reason, a so-called "disconnection syndrome" can very well lead to the loss of a function simply because the connections become interrupted or blocked. For perceptual memory, the connections between limbic structures (hippocampus) and the cortical areas for perception (visual cortex and visual association cortex) in particular are essential for processing perceptual memory (Adair et al., 1997; Hof, Vogt, Bouras, & Morrison, 1997), and this is thus similarly the case for episodic memory (Shastri, 2002).

In spite of the long-protracted development of some of its individual areas, the limbic system already makes a certain level in memory performance possible at a very early age, and this would be thoroughly impossible without a certain degree of communication taking place between the individual structures, something which presumes a minimal level of functional maturity. Examples of such early performance can be seen in acts of recognition and, as we will see later, in delayed imitation. Recognition is a form of passive memory and, in the case of infants, is not necessarily a conscious process. The conscious recall of facts or past events – which is what we usually mean when we refer to "remembering" or explicit memory – develops at the earliest in late infancy and requires the entire period of childhood for full development.

Working memory

A major turning point in memory development is brought about by the appearance of the first *active* forms of remembering. As opposed to mere recognition, this form of memory involves a conscious process, which most children initiate by the age of 8 or 9 months. This system, which forms the basis of all active remembering, is referred to as working memory and frequently, though inexactly, as short-term memory. Short-term memory properly only designates a person's ability to hold information "online" for a short time span after having been exposed to the information (Cowan, 2000), whereas working memory refers to actively processing this informa- tion on several levels in its various components together with other information that has already been stored, and then to transferring all of this material into a temporally limited storage site, for the sake of later recall (Baddeley, 2002).

Working memory occupies a unique position compared to all other mem- ory systems. First, the amount of information that can be stored here is limited, and second, this information is rapidly lost if it is not repeated and thus transferred to long-term storage. We make use of our working memory when looking up, for example, a telephone number which we keep in mind only long enough to dial it. If we do not repeat the number a few times beforehand, we usually forget it within less than a minute.

With the development of working memory, children are finally able for the first time to form mental images of objects and persons for short times and recall them actively. As a result, they understand that objects continue to exist when they are not physically present. Jean Piaget coined the term "object permanence". The child thus begins to realize that things in the immediate surroundings have an existence of their own, independent of whether the child directs his or her attention to it at all. Consequently, these surroundings can be represented mentally better and better and the child in turn can coordinate its behavior according to mental images. At this age, children stop crying out of frustration when they cannot see a toy hidden from view, and instead start actively looking for it.

Storing, preserving and then recalling a mental image are, just like behavioral control, performed mainly under the influence of the frontal lobe. The dorsolateral area of the prefrontal cortex, situated in the anterior region

Box 5.2 Brain structures relevant to working memory: dorsolateral prefrontal cortex and associated areas

Functions of working memory can be observed in the lower mammals, although the diversification within the working memory seen in adult humans is far more complex than that seen in babies or other mammals. As we describe in Box 6.2, testing for short-term memory and working memory traditionally makes use of certain learning tasks that require remembering whole motor sequences (such as, "After seeing the stimulus on the left, wait 7 seconds, and then head down the left passageway, or else after every trial down any one passage, take the other passageway not chosen in the previous trial"). Studies on animals have shown that several regions of the brain are relevant to functions of working memory. In humans, however, one region seems to play a dominant role, the dorsolateral prefrontal cortex (see Figure 5.6, p. 134). Phylogenetically, this region matures earlier than the companion area, which is situated immediately inferiorly, the orbitofrontal cortex (see Figure 5.6). This is related to the fact that the orbitofrontal cortex is more strongly involved in social functions that require interaction with other persons over many years. Nonetheless, working memory only starts to function after (1) a child has learned to diversify and to coordinate his or her functions of attention (sustained, selective and shared attention and vigilance) and (2) the process of myelinization (see Box 4.5) in this area has advanced far enough to allow rapid connections with posterior cortical structures. Of course, in this case, too, just as with the procedures which function unconsciously in the procedural memory system, subcortical structures, the basal ganglia, play a particularly relevant role by coordinating components between (cortical) sensory and motor areas (compare Figure 4.27, p. 99).

Working memory denotes the ability to hold information online for a short time so as to then subject it to further processing, either reproducing it in the form of recall or encoding and storing it long-term. Correspondingly, nerve cells have to perform synchronous activity within an extremely limited space (the dorsolateral prefrontal cortex) and at the same time establish connections to other brain regions. Myelinization is thus once again a prerequisite for establishing synchronized activities. At the age of 1 year, the brain of children already has sufficient neural connectivity to maintain conscious representations of several stimuli for a short time.

of the frontal lobe, is particularly involved in working memory, while in behavioral control further prefrontal cortical areas are engaged as well (Figure 5.6; see also Figure 4.1, p. 53). Interestingly, the age at which object permanence first occurs coincides with a strong surge in the growth of the dorsolateral prefrontal cortex. Between the eighth and twelfth months of life, we also see the first signs of a metabolic activity that will increase up to the fourth year. This increase is related to a massive growth in the number of dendrites and synapses during the same period of time. Initially, the performance ability of the dorsolateral prefrontal cortex is considerably limited. When a small toy has been hidden under a cup, an 8-month-old child can only remember for 2–5 seconds under just which one it can be found, whereas a 12-month-old remembers this twice as long, namely up to 10 seconds (Goldman-Rakic, 1987, p. 615). Working memory is also involved

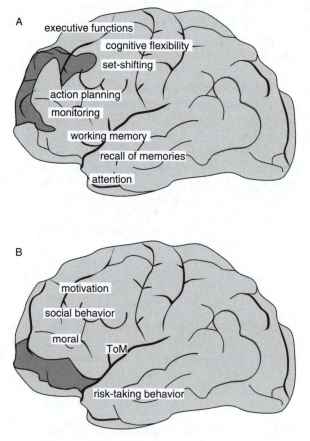

Figure 5.6 Lateral view of the human brain. Panel A sets off (in dark coloring) the position of the dorsolateral cortex. B sets off that of the orbitofrontal cortex. Both panels designate the functions attributed to the different areas. ToM: theory of mind.

in strategies of encoding and recall, which are based mainly on experience and go through a long period of development extending into adolescence. Within the whole of the prefrontal cortex, we see use-dependent selection of synaptic connections and the concomitant restructuring of neuronal connectivity patterns even up to the age of 16 years (Huttenlocher & Dabholkar, 1997). The gradual refinement of synaptic connections in the prefrontal cortex coincides with the development of a whole series of memory-relevant functions.

Contemporaneously with object permanence, the child gradually develops a genuine bond to another person, a caregiver, and starts reacting to strangers with "stranger anxiety". This indicates a considerable jump in emotional development and is probably due to rapid advances in the functionality of the prefrontal cortex. The gyrus orbitofrontalis, an area within the prefrontal cortex, is part of the (extended) limbic system (Nauta, 1979; Nieuwenhuys, 1996) and is decisively involved in processing emotions. Slowly, through the years of development, emotional information comes under increasing control from cortical areas, that is, children gradually become more aware of their own emotions. They now experience the emotions that up to then only gave them a signal (for something else happening within them) and that were visible to others only in some physical expression. When the frontal lobe continues to develop, we see the first signs of behavioral suppression, that is, children now demonstrate the ability to control their feelings and activities (Schore, 2001). However, at the age of 8 months, this ability is still very underdeveloped and only substantially progresses in the following years when the frontal lobe slowly matures.

An important developmental advance can be seen when a child starts to

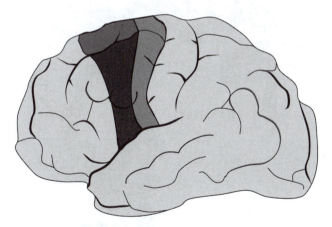

Figure 5.7 Position of the primary motor cortex (light gray) and of the premotor cortex (the two darker gray areas) in a lateral view of the cerebral cortex. Both the primary motor and the premotor cortices extend for a few centimeters over their border on the uppermost part of the brain onto the internal surface.

crawl, which usually occurs around the eighth month. Crawling is a comparatively independent form of exploring the world and the environment, and the relatively complex series of movements necessary for such exploration requires a certain level of maturity in the most important motor centers: the primary motor and the premotor cortex (see Figure 5.7).

The primary motor cortex, situated in the posterior part of the frontal lobe, controls all voluntary movements. Each point along this cortex controls the movements of a certain group of muscles (see the "homunculus" in Figure 5.8) and receives feedback on these movements and the position of the joints from the somatosensory cortex. The tracts and nerves of the primary motor cortex initiate their myelinization at the time of birth and do not complete this process until the end of the second year.

Myelinization in the premotor cortex requires an even more extended length of time. This area is essential for planning motor sequences. Myelin cannot be found in the area until the sixth month, and several years are needed until the axons are completely insulated (Eliot, 2001, p. 388). This slow development in the premotor cortex explains why children need such a long time to perform tasks which require "complex planning strategies" such as drawing a circle, or sitting on a tricycle while pedaling and steering at the same time (Eliot, 2001, p. 388).

Figure 5.8 The so-called homunculus: the representation of the different regions of the body on the surface of the brain in the motor cortex.

The plan for conducting a certain movement arises in the premotor cortex, whereas the primary motor cortex then takes charge of the control of the movement moment by moment and gives commands for executing the movement to the individual body muscles. Generally, these commands project down the most important descending pathway of the motor cortex, the tractus corticospinalis or pyramidal tract. The insulation of this important tract with myelin begins prenatally and continues to the end of the second year. The maturation of this tract is seen as primarily responsible for the development of the ability to bring the movement of the limbs under increasing control of the cortex, so that an infant slowly becomes capable of coordinated, purposeful sequences of movements, such as crawling (Konner, 1991). The primary motor cortex gives commands to the muscles through the pyramidal tract, but the program for this movement has to be decided at some other, higher level. The cerebellum and the basal ganglia are likewise involved in planning movements; their role in procedural memory has already been discussed above. The subcortical centers for planning movements are connected with the motor areas of the cerebral cortex by two large loops and thus have a major influence on every single movement. It is assumed that a sequence of movements such as crawling and, later, walking is primarily under the control of the motor cortex in initial phases, but that, once they have been successfully learned and have become automatic, they are increasingly under the control of subcortical structures,

As we have already pointed out, the age of 8 months marks a milestone, in the emotional, the cognitive, and the motor development of a child. Once a child has the ability to move around independently of the mother, a strong emotional bond to the mother becomes a necessity, as only such a bond can guarantee some protection for the defenceless child whenever it goes off a bit from her immediate vicinity. One element that, among others, prepares the child for such a close bond is the sense of object permanence, which enables a child to understand that the mother does in fact continue to exist even when she is not physically present at any one moment. The development of memory thus cannot be properly understood in isolation, without taking into consideration progress in other important abilities that are influenced by developments in memory and also in various other behavioral domains of human life.

The development of a system of knowledge and the early precursors of episodic memory

The active recall of the contents of memory is what makes conscious remembering possible at all. Before the time of active recall, remembering only occurs in the form of an unconscious series of movements, or it is coupled to the presence of specific environmental stimuli. When working memory has finally developed, remembering enters the phase of a conscious process. However, this form of memory is nonetheless an exceptional case within the different memory systems. Its contents, namely, can be lost in a matter of seconds. When do children start forming long-lasting memories that can be actively recalled later?

The metabolic activity in the prefrontal cortex increases strongly at the end of the first year, and this is related to an accelerated growth in dendrites and synapses in the area. This metabolic situation leads to a corresponding improvement in functional abilities in the dorsolateral prefrontal cortex and thus in working memory and active recall. An 8-month-old child can, for example, remember where a toy has been hidden from view at the most for 5 seconds, while a 12-month-old child already maintains this information for 10 seconds (Goldman-Rakic, 1987, p. 615). When children have a memory task to perform that does not rely solely on observing something, but also includes procedural activity, their memories in fact last longer, but, interestingly, over several years this increase is merely linear. Testing memory in such cases traditionally makes use of the "train task", whereby children have to learn to press a lever in order to set a small train in motion. The results of this task and similar ones in age-related improvement in memory span have been reviewed by Rovee-Collier and coworkers (2001, p. 112), and are shown in Table 5.1.

The overview shows a rather slow improvement in long-term memory in children up to the age of a year and a half, which is certainly related to the continued growth and maturation in the frontal lobe, hippocampus and additional structures in the limbic system.

Tasks of "delayed imitation" can be used to determine the level of development in children. The tasks are characterized by somewhat complex requirements for memory performance. They call for a series of motions to be seen by a child, without having the opportunity to imitate them immediately. That comes after a certain delay. In this way, it can be determined how long an infant can maintain the series in his or her memory and then recall them actively.

During the 1990s, it was assumed that children could not succeed at such tasks until the ninth month, that is, that they would not remember the series of motions which they have observed and then finally imitate them before they reached 9 months of age. More recent studies, however, have demonstrated that children at the age of 6 months are already capable of

Table 5.1 Memory rate as a function of age
(Rovee-Collier & Hayne, 2001, p. 112)

Age	Memory
6 months	2 weeks
9 months	6 weeks
12 months	8 weeks
15 months	10 weeks
18 months	13 weeks

imitating a series after a delay. The memory spans reported in the studies vary, however, from study to study: Barr, Dowden, and Hayne (1996) and Hayne, Boniface, and Barr (2000) reported a memory span of 24 hours, whereas Barr and Vieira (1999) reported a delayed imitation even after 14 days.[1]

As of 6 months at the latest, children can retain a series of events in memory over a certain length of time – and this span of time increases with advancing age. In the view of Nelson (1996; Nelson & Fivush, 2004), forgetting can be called functional, insomuch as in normal, everyday life only the repetition of the contents of memory determines their significance. If episodes are repeated – for example, the exact course of events connected with the evening bath or with eating – infants form scripts or "mental event representations" (Nelson, 1996) that enable them to get along in their daily life. Episodes which fail to be repeated are forgotten because they have no practical significance for daily living.

It is generally accepted that explicit memory plays a role whenever children can imitate a series of actions after a certain delay if these actions have been presented to them only once before. Delayed imitation is thus considered an indication for whether explicit or declarative memory is already functioning. Nonetheless, according to Nelson and Fivush (2004), there is still debate as to whether the phenomenon of delayed imitation is associated with semantic memory (that is, with general knowledge of facts and motor acts; see Figure 4.11, p. 69) or rather, already, with episodic memory. "Thus, deferred imitation studies have documented a clear move to declarative (or explicit) memory skill by about 1 year but have not provided evidence of the beginnings of autobiographical memory" (Nelson & Fivush, 2004, p. 492).

In reality, however, imitation does not constitute proof of the functioning of episodic memory. It is perhaps more the case that the objects infants see simply place an exceptionally high demand on their attention at an age when their processes of inhibition are still very underdeveloped at the level of the brain. There is also debate on the extent to which an infant remembers an experience in a laboratory or rather only remembers what is expected about how to treat certain objects. It is also possible that infants do not imitate a particular set of actions because they remember the specific situation in its matrix in time and three-dimensional space, but simply because they much more remember, perceptually, procedurally and semantically, just how the objects can be treated which were already once presented to them (compare Chapter 4 on the different systems of memory and the corresponding Figure 4.11, p. 69). The ability of delayed imitation can probably be better described therefore as an

---

1 According to Rovee-Collier and Hayne (2001, p. 114f.) the study by Barr, Dowden, and Hayne (1996) also showed that quite frequently inadequate tasks were in reality the reason for assuming that delayed imitation could not be seen in infants. The study showed that 6-month-old children could imitate a series of motions (a glove is taken off a doll's hand, the doll is then shaken, a bell is rung, and the glove is put back on the doll's hand) even after a delay of 24 hours, but only if the demonstration phase lasted at least 60 seconds. The children were not capable of remembering the motions when the demonstrations only took 30 seconds.

indication that a system of knowledge or semantic memory has slowly developed, rather than as an early hint of the functioning of episodic memory, as suggested by some researchers (e.g., Bauer & Wewerka, 1995).

A further argument for this view is the idea that in the final analysis we are probably treating a form of emulation learning, that is, learning which is targeted on the result and not on the strategy with which it is performed (Tomasello, 2002). In the course of evolution, this form of learning is observed in non-human primates and is in fact older and more "primitive" than fully developed imitation learning, which is limited to humans. Delayed imitation can thus hardly be considered an indication of the presence of episodic memory because it can well function without any reference to time, self-identity or emotions, which are all characteristic of episodic memory.

In just which form is information stored in semantic memory? It is assumed that the brain can only supervise the large quantity of incoming information by ordering it according to categories, that is, by deciding on an appropriate category for several objects based on a common characteristic (such as that all cars have wheels). To date, there has been no final, convincing explanation of how children form categories, although it is considered relatively probable that they do this. First, when they repeat whole series of actions and, second, when they experience situations in an intermodal way, that is, when meeting other persons is accompanied with joy, elevated moods, touching and being touched, and being teased or rocked back and forth, or when feeding takes place at the same time as touching the different spoons or bowls or feeling the difference between warm and cold things. In addition, as Grimm and Weinert (2002) pointed out, children already seem to form dif-ferentiated knowledge of the phonological-prosodic categories and rules of their mother tongue during their first year of life. While doing this, they are continually processing from the very start, not only isolated auditory infor-mation, but also visual-social material. This can be impressively demon-strated by observing 4-month-old children "lip reading". In a study by Kuhl and Meltzoff (1982), infants stared at a face for a longer length of time when movements of the mouth coincided with a tone presented close by, whereas when the intermodal sensations (movements and tone) were discordant, the infants actually watched the face for significantly less time (Grimm & Weinert, 2002, p. 525).

Basically, the same brain structures are involved in the encoding, storage and recall of information from the knowledge system that were described in connection with perceptual memory. In the system of knowledge, information is stored for a considerably long time. The more relevant this information is for us, and the more frequently we make use of it, the more probable it is that we will remember it for a long period of time. Information receives its emo-tional coloring from the limbic system, which is also the site where the transfer takes place from short-term to long-term memory. When children with advancing age remember for longer and longer times how they are expected to handle a certain object and when they are gradually capable of forming lasting categories for objects and activities, processes of maturity are involved in the limbic system, most particularly the rapid increase in volume in the hippocampus during the first 9 months of life and the improvement in insulation of the fornix with myelin, the most important limbic tract. However, in studies on the ability of recognition, children have shown lasting memories even before that time, even though they still cannot recall them actively.

Importantly, only when children are capable of actively referring to stored information has the basis been developed for semantic memory. The prefrontal cortex is always activated when the contents of memory are being actively processed. This cortex matures far more slowly than the limbic system and does not take up its function until the eighth month when the network of its synaptic connections reaches a critical density (e.g., Goldman-Rakic, 1987, p. 615). Recall of information from the semantic memory system is controlled in adults mainly by the left hemisphere – or, to be more exact, from portions of the left hemispheric prefrontal cortex and the left-sided temporal lobe (Markowitsch, 2002a). The left hemisphere is active especially in analytic, logical thought processes, whereas the right hemisphere is more strongly involved in processing emotionally weighted information (Markowitsch, 2002a). Results in adults, however, cannot be generalized to infants. For example, the right hemisphere develops more quickly than the left up to the second year of life and can thus assume a large part of its final functions much earlier (Chiron et al., 1997, p. 1057). Recall from the system of knowledge is possibly performed by both hemispheres in infants, later in life possibly only by the right hemisphere.

The prefrontal cortex is not only involved in the recall of stored information, it is also activated in important ways in encoding this information. After we have received information from the sensory organs, it passes through working memory. As we showed in the previous section, working memory is mainly localized in the frontal lobe. One other region, which is likewise activated, is the lateral part of the temporal lobe in the left hemisphere (Markowitsch et al., 1999a). The importance of both regions and their alterations over the course of development of working memory in children and adolescents between the ages of 8 and 18 was highlighted recently by Nagy, Westerberg, and Klingberg (2004). They made use of a new methodology – diffusion-weighted MR imaging (a variant of magnetic resonance tomography) – with which the microstructural portions of the white matter (the network of axons) can be measured.

From the frontal lobe, the information proceeds in several pathways to the limbic system, where it is analyzed, combined with analogous information already stored, and then evaluated for its social and biological relevance. Information that is classified as important enough to be kept is then stored in the form of lasting synaptic alterations in extensive cortical networks in the higher sensory cortical areas (Markowitsch, 2002a). It is possible that the final step – the long-term storage of memory contents – takes place in the first years of life in other regions of the brain than those where it occurs in adults.

Studies on monkeys have shown, for example, that during the first months of life the visual association cortex (see Figure 4.27, p. 99) is not yet involved in memory processes in the same way as in adult monkeys (Bachevalier, 1990). Other findings, too, on the development of the brain suggest that the storage sites for lasting memories in early childhood are possibly different from those in later life. The so-called polymodal association cortex, in which information is integrated from various sensory modalities, is not fully developed until relatively later in life, around the thirtieth year (Benes, 1994). During the first years of life, every minute thousands of new contact sites arise between nerve cells, which are either consolidated or canceled depending on whether they remain in use or not. Altogether, a considerable "reorganization" takes place in the neuronal structures for connectivity, and it is probable that this actually chaotic condition among newly established connections does not permit any lasting storage of memory contents. Furthermore, the left hemisphere – which is the usual area for storing information in the system of knowledge in adults – has a rather slow development and is thus possibly not yet mature enough in the first years of life for long-term storage.

Summarizing, we can conclude that infants first take in and store information through processes of habituation, conditioning and priming. This indicates that learning at this early stage in development is characterized by feelings of familiarity and by associative stimulus linkage. These forms of learning are classified as implicit learning and are almost universally found in the animal world. The brain structures involved are phylogenetically old and ontologically they develop early. In addition, at an early age, human infants are quite capable of memory performance on the level of perceptual memory involving structures in the brain that (later) play a role in both the conscious storage of information and its transfer from short-term into long-term memory (Markowitsch, 2002a). As a case in point, infants can already recognize certain stimuli a few days after birth. Recognition involves a passive form of memory and does not require conscious activity. The active (and conscious) recall of the contents of memory presupposes a certain degree of maturity in the prefrontal cortex, a region which in the majority of children has developed far enough by the eighth month so as to form mental images of objects and persons and to recall them actively. At the same time, the children start developing an understanding that things exist independently of their own attentiveness to them, as autonomous entities in their own right. And by acquiring a sense of object permanence, children establish the basis for an accelerated system of knowledge. As soon as they realize that objects are components of the environment that continue to exist on their own, children also start acquiring knowledge of these objects, such as their function or a more general heading or concept for them. In addition to lifeless objects, persons are also seen as entities with the ability for independent survival. The age of 8 or 9 months thus marks a milestone in the cognitive, motor and emotional development of a child, although more time will be needed until autobiographical memory develops.

6 The first quantum leap in memory development: the 9 months' revolution

One of the most fascinating, and at the same time one of the most inexplicable phenomena in human life, is our ability to recognize the feelings, desires and intentions of other persons by merely gazing into their eyes, even when we do not know them and never had anything to do with them before. It is quite possible through eye contact alone to reach a common understanding about the behavior of another person, as when someone else on a train talks on a mobile phone very loudly about embarrassing things, or when somebody has a slight mishap and one smiles with the other bystanders. Such understanding can occur completely without verbal communication or any idea of just who the other persons sharing our impressions are, simply through a minimal use of facial expressions and eye contact. This is truly astonishing, especially when we consider how many words of speech would be necessary to achieve the same degree of understanding about something we have seen.

This obvious ability of affective social understanding is completely impossible for babies until the eighth month. Of course, as the examples from the last chapter have shown, infants are quite capable of astonishing behavior themselves, initiating and maintaining a variety of forms of communication, but this communication remains, as we have already pointed out, one-sided to the extent that an infant's consciousness and memory have not yet attained a reflexive or autonoetic dimension, something which permits a conscious relation between one's self and another person.

That is precisely what takes place in the phase that we designate as the first quantum leap in the development of memory. At the age of 8 or 9 months, namely, babies start developing shared attention, that is, they direct their attention to some object or other at the same time as another person and – under the control of eye contact – reach a common understanding that this attention should continue. Thus, approximately between the ninth and the twelfth months, children start checking on whether the adults in their immediate vicinity are actually directing their attention to the same object that the children themselves are viewing. Then, between the eleventh and the fourteenth months, they start following the gaze of an adult; and between the thirteenth and the fifteenth months they start directing the attention of adults to objects (usually through gestures) (Tomasello, 2002, p. 78).

A continual emotional "monitoring" is inherent to interactions such as these – as long as attention is shared, common to both the child and the adult, children as well as their mothers experience a sense of joy; and when the shared attention threatens to get weaker or to cease altogether, unpleasurable states and feelings, such as uneasiness, frustration and strong anger, arise (Trevarthen, 2002, p. 222). Shared attention presupposes both a direct social relationship in an interactive medium, with the help of eye contact or gestures, and emotional control over the entire course of the transaction. And to achieve this, new conditions have to be first established in the brain, as it is no longer simply a process of education, in which a child learns something existential or physical, but rather a process in which he or she begins playing an active role. Martin Dornes aptly described this new situation thus: "It is not simply a case of mother and child both seeing the same thing (which is joined attention) but rather that they see the same thing together (which is shared attention)" (Dornes, 1993, p. 153, our translation).

In this phase, a completely new interface evolves between the babies and their social environment – they now participate in their social world not merely by having most of their own needs satisfied by their parents or caregivers, that is, not merely by evoking behavior from others that is related only to the children themselves. Instead, they now start entering into a genuine affective and mental exchange, a completely new form of give-and-take with the outside world. The earlier "person to person games" and "person to object games" (which infants were already capable of by this age and by which, as we have been describing, they practiced preliminary forms of communication, emotionality and memory abilities) are now replaced by "person–person–object games" (Trevarthen, 1998), and this constitutes a major advance in personal development: namely, entering into a social world in which the children now participate consciously. The significance of this advance can be clearly seen by considering the fact that this also represents the borderline for the mental abilities in other primates. They certainly have a large number of abilities, but not the ability of sharing attention or directing the attention of someone else to something of interest (Tomasello, 2002, p. 47). There may be exceptions here, as in the case of primates that have been brought up by humans in a purely human environment, but in their normal environment nonhuman primates do not show any sign of these social abilities and thus do not develop any degree of intersubjectivity. This then constitutes the social borderline between animals and humans.[1]

This quantum leap makes all further ontogenetic steps in development possible, from the passive understanding, as well as the active acquisition, of

---

1 Tomasello, too, emphasized that pointing is a uniquely human communication behavior. Interestingly, the lack of the ability to point is an early symptom of autism (Tomasello, 2002, p. 91), a severe developmental disturbance in which the main characteristic seems to be the lack of participation in social events.

speech and the genesis of a self-concept. And so that such a major leap can be effected, a number of other developments apparently must have already been completed. A basic feeling of selfhood, or what Daniel Stern calls a "*core self*" (Stern, 1985), must have arisen and become stable, so that the self realizes that it is an entity separate from others (Dornes, 1993, p. 90). This core self develops by the age of 2 or 3 months. It lacks any form of reflexive dimension, but is based on different components in infants' experiences of the world and of objects, enabling them to experience themselves as an entity. The most important of these components are the realization of self-agency (when infants know that they themselves can cause things to happen) and the feeling of self-coherence. The most apparent source for the first component, self-agency, is "proprioceptive feedback", the fact that the actions of a baby not only affect something in the environment but also coincide with a different sensation in the body. When children kick off a blanket, they not only feel a difference in temperature in their skin as a result but they also "felt" their own kicking movements that led to the change in temperature. When the two effects are thus felt in association with each other, they have a very different meaning for the children than when, for example, a change in temperature is brought on by their mothers removing the blanket. Or, in other terms, "Self-executed actions result in a proprioceptive feedback that is usually missing when actions come from the external world. When a mother vocalizes, the child hears a tone. But when the child vocalizes, he or she clearly hears a tone, too, but in addition to that, there are also sensations in the chest, the throat and in the vocal cords, all of which are only experienced when the child produces the tone. The difference between the two experiences lets a child notice when he or she has done something or somebody else, and this ability for making such a differentiation contributes . . . to experiencing the self and the object as separate entities" (Dornes, 1993, p. 91, our translation).

Dornes also remarked that self-executed actions produce a "contingency relationship" between the action and the effect, whereby a person's own actions always have an effect on himself, but not necessarily on anyone or anything else: "When the infant vocalizes, he or she always hears a tone (a perfect contingency), but the mother comes only every second or third time (an imperfect contingency)" (Dornes, 1993, p. 91, our translation). This experience, too, contributes to the basal feeling of seeing oneself as different from the environment. The second component, self-coherence, is based on the fact that a mother is recognized as the mother independently of whether she is seen in profile, in half-profile or full-faced, or, put in more abstract terms, this is an ability founded on (1) coherency of form combined with (2) a sense that time is the same even when making different movements (in the hand and foot simultaneously) or perceiving different stimuli at the same moment (hearing and seeing things), and (3) common "intensity contours" (in the term of Dornes) or "vitality contours" (in the term of Stern) for gestures and sounds.

Tomasello (2002, p. 76) also holds that proprioceptive feedback while getting to know the social and physical environment leads to a form of physical understanding of oneself (see also Nelson, 2002; Nelson et al., 2002). In discussing what happens between the ages of 2 and 9 months to construct a feeling of core self-identity, we always have to keep in mind that this is a non-reflexive self, an "existential", as Dornes calls it, or an "experiential" self in the terminology we suggest. This is a self which is built up through the help of experiences that accumulate over time and continue the development further, but which is in no way already capable of accounting for these experiences. Nonetheless, the fact that such a core self arises is the prerequisite for shared attention to be possible. What occurs when attention is shared is the focusing of two self-entities on some third one. And that, in turn, is the prerequisite for the later ability to internalize other perspectives, and that is the basis for genuine intersubjectivity: the ability to see the world from the viewpoint of someone else.[2]

At the end of this section, we will come back to the concept of the *core* self. At the moment, we want to treat some of the other important requirements for the interactive jump seen in shared attention. For example, there are communicative behaviors, both preverbal and verbal, that prepare for the later relationships of extensive interchange: rhythmic mirroring (or attunement), protoconversations, turn-takings, etc. In the early stages, the behavioral interactions only have a one-sided communicative significance, meaning that the imitated person feels as though he or she were being directly addressed by the infant, something which has a very positive effect on the general caring behavior. At the same time, long-lasting patterns of communication are being initiated in this way that in a short time become mutual, two-sided communication or genuine interaction (see Chapter 7, pp. 165ff.), which then prepares the rhythmical and syntactical patterns for the verbal interaction that develops much later. It is important to realize that the later, usually more complex and

2 Neuroscientific research has made use of a concept ("the self-condition") similar to that of the core self. Antonio Damasio described the neuronal foundation for the self as the continual reactivation of two forms of representations. The first form comprises those facts that define one's own personhood and which later are seen as one's own preferences, habits, routines, specific experiences, skills and relationships. All these facts are constantly being reactivated and then configurated anew in accord with the more recent experiences. The second form of representation (that interacts with what Damasio designates as "part of the self condition") consists of those representations of changes in bodily state which result from activity. Damasio assumes that "subjectivity depends in great part on the changes that take place in the body state during and after the processing of object X. [. . .] Early body signals, in both evolution and development, helped form a 'basic concept' of self; this basic concept provided the ground reference for whatever else happened to the organism, including the current body states that incorporated continuously in the concept of self and promptly became past states. [. . .] What is happening to us now is, in fact, happening to a concept of self based on the past, including the past that was current only a moment ago. At each moment the state of self is constructed, from the ground up. It is an evanescent reference state, so continuously and consistently reconstructed that the owner never knows it is being *re*made unless something goes wrong with the remaking" (Damasio, 1994, p. 318).

more synthesized forms of communication do not replace the older ones, but rather they are added onto them. Even when we have long become capable of communicating on a verbal-symbolic level, we can still exchange information with others through direct bodily contact, eye contact and gestures.

The socialization of emotions

One particularly significant marker on the way to intersubjectivity is seen in affect attunement between a child and his or her caregiver. By seeing a mother's eyes, a child can find assurance that a small rabbit hopping nearby is there to make everybody happy, while a dog growling is something that makes them frightened. These simple examples show what dimension this phase of shared attention already opens up: During this phase, infants get to learn not only the social reference associated with some third thing or person, but all the accompanying vocalizations and affective expressions, and this brings us to the topic of the social shaping or molding of primary emotions.

In such situations children learn, together with others from their age group, what "someone" is supposed to be afraid of and when "one" is supposed to be happy (social referencing). Dornes pointed out that the ability to recognize an emotional expression in the face of another person is in no way a matter of course, but instead has to be learned. For example, infants between the ages of 2 and 5 months register the difference between happy and sad facial expressions, although this difference is basically insignificant to them inasmuch as they do not react emotionally to the one or the other. Later on, however, and, according to Dornes, that means between 5 and 7 months of age, they "start reacting emotionally themselves to the emotional expressions in another person's face, reacting with a smile to a happy face and with a sad face to a similarly sad look from someone else. At the age of 9 months, such reactions can definitely not be referred to simple imitation, but rather to a real, affective understanding. The children now compare their own feelings with those perceived in others" (Dornes, 1993, p. 154).

At the age of 9 months the "socialization of feelings" begins (Dornes, 1993, p. 154). We can see how absolutely essential the ability of "affect attunement" and "social referencing" is when we take into consideration the fact that fully developed intersubjectivity (as it can be seen in an intimate conversation between adults) is founded on continuous control over whether we properly understand the other person we are talking to (and not just on a verbal level but also on an emotional one, through modulating the tone of voice and eye contact). These abilities remain functional throughout life and consolidate the basis for the social synchronization of humans living together.

In our view, before the age of 9 months, it is not possible to talk about an intentional subject starting to develop, while Tomasello, for example, is convinced that all developments as of this age take place *because* the infants already perceive their caregivers as intentional and thus as basically similar to themselves (Tomasello, 2002, p. 53; compare Stern, 1985, who has a similar

Box 6.1   Primary and secondary emotions

Primary emotions are, first, signals that accompany situations in which the organism reacts to certain cues, whether it wants to or not, whereby in humans (and probably in many higher mammals) a level of emotionality is reached in direct association with the physical changes in the body that take place, no matter how conscious these changes become. This level of emotionality functions as a feedback for the organism, as a marker that something of significance has happened. The primary emotions are traditionally considered to include fear, happiness, anger, disgust and sadness; often surprise is counted among them as well. As opposed to a young chicken that hides after spotting a hawk, thereby demonstrating a reaction of fear, in humans the situation is not exhausted merely by the association between cue, autonomous reaction and emotional excitement, but also involves experience of the emotion. What is more, as Damasio has said, the association is consciously perceived between the object that induces the reaction and the emotional and physical condition that is regulated by the object. That is, a consciousness exists for what the person is feeling. In the view of Damasio, the evolutionary advantage in having such a consciousness is that an emotion which is not only part of an autonomous pattern of reactions but also supplies data for the evaluation of a bodily state allows for a much broader variation in possible actions after the first, immediate reaction. In addition to the innate and preorganized ways of reacting, humans have an acquired, experience-dependent reaction which is well suited to distinguish between the outline and typical movements of a real eagle and an almost identical silhouette of a child's kite, and then to react correspondingly. Furthermore, the ability to experience emotional reactions consciously can also serve to form categories as to just which form of appearance in the cue should be evaluated as dangerous or not. In other words, as opposed to the situation in which an emotional reaction remains unconscious, actually experiencing that reaction consciously means an economical gain as far as further actions are concerned and thus has a survival advantage. One's own reaction can itself be evaluated, and from this evaluation additional conclusions can be drawn as to which action is appropriate in facing analogous situations in the future (Damasio, 1994, p. 186). Such secondary emotions, precisely because they are experience-dependent, are subject to considerable cultural and social imprinting, and thus function in a completely culture-specific and period-specific way.

conviction). But, in our view, this is equivalent to putting the cart before the horse. If I want to identify myself with something "similar to myself", I have to have a concept of self already that I could compare to myself, that is, a concept that I can raise to an abstract level and objectify. And that ability is only possible much later in ontogenesis and is itself a product of social intercourse, in which I learn what distinguishes me from the others and, vice versa, what I am in their eyes. A similar error in logic is at the root of Meltzoff's conclusion that early imitation behavior in neonates and infants can be referred back to a similarly vague category of similarity just being felt or sensed ("like me"; see Meltzoff, 1999; Rochat, 2001). We would prefer to express it this way: Infants mean a lot to us when we observe their truly impressive communicative and motor abilities, but at the same time these infants mean nothing to themselves. They are quite simply a part of a social and physical environment which is primarily responsible for the well-being or the discomfort of their core self.

The hypothesis of intentionality has a very weak standing inasmuch as it tries to explain a phenomenon, as it were, with itself. We thus suggest a different mechanism as an explanation. In this exact phase of development, children can acquire and make use of that decisive social competence that will later make them full-fledged members of their social community because the prerequisites are not yet functionable on the level of the brain until the age of 9 months, and even here interactive processes play an important role. Schore (2000, p. 162) aptly made the point that early bonding behavior is regulated by the emotional processes of exchange between the mother and her child, which, in turn, have direct effects on biochemical and metabolic processes in the child's developing brain.

> This conception, congruent with nonlinear dynamical models, focuses on reciprocal affective exchanges in which the caregiver psychobiologically regulates changes in the infant's state. [. . .] The creation of this dynamical system of "contingent responsivity" occurs in the context of face-to-face interactions, and it relies heavily upon the processing of visual and auditory (prosodic) information emanating from the most potent source of stimulation in the infant's environment – the mother's face. The human face is a unique stimulus whose features display significant information, and it functions as a continuous real-time readout of internal processes.
>
> (Schore, 2000, p. 162)

According to Schore, neuronal loops are set up that, on the one hand, process environmental information on the level of the cortex and, on the other hand, register and process changes in bodily states on the subcortical level (2000, p. 169). Such "cortico-limbic association patterns" arise in the second and third quarter of the first year of life. Toward the end of the first year, the "orbitofrontal system" matures and is responsible for a series of those new functions, which start to reveal themselves as of the eighth or ninth month.[3] Precisely at this moment, new "convergence zones" (Damasio, 1994) form on the neuronal level in which emotional conditions, new cognitive abilities and social interactive processes start to cooperate. Once again we cannot fully understand the full process involved as long as we consider it under the aspect of a purely individualistic "development" only of the child. Of course, biological processes of maturation have to be completed for further growth in this phase, but these alone would not lead to the establishment of convergent loops if ever the stimuli from social interaction, for whatever reason, fail to occur. And these stimuli are usually of a particular intensity at this age.[4]

Social interaction and neuronal development

Considering neuronal organization, we see yet another sign that, with the end of the first year, the child is entering a decisive new phase. At this time, the synaptogenesis reaches its apex in growth, after which use-dependent and experience-dependent pruning processes come to the fore (Huttenlocher, 1979, p. 202). Based on studies of synaptic density and dendritic sprouting, Huttenlocher divided postnatal cortical development into two phases. The first extends from birth to the end of the first year and is characterized by "rapid decline in neuronal density, by an increase in synaptic density and in number of synapses per neuron, by dendritic growth, and by expansion in the total volume of cerebral cortex. Phase two extends from age 1 year to adolescence. It is characterized by a slow decline in both synaptic and neuronal density. Dendritic growth continues, and the density of synapses along dendrites declines" (Huttenlocher, 1979, p. 202).

This picture once again describes central events of childhood development on the level of the neuronal structures of connectivity. In the first months of life, the baby accumulates more and more possibilities of exploring the world through habituation, interaction with caregivers and objects, and proprioceptive feedback – and at the same time the child takes in a large quantity of information that is nonetheless relatively minimally structured. The

---

3 "Although the amygdala, a limbic structure that appraises only crude information about external stimuli, is on line at birth, a critical period for the development of corticolimbic association areas onsets in the second and third quarters of the first year, involving maturation of the anterior cingulated cortex, an area involved in play and separation behaviors, laughing and crying vocalizations, face representations, and modulation of autonomic activity [. . .]. By the end of this year the orbitoinsular region of the inferior prefrontal cortex, an area that receives information from the ventral object-processing visual stream and contains neurons that fire in response to faces [. . .], becomes preeminently involved in the processing of interpersonal signals necessary for the initiation of social interactions and in the regulation of arousal and body states, properties that account for its central involvement in attachment neurobiology" (Schore, 2000, pp. 170–171).

4 Webb, Monk, and Nelson (2001, p. 154) assumed that the greatest density of synapses is reached at 15 months of age and then begins to decrease.

oversupply of neurons is meaningful for this phase because they are soon to be reduced by experiential and usage considerations. These experiences that the child has in the expanding social environment after the ninth month of life reflect the increasing numbers of synapses and the growth in dendrites – mediated among others by social interaction in which the child participates in an active way. The quantity and the level of complexity of these experiences clearly increase, and they have to find a form to become efficiently useful and socially fitting. Once that succeeds, the following phase becomes one of increasing consolidation and improving the structure of these early experiences – and this is when use-dependent processes of reduction take place on a large scale, and the structures of connectivity provide increasingly stable patterns that can serve as the foundation for new experiences and progress in learning and memory.

A further key to the social revolution that takes place in the last quarter of the first year of life is the maturing of the hippocampus, the central organ for the long-term storage of memories (see Chapter 5). Coinciding with the maturing of the hippocampus, there are two other developments: the capacity for long-term storage of semantic information and holding information online in short-term and working memory. This is the first time that processes of information selection become apparent, with some aspects or parts of information remaining in working memory while others are deleted there. And for such information selection, cortical regions are particularly important where final maturity is still far off, but where after 9 months a first surge in myelinization occurs. This is the case in parts of the temporal lobe (spatial orientation, spatial memory as a precursor of memory for time) and parts of the frontal lobe ("chunking" or "parsing" information into portions more easily handled; Pribram & Tubbs, 1967).

When an infant remembers for longer lengths of time how certain objects can be handled, a considerable advance in memory development has occurred. Semantic memory can store, at least theoretically, an unlimited quantity of information, namely all the things we learn about the world over our whole lifetime. And, frequently, we only need to come in contact with some piece of information once to remember it for as long as we live. What is also typical of semantic memories is the fact that in the majority of cases we do not remember when and where we originally experienced the material; for example, when we first learned that the yellow ball in the sky is called the "moon" and that London is the capital of Britain.

Nelson (1996, p. 228) maintains that for infants, the function of objects is the decisive criterion for placing them in a specific category. Thus, once again we are treating a form of practical usage that reappears as a cognitive achievement. At the age of 1 year, children show the first indication that they have formed global categories (such as "animal" or "vehicle") (Nelson, 1996, p. 110). During the formation of these categories, "mental event representations" probably play a major role, since various undercategories of events (bathing, playing, eating, etc.) already make up the corresponding memory scripts. Such event categories possibly precede the formation of object categories, probably indicating that social events and their time course play an earlier role in memory development than object-related ones.

Most of the events in a child's world are daily routine activities in which the child either plays a central role or functions as observer. Toward the end of their first year, children have learned the sequence of most of their routines well enough to take an active role and anticipate certain actions, without having to be guided by adults through every single step (Nelson, 1996, p. 96). When new experiences can be referred to categories that have already been established, some of the details that make up the uniqueness of the experience are lost. Thus, as a child, but also as an adult, people do not remember any one specific dinner or breakfast from the previous week, but they still have a general idea of the sequence of events during such a dinner or breakfast. What is relevant here is the fact that through the memory of general sequences, that is, for routines and scripts that give structure to everyday life, it is possible to anticipate the next, expected steps in a sequence, that is, we can form an ability for prospection. With the slow dawning of prospective memory, an incisive foundation is laid for living in the three temporal dimensions of the past, the present and the future, thus making possible the development of an autobiographical memory that positions one's personal identity within these time zones.

All in all, the first 8 months of life involve revolutionary changes in almost all levels of the life of a child, and it has been speculated that at this time in development a kind of redistribution of emphasis takes place, away from genetic determinants in favor of social ones (for example, Webb, Monk, & Nelson, 2001, p. 165). While, on the one hand, as we have already seen, major influences on children's development have already come from processes of interaction with their parents or caregivers, on the other hand, Webb and coworkers were correct in emphasizing that the interplay between neuronal and social events is still far from being deciphered completely or even only approximately. And, to be precise, even the neuronal background is far from being explained satisfactorily. This is due, among others things, to the fact that our methods are quite limited, since we still have no way of measuring activation at the level of the brain in concrete interactions between a mother and her child, with the help of imaging procedures, and this is obviously all the more so when we try to map pruning events *in vivo*, at the precise moment when a child is having new experiences. This is one of the reasons why collating the results from different fields (neuroscience, developmental psychology, research on interactions, linguistics) remains a mere attempt to relate results of completely different types that were all obtained with very different methodology. They are nothing more and nothing less than that. What we can conclude from all these different approaches is that the development of memory is a multimodal process in which biological factors interact with social factors, and only when they act in unison can their interplay, which reconfigures itself over the course of time, guarantee success to the endeavor.

Box 6.2   Chunking

Research on mammals and birds has shown that a series of especially adapted tasks, known as "delayed-response-type tasks", is available for investigating short-term memory. We have already described the work of Goldman and Galkin (1978) in Chapter 4 on the Kennard principle in young monkeys (see Figure 4.25 on p. 93) and in Chapter 5 (pp. 120ff.) we discussed gradual learning as opposed to all-or-nothing learning. As these examples illustrate, delayed-response-type tasks are applied in order to find out whether and, if so, for how long animals can remember where they were before (or in monkeys in which direction they used their hand) or which direction they will be expected to run in the next trial (or use their hand). Rats are usually only tested by tasks that demand a delay of around 5 seconds, whereas monkeys can in fact be relied on to work with delays of as much as 30 seconds.

The results show that when parts of the frontal lobe have been surgically removed bilaterally (in monkeys a region in the dorsolateral prefrontal cortex; Jacobsen & Nissen, 1937; Mishkin, 1957; Rosenkilde, 1978; see Figure 4.1, p. 53, and Figure 5.6, p. 134) in adult animals, they are no longer capable of performing this type of task with even very short delays. This kind of deficit has been attributed, in both animals and humans, to a loss of short-term memory after damage to the frontal lobes (Butters, Pandya, Stein, & Rosen, 1972; Wiegersma, Scheer, & Hijman, 1990). But then Pribram and Tubbs (1967) changed the time intervals between "grab towards the left" and "grab towards the right" in such a way that every second time a long pause ensued ("chunking"). Because of this alternation, consecutively correct reactions after a short pause entailed grabbing in only one direction, the left, and consecutively correct reactions after a long pause meant grabbing in the other direction, the right. With the help of this "trick", the monkeys that had been severely disturbed postoperatively could now perform the task almost perfectly again.

This example demonstrates, first, the significance of the frontal lobe as a timer, and thus as a controlling instance over short-term memory, and, second, how use of an external pulse generator can improve performance, a method that has also been found useful for patients with brain damage (Thöne-Otto & Markowitsch, 2004).

Returning to the topics of shared attention and what Tomasello has called the "9-month revolution", we can see that the ontogenetically revolutionary event consists in the very first appearance of a triadic constellation, which, in the terms of Tomasello, takes on three, age-correlated forms: testing, following, and controlling attention (Figure 6.1).

If, as Tomasello describes, this sequence of behavior reflects "the dawning understanding of other persons as intentional actors" (1999, p. 69), this would still appear to us to be only one side of the coin, and probably in fact the lesser side, from the ontogenetic point of view. This other side, the more important one for the developing child, is the ability of shared attention and with this ability, the child can now experience that someone else sees and treats the child as an intentional actor: Children see themselves then for the first time practically as a social being. In the hierarchy which Carpenter, Nagell, and Tomasello (1998) worked out empirically, the necessary preceding steps were the abilities to check for and then pursue the attention of someone else. The children check on whether the caregiver is interested in the same thing as they themselves are. Viewed thus, the way a child handles an object gets a new format when the object, at first only structurally or superficially, is viewed from the eyes of the other person, or, put metaphorically, when the child sees his or her own actions with the eyes of the other. Without doubt, the ability to understand oneself as an object being observed by others is a significant foundation for the concept of self which subsequently develops.

The third element of the triad – guiding the attention of another – is decisive in that the child can now assume that the other person also finds something interesting in what the child is occupying himself with at the moment. This presupposes not only a potential conformity between the two perspectives, but also the idea that the child is becoming an active participant in a social event by explicitly performing actions, and that constitutes the difference between the time before the 9 months' revolution and the time after that. To that extent, we come to the conclusion that the decisive element is not under-standing others as intentional but rather seeing oneself as an intentional being and becoming an active participant in a common social space.

When we look at shared attention in a little more detail, we notice that it sounds rather simple to state that a child "checks on" another person's attentiveness. What does that mean in reality? What does this "checking on"

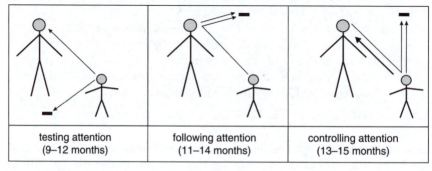

| testing attention (9–12 months) | following attention (11–14 months) | controlling attention (13–15 months) |

Figure 6.1 The triads of attention (Tomasello, 1999, p. 79).

entail? Gazing, gestures, emotional facial expressions, mutual signals of joy, for example, are involved. But an interaction on such presymbolic levels represents an extraordinarily complex achievement because it presupposes that these gazes, gestures, expressions and signals are deciphered correctly, and that, in the long run, is certainly not simple. Daniel Stern emphasized that the basic processes underlying shared attention are insufficiently understood when they are viewed as temporally distinct acts, in the sense that a child wants feedback on whether what he or she is doing at the moment meets somebody's approval, and then a smile signals exactly that. In reality, however, the processes concerned here are those that are temporally sequenced when children check on or pursue attention in others. And even what conveys approval in the smile has a temporal structure (Stern, 1999, p. 71). Stern calls the different intensity and sequence of an emotional expression "vitality contour" and ascribes such vitality contours to all activities with a temporal structure that are felt and perceived. In this respect, Stern attributes both a Darwinian function to every emotion (in the sense of primary emotions: the function is joy or fear) and a vitality contour, and "each adds a different meaning to the experience, as acted or perceived" (Stern, 2002, p. 71).

If we view emotions as internal and external communicators in which the valence of an experience is passed on, then the meaningfulness of vitality contour and Darwinian function can vary. Thus, if children want to examine whether they are being encouraged in what they are doing, the Darwinian function (a smile signals joy, which in turn signals approval) is meaningful, conveying the message, while in longer social interactions serving to establish a sense of mutuality, the vitality contour in the smile conveys the pivotal message, which is basically still the same in adults. Ironic remarks, exaggerated disappointment, etc., would be impossible without the mutual give and take of emotional expression and vitality contour.

Vitality contours certainly play a role in communication and in the experiential world of children before the 9 months' revolution; after all, they can be considered the microsequences of those daily routines of bathing and feeding which form the first more complex memories of the children. With the 9 months' revolution something new occurs in that the vitality contours that index and regulate the emotional exchange between mother and child are perceivable externally (for the one person) and internally (for the other). Children not only evaluate the (mirroring or correcting) reaction of their mother to what they are doing at the moment, but also feel the mother's reaction to the signals originating in the children, and this is precisely the start of genuine interaction, which means that the assumed reaction of the other person is always a part of one's communicative actions. In developed speech, the same rule still holds: I speak the way I assume my partner expects me to speak. This basic principle of interaction is regulated in mutual, modulated and sequenced exchange of eye contact, sounds, gestures, etc. It is rather interesting to note that, in the view of Stern, vitality contours are immanently temporal. They mark an emotion as a course in time or as a sequence by giving it a beginning, a middle and an end. Smiling or laughing starts, remains visible for a while, and then gradually disappears, and the same is true of anger or crying. As Stern described, the temporal structure is, in principle, completely immanent for the vitality contours of a child's early experiences: urinating, feeling hungry, sucking, etc., all show a standard course over time, which can be called prototemporal sequences in a child's physical world of experience.[5] To that extent, children experience how, with the help of early imitations (as described by Meltzoff & Moore, 1977), they can register their environment within the frame of a sequential structure, not merely as a succession of individual actions, taking into consideration both their inner proprioceptive experience and the perceptions of the other person. The key to understanding this idea is to assume that by the age of 8 or 9 months, temporality is a procedural and psychological-physical basic experience that at the stage of the 9 months' revolution takes on an autonoetic dimension that can become conscious and is thus the basic format for the ability that does not develop until later to differentiate the past, the present and the future.

The vitality contours of early experiences thus make up the precursors of both autonoetic memory and, at the same time, those regulators and indicators of communicative actions that turn the children more and more into social actors. This process, of course, does not occur abruptly; it is probably associated with the new functionality in working memory already mentioned. The conscious monitoring of an emotional interaction, together with the accompanying vitality contours, requires a short-term memory with a certain capacity, and this is probably the case, as we mentioned, only as of the age of 8 or 9 months. This is the age when the proper functioning of working memory (presupposing a certain degree of biophysiological maturity) collaborates with the temporalizing of activity sequences (presupposing a certain degree of maturity in psychological development) so as to make a new social ability possible: shared attention, which is the key to all further developmental steps.

In addition, Stern emphasizes the fact that vitality contours are closely associated with intentionality because the temporality of actions and processes of exchange (which are clearly demarcated by time) automatically introduce an immanent intentionality in the very moment when it allows someone to anticipate the end of a sequence (Stern, 1999, p. 75). Then the temporal sequence attains significance: One starts trying to attain something, and the time that passes becomes a measure that reduces the distance to reaching the goal. In that way, vitality contours have an intentional aspect from the moment that they are perceived and felt, and that is the moment when children learn to see themselves as intentional beings. At the same time, something quite new originates on the psychological level. The child no longer exists only in a state of an ever-continuing present, but rather begins to

---

5 In a further publication, Stern designated such temporal sequences as "protonarrative" (1998; compare Welzer, 2002, p. 76).

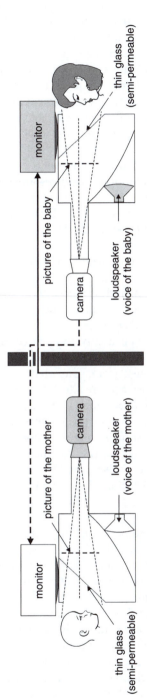

Figure 6.2 Double video experiment (Trevarthen, 2002, p. 222).

live in a present filled with experience (Stern, 1999, p. 72), which is doubtlessly a prerequisite for the later differentiation between a "before", a "now" and a "later". Thus, the 9 months' revolution marks a fundamental step away from unconscious existence in a permanent and asocial present toward a social space characterized by tenderness, interaction and intentionality.

Existing in a permanent present does not mean that the infant's self would not be differentiated through the action of the social and physical environment. Recent research on infants offers considerable evidence that infants perceive their own bodies very differently from other objects or persons, making possible the foundation of an early core self, which, in turn, is a prerequisite for the 9 months' revolution. Without a concept of self, if only an incomplete one, the triadic attention sequences already described could not develop. In fact, there is general acceptance today of the idea that infants possess an ecological self (Neisser, 1991), a physical one (Nelson, 2002; Nelson et al., 2002), a bodily one (Rochat, 2001), or a core self (Stern, 1985), which is based essentially on the fact that children can have proprioceptive experiences, as when they make a movement with their hand and at the same time see and feel this movement, or when they utter a sound that they both produce and hear at the same moment. It is precisely this aspect of a feedback in which proprioceptive experiences clearly differ from experiences with objects or other persons. A number of studies confirm that infants have already developed a feeling for their ability to elicit certain effects actively (Rovee-Collier, Hayne, & Colombo, 2000) (see Figure 5.1, p. 120).

If they thereby see themselves as "agents", in whatever sense of the word, in a physical environment, they also acquire a feeling of being "social agents" (Rochat, 2001; Rochat, Querido, & Striano, 1999), by communicating with their caregivers (as numerous studies on protoconversations have shown). This is also apparent when they show strong irritation at a communication that does not develop in the expected way, as when the mother suddenly stops communicating and instead shows a blank, expressionless face (still-face test; see Trevarthen, 2002). A technically rather complex experiment (see Figure 6.2) that had the mother and child communicate in real time but over a video monitor, also evoked strong signs of discomfort in the child, even when the mother's part of the conversation was heard, but time-delayed and thus no longer fitted the actions or the initiatives of the child. That the child registered the desynchronization in uncomfortable ways doubtlessly reveals the fact that he or she has quite specific expectations as to what should come next in this form of communication.

The interpersonal and the physical self do not constitute any form of conscious or reflexive self-perception, rather in early development a "protorepresentation" of the self already originates that is the product of interpersonal and physical experiencing. Rochat, working on proprioceptive perception, dated this early development to the age of 3 months (Rochat, 2001, p. 199). The next steps in the development of the self-concept are seen in the second half of the second year of life when children recognize themselves in a mirror or at the age of 3 years when they recognize themselves in photographs.

The representation of the self is established at the latest at this age, and it is not merely a coincidence that children start using personal pronouns with a sense of confidence. And at the same time, the origin of empathy can be seen, the "vocabulary spurt" starts, and children begin to play imaginative games as if they were somebody else, that is, role-playing, a reliable indication of the presence of a cognitive self-concept (Howe et al., 2003, p. 474). Howe and coworkers hold that the cognitive self is the decisive prerequisite for the development of autobiographical memory because, by this stage, children have the ability to center their experiences and events on one single reference point, and that is their own selves. Every new experience can now be organized within the "knowledge structure" of the self (Howe et al., 2003, p. 480). At this age, as all parents know, children already have very lively episodic memories, but they still lack the ability to arrange these memories along temporal lines. Things happen and events take place, but as long as the children still lack the temporal frame of reference of a continuous self, it makes no difference whether these things and events happened yesterday, a month ago, or whenever. And related to that is the fact that children cannot reliably classify their memories according to their sources, once again revealing that a self situated within a time frame is clearly still lacking.

Howe and coworkers (2003) emphasized that the prerequisite for autobiographical memory is already found in the cognitive self-concept, and not just when elaborate speech acquisition is possible. In their view, the organizing structure of the cognitive self constitutes the precursor of autobiographical memory, a precursor which finds its conceptual form to a certain extent through symbolic language. But in our view, they have overlooked the fact that language as a representational medium does not just simply make a translation of inner experience into the outside world possible; rather, it establishes in its own right a new structure for the self in which children can look back at themselves in their imagination, see themselves in different times, places or situations, and thus engage in the "mental time travels" that Tulving identifies as the decisive characteristic of autobiographical memory. Thus, it is in the cognitive self that we locate a necessary precondition for autobiographical memory, which, however, cannot be organized before a symbolic language is mastered. We treat this topic in more detail in the next chapter.

7 The second quantum leap in memory development: language

"In the beginning was the word" is true of the development of human culture, for the evolution of human concepts opened the door to all further organizations and achievements of man's thought.

Julian Huxley (1953, p. 35)

The origin of symbolic language belongs among the most fascinating enigmas of phylogenesis. Just as, in ontogeny, the development of language competence makes the unfolding of autobiographical memory possible and thus raises all other further progress in competence to a new, self-reflexive level, so, on the phylogenetic level, the origin of symbolic forms of communication had the effect of a developmental accelerator *par excellence*. Only by possessing communicable symbols is abstraction from concrete situations possible, permitting the transfer of information, knowledge and learning over the expanse of space and time. Within the frame of this book, it would not be possible or necessary to speculate on how language may have originated in the course of human evolution, but we want to allude briefly to our basic assumption that language originated from the successive extension of communicative techniques and competences and that probably, at least theoretically, a course of development can be hypothesized from nonsymbolic communication through sounds and gestures all the way up to symbolic communication through linguistic symbols and words. This assumption is sound because the ontogenetic path toward language progresses from presymbolic forms of communication. Communication, that is, social exchange about one's well-being and needs, functions before language in infants, and so we do not find it convincing to "explain" the phenomenon of human speech capacity by the assumption of a single, simple origin, such as the existence of a so-called language gene (compare Chomsky, 1998 [1975]; Pinker, 1994).

In common with many other workers in the field (e.g., Donald, 2001; Nelson, 1996), we assume that basic protolinguistic competence is made possible by early communicative experiences, that is, the daily, practice-oriented exercises with question-and-answer sequences (see Welzer, 2002, p. 83), scripts (routinely repetitive actions), and naming and expressing things that accompany various actions. The final acquisition of speech can then grow out of these basic competencies later. Social practice itself makes possible a structure in which learning a symbolic language can be organized. This highly complex and, at the same time, uniquely human competence appears in the course of early childhood when forms of nonrepresentational and nonsymbolic communication are practiced, systematically refined, and extended.

Because autobiographical memory, in our definition, has to have a temporal, spatial and personal reference, it cannot originate without a representational medium. For this reason, we will now give a brief review of the ontogenesis of speech acquisition. The ability of mental time travel, to plan future actions, and go over different alternatives for an action presupposes a representation of precisely these acts and the objects, conditions, time frames, etc., connected with them. In that respect, the origin of autobiographical memory is very closely associated with acquiring a symbolic language, which of course is preceded by more basal forms of communication and interaction that have a preparatory function even before birth.

Acquisition of protolanguage

Expressed more exactly, we would have to say that, however strange it sounds, language acquisition begins in the fetal phase. Indications of the prenatal active and passive competency in the sounds of language can be seen in the ability of neonates "to perceive contrasts which are relevant for the differentiation of phonemes" (Dittmann, 2002, p. 18; see also Howe, 2000, p. 5), or the ability of "categorial speech perception", a term for infants' distinguishing, for example, between the sounds of *b* and *p*. Intriguingly, infants have an even more universal ability for categorial speech perception and for distinguishing between phonemes than do adults. One study (Werker & Tees, 1992) showed that children who grow up in an English-speaking environment can distinguish phonemes that do not occur in English (Howe, 2000, p. 5), but this ability is lost after the sixth month. Dittmann concluded that "in the course of the first year of life, the perceptual ability adapts itself to the language that is spoken in the environment of the infant, whereby the ability of 'excessive' categorial differentiations decreases. Early speech acquisition should not be viewed as the sensibilization of an infant to specific differences within his mother language, but rather as the de-sensibilization to possible differentiations which the infant could perform from the beginning" (Dittmann, 2002, p. 18; our translation; see also Nelson, 1996, p. 106).

This finding is an indication of a principle of development that is probably fundamental to human ontogenesis, that is, that a basically inherent, though unstructured, surplus in developmental potentials will become specialized under socio-cultural influences, and potentials that are not made use of in the individual developmental environment are excluded irreversibly and disappear. This process shows a highly interesting parallel to the ontogenesis of synaptic connections in the brain: here, too, a considerable surplus in synaptic connections (see "Synaptogenesis", Box 4.5) goes through a process of specialization and is reduced in number depending on the environmental experiences that the child has (see "Pruning", Box 4.5). At the same time, this principle shows to what extent the social and cultural conditions of the individual environment of the child are responsible for just which pattern of connectivity will establish itself in early development.

This principle already plays an important role in transnatal learning processes. The perception of sounds in general and specifically those of spoken language already occurs before birth, and neonates can "remember" many acoustic impressions (see Chapter 5: "Prenatal and transnatal development of memory: earliest forms of learning", p. 113ff.). As a result, they are able to distinguish different voices, languages, and, in fact, different rhymes and stories with the help of elements of prosody (melody, intonation, rhythm).[1] The ability of neonates to distinguish the voice of their mother from other voices is well documented and is probably related to their remembering these prosodic elements, although something else certainly plays a role here. The experience of the mother's voice is not a purely acoustic one perceived through the skin and muscles of the mother's body, from the outside world, but, more specifically, it is perceived through the pattern of vibrations within her body.

These are all phenomena of passive acoustic perception. That babies are quite capable of producing a series of active, rather loud sounds by themselves is, of course, well known. Dittmann (2002, p. 20) distinguishes the following stages of "pre-linguistic sound development":

- from birth onward different types of crying out;
- from the sixth to eighth week, vowel-like cooing sounds start, often accompanied by hand and finger movements, smiling, excited facial expressions, etc. (Eliot, 2001, p. 432);
- from the fourth month (or the fifth to sixth month, according to Nelson, 1996, p. 107), babbling appears, and somewhat later, usually around the seventh month, children begin forming combinations of precursor consonants and vowels, such as *ba* or *ga*, which in time, through repetition, give way to the typical *babababa* and *gagagaga* all parents know, which is a "preliminary stage for the later consonant-vowel-syllable structure". At the same time, "with these sound chains the infant experiments with different prosodic patterns, that is, with variations in pitch (basic frequency), loudness, syllabic rate and other temporal parameters"

---

1 In a study by DeCasper and Spence (1986), pregnant women were asked to read out loud a particular story twice a day during the last 6 weeks before delivery. Shortly after their birth, the infants were given tape recordings of either the same story or a different one read by their mother and a complete stranger, in every case a woman. The intensity of children's sucking on a pacifier (which was connected to the tape recorder) allowed them to "decide" which story and which voice they wanted to listen to. The infants clearly preferred the story they already knew, irrespective of whether their mother or the other woman did the reading.

(Dittmann, 2002, p. 21, our translation), which most probably sets the stage for the "prosodic structures" of the symbolic language that is only mastered much later.

An interesting aspect of these developments is the fact that at this stage babies are not conscious that their ability to utter sounds constitutes communication and has an informative character that another person can make sense of. For the babies, the sounds probably only have importance as communication inasmuch as they can interact with their mother at the level of rhythm, pitch and prosody; otherwise, these early communications are rather more one-sided, in the sense that the caregivers feel as if they were being directly, personally "addressed". And in fact this is the way the caregivers react: by communicating, repeating, and so on.

A very similar form of one-sided communication can also be seen in early childhood in the development of facial expressions: All emotions have an expressive character which can be deciphered by the person taking care of the baby. In evolutionary terms, this primarily communicative association between the emotional expression of an infant and the reaction of the caregiver initiated by this expression should not be interpreted as something without function, as if it were a mere accidental accompaniment of bodily excitement. On the contrary, emotional expression in neonates has immediate survival advantages. It is obviously quite apparent that, when an organism is incapable of autonomous survival, there is high functional value in being able to get its own state of well-being and needs across to the caregivers and thus in securing adequate care. At the same time, in humans, the primary purpose is not just to signalize basic needs and whether or not they have been satisfied sooner or later, but also to get the attention and arouse the feelings of the person who feels responsible for the well-being of the baby when it starts crying desperately. This means that, through the emotional display that infants show about their condition, something happens to the persons caring for them, something which releases an emotion in them, as well. Emotions not only play a role in what happens *in* a person but also in what happens *between* persons (Trevarthen, 2002).

When we view emotions as being primarily an expression of reciprocal relationships, of a give and take that is triggered and regulated through emotions, they can also be seen as early communication or the medium of communication that prepare the way for later processes of communication and interaction. One interesting point in this discussion is that communication and interaction obviously function perfectly well, although infants have no self-concept or autonoetic consciousness, and do not have the slightest awareness that they are communicating. This fulfills, in the simplest way possible, the basic assumption of communication theory that it is not possible *not* to communicate. Thus, infants set in motion a behavior in their caregivers that is directly related to the infants and from which they directly profit.

In other words, even if this communication is rather one-sided at this point in early childhood, it is still genuine communication and creates consequences for both sides in that communication. At the same time, in the early development of both articulation and emotional expressivity, the ontogenetic principle of developing preliminary rudiments for future (communicative) skills is evident in a social process. Even though infants have no awareness for their being a part of a process of social exchange, it is precisely this lack of awareness that functions as a precondition for practicing the many different sequences, patterns and rhythms of such exchanges, which later, with the emergence of intersubjectivity, develop into genuine, two-sided interactions and which, at an even later stage, after speech acquisition, finally attain the form of verbal, symbolic interaction. The ability to express emotions and sounds belongs to the biological prerequisites of social exchange, which determines the entire course of ontogenesis and gives it the individual stamp of each different historical and cultural environment.

Protoconversation

In our cultural world, adults speak with their infants and young children in the first year of life in "motherese", the first form of "infant-directed speech" (IDS). This speech is "usually characterized by a high pitch of voice, clear articulation, exaggerated melody, pauses between the individual phrases, emphasizing especially important words, repetitions and avoiding complex sentences" (Dittmann, 2002, p. 28; our translation). Through these means, apparently, the attention of the child is regulated in early dialogue situations or "protoconversations" in which caregivers interpret the sounds that a child makes, or reconstruct them from the actual context, and then repeat them in their own voice and thus give them social "meaning". In this way, presumably, a "foundation is established for the acquisition of word meanings", as Dittmann put it (2002, p. 29).

Later communicative abilities go through preliminary stages when, for example, early interactions between a mother and her child are structured while talking or singing through precise rhythms which the two interactors follow. Recent work on early musical ability has used sonographic recordings to show that infants already harmonize with a "song" that their mother "makes up" for them. The infants fill in rhythmical syncopes or empty pauses with their own tones, which fit the pitch and melody of what the mother is singing (see Figure 7.2).

Protoconversations are, however, nothing like communicative "one-way streets". It is not only a case of the mother addressing her child (and adapting the level of her vocabulary to the needs of the child), but the children themselves also imitate such elements from such conversations in their gazes, gestures and sounds (Trevarthen, 2002). The mother and child direct their attention to each other, the infant smiles, makes sounds, and moves his or her legs. Interestingly, infants imitate facial expressions and particularly the movements of the lips of the other person, and they have this ability from the

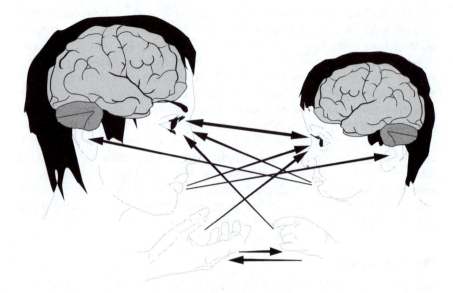

Figure 7.1 Channels of early communication (Trevarthen, 2002, p. 217).

moment of birth (see Meltzoff & Moore, 1989). Infants are apparently very sensitive to the emotional expression in their mother's voice and to changes in her facial expressions (see Trevarthen, 2002, p. 214). In addition, role-playing, mutual, friendly teasing, etc., are all a part of these protoconversations, whereby conversational patterns are slowly prepared which will become effective later in verbal communication. At the same time, there may be an unfortunate temptation to read too many cognitive abilities into these

Figure 7.2 Coordination between a mother and her child while singing (Malloch, 1999).

protoconversations, or to conclude that, at this early stage, infants are capable of reacting consciously to the actions or emotional expressions of others: "These early conversations are certainly important preliminary steps for learning language", according to Lise Eliot (2001, p. 432), "but in their essence they are emotional expressions, and the basic behavior originates in the emotional centers of the brain" (our translation). For this reason it would be incorrect to describe protoconversations as an arena for "primary intersubjectivity", as Trevarthen has suggested. Intersubjectivity includes an ability, at least in a rudimentary form, for seeing the world with the eyes of the other person, and at this early stage in life this ability has not yet developed. That only occurs, as we have described, as of the age of 9 months. Until then, it is better to refer to "primary communicability", as there is no doubt that infants are well able to communicate from the beginning of their lives.

Speech acquisition

The age of 9 months also marks the end of the phase of babbling. The trains of different sounds become more and more variegated, and we can safely assume that by this stage certain patterns of intonation, typical of the mother tongue, are being repeated and practiced (Dittmann, 2002, p. 22). Approximately at this same time, children start reacting especially to particular words such as the names of family members (Nelson, 1996, p. 112).

Around the age of 1 year (in some cases 2 months before then or 9 months later), children utter their first words (protowords: *mama*, *papa*, *tata*, etc.), usually in connection with repetitive everyday acts (so-called routines; see Nelson, 1996, p. 113). At the same time, they acquire a form of knowledge of the rules that enables them to distinguish words from other combinations of sounds (see Dittmann, 2002, pp. 27f.). As Katherine Nelson put it, the first words that children speak fit the activities in which the children are involved and which are structured by the parents; when the parents give the children specific objects, or take them away, the objects are typically named as well as the respective verbs ("give" and "take"; Nelson, 1996, p. 115).

At the age of 15 months, the children have a vocabulary of about 10 words, whereby individual differences can be marked (Nelson, 1996, p. 112). In the child's second year, we can observe adults making use of a "supportive language" (Grimm, 1998; see also Dittmann, 2002, p. 30), which is comparable in function to "motherese". Dialogue structures are provided; the child's attention is directed to certain aspects of the situation at the moment or segments of reality; utterances from the child are repeated, corrected, and commented on; and imperatives and questions predominate. It is interesting to note that some children speak in small "sentences" rather early; even as early as only a few months after speaking their very first words, they construct sentences with a higher degree of complexity. These sentences appear to be partly understandable, although they usually remain undecipherable, and only the intonation gives the impression that sentence structures are being imitated.

Quoting Nelson (1973), Dittmann (2002, p. 33) mentions two different strategies or styles in children's speech acquisition at this age. Children can designate certain things in the environment with the help of individual words (in the broader sense of the word), and this style is referred to as the "referential style", or they can practice social communication, and this is called the "expressive style", in which they "maintain their role in a dialogue and fulfill the demands for mutuality in speaking even when their sentences often remain unintelligible and they do not yet have the necessary words" (Dittmann, 2002, p. 34; our translation). From the functional point of view, we can once again see that speech acquisition is not an end in itself, but rather serves most particularly social synchronization, which at this age can very well be subject to imitation by the children.

Usually, children make use of both strategies or styles one after the other, and this makes perfect sense considering the successive unfolding of verbal communication abilities: "While the expressive style has more of a social communicative function, the referential style has more of a designatory one" (Dittmann, 2002, p. 35, our translation). Nelson (1996, p. 113) also refers to these aspects and mentions the high degree of interindividual variability in the phases of learning a language, including the different styles. She attributes these differences to social and cultural differences in the manner people communicate with children generally or, specifically, in the mother–child dyads. Nelson thus rejects two earlier assumptions in the research on speech development: that children always first learn names for objects and that speech acquisition always passes through the same stages in all children. Because, according to her, language is acquired in an "adult–child communicative system" (Nelson, 1996, p. 113), intercultural and interindividual differences are unavoidable in the process.

An ability closely associated with speech acquisition is categorizing the environment (Nelson, 1996, p. 107). Recent research supports the hypothesis that children start categorizing objects in the second half of the first year of life (see Dittmann, 2002, p. 36; Nelson, 1996, p. 108). Thus, even before learning words such as "dog" and "car", they have already developed categories for these objects (although they also somewhat "overly extend" the categories to include, for example, all small animals in their word "wawa"; see Dittmann, 2002, p. 38; Nelson, 1996, p. 108).

Nelson (1996, p. 109) differs from Piaget's research tradition and emphasizes that the ability to construct linguistic symbols originates from collective symbolic practice, and not from individual cognitive acquisition. Of course, she writes, "there must be a preparation on the individual level in order to make the interpersonal possible" (Nelson, 1996, p. 109). Her argument is that children form categories based on their own direct experience with objects *and* on interaction with adults. This idea is important because here (as in so many other points of time in ontogenesis) it is once again possible to see, first, various modules of experiential learning in children and, second, social modulators working together through the caregivers so that the process of development can progress properly. If components of this modulary system fail, developmental disturbances result.

When the children's vocabulary reaches approximately 50 words, usually around the eighteenth month, we can see two new developments. First, the so-called vocabulary spurt occurs (see Dittmann, 2002, p. 40; Nelson, 1996, p. 122), that is, the size of the chidren's vocabulary grows markedly in the following months. And second, children start speaking in two-word sentences, and at around 2 years of age they form sentences with three words and more, and begin using prepositions, pronouns, tenses and auxiliaries (Nelson, 1996, p. 113). As Dittmann (2002, p. 42) also points out, children at the age of 18 months already use words "which designate activities (such as eating) or qualities (such as nice)", as well as proper names, and "words for events (party), substances (water) or temporal units (day)".

Admittedly, the two-word utterances cannot be called sentences in the sense that we find them being used by adults, but their word order is an indication that at this age children already effectively use such structures found in adult language ("protolanguage"; Bickerton, 1995; see also Dittmann, 2002, p. 53). In addition, "they already possess considerable grammatical knowledge which is seen in their performance in understanding others" (Dittmann, 2002, p. 57).

Between the ages of 2 and 3 years, children start opening up the world of symbols for themselves more and more, and so demonstrate the development of autobiographical memory, which will help them (at first with the help of their parents) to relive events from the past that they have directly experienced themselves. Passive and active speech skills, a slowly evolving consciousness of their own self as different from others, and better and better ties to a sociocommunicative environment in which they are growing up form different aspects of the same developmental process that is intimately connected with specific advances in brain maturity.

For speech production and processing, the two main areas described in Chapter 5 in some detail are pivotal: Broca's area subserving speech *production* and Wernicke's area, which is essentially responsible for *understanding* speech. Completely unexpectedly, language is not processed in the same areas in children as in adults, meaning that processing communication in children at a prespeech age is not an immature form of the later system for processing symbolic language; rather, it is principally distinct and has to go through different developmental stages to reach functionality. As shown by the studies described in Chapter 4 on hemispherectomy and the Kaspar Hauser experiments, there is also a time window for language development. If the first language is not learned within a critical period, the neuronal connectivity necessary for speech cannot develop along normal lines, and permanent damage is the result. Eliot (2001, p. 516), for example, described a case of severe child abuse in which a young girl was locked up for years and experienced absolutely no verbal communication, and in this and other tragic cases, such as that of Kaspar Hauser or "wolf children", the essentially social character of speech acquisition becomes quite apparent. Without a well-functioning communication system between adults and their, as yet immature, children, speech acquisition is impossible, or, put technically, the respective neuronal connectivity cannot be established.

After these considerations we can return to the topics of speech acquisition within a sociocommunicative setting and autobiographical memory, which only begins to develop when speech acquisition (in the fuller sense of the term "speech") is also developing. Up to the age of approximately 2 years, language functions as an emotional-communicative medium that can be viewed as one of the regulative rhythmic elements in the social universe of the child and that, at that time, already contains many elements of later symbolic communication such as taking turns and even prosody. This medium makes social communication possible even when the ability of reflexivity has not been developed yet. In this case, language becomes a symbolic medium with which a child can call things into mind and can also demonstrate some achievements in social understanding that were completely impossible before that time. Communication at the level of symbolic language is the ability which, for the first time, makes social exchange possible with respect to one's own feelings, perceptions, experiences and opinions and those of others, and as such it is the most important factor in cultural transmission in the sense of the "ratchet effect" in cultural evolution mentioned earlier (Chapters 1 and 2, pp. 8f. and 25). Moreover, symbolic communication facilitates those concepts and interpretational frames with which children learn to understand and define themselves. Again, we see how fundamental the acquisition of symbolic language is to the development of autobiographic memory.

Memory talk

The emerging ability of speech alone is not sufficient for autobiographical memory to develop; of essential importance is also the ability to distinguish between distinct zones of the past, present and future: between a *before*, a *now* and a *later*. Autobiographical memory presupposes an awareness of time, and for the origin of such a concept it is necessary that memories have a reference to the individual person; this is demonstrable at the age of approximately 2½ years, the age at which children can recognize themselves in the mirror and start making use of personal pronouns. In line with work by Howe and Courage (1993, 1997), Povinelli (1995; Povinelli et al., 1996) assumes that the ability to recognize oneself plays a central role in the development of autobiographical memory. But as opposed to Howe and Courage, he holds the view that autobiographical memory does not originate before children develop a feeling for themselves as being within a time frame.

How can research establish the fact that children do in fact recognize themselves? Usually, a colored sticker is placed on their forehead while playing a game, but so that they don't realize it, and this scene is either photographed or recorded on video. After a short time (averaging 3 minutes) the photo or video is shown to the children. If they then reach up to their forehead, it is assumed that they recognize the association between themselves in the past and themselves now in the present (delayed self-recognition).

The study by Povinelli and coworkers (1996) showed that no child of 2 years of age tries to touch the sticker on their forehead, but that 25 percent of the 3-year-olds and 75 percent of the 4-year-olds do so when viewing the video, and similar results were obtained when they looked at their photos. Interestingly, there is an association between the performance of the children in delayed self-recognition and the quantity of their memories of past events (Welch-Ross, 2001). Three-year-olds who reach for the sticker while looking at the video or the photo remember, on average, more episodes than children who do not try to touch it. However, this phenomenon can be seen only in children of mothers who, in their mother–child dyads, practice a specific style of communication ("highly elaborative mothers"). This also confirms the thesis (see Reese, 2002) that a close connection exists between cognitive abilities and interactional experiences and competencies.

Welch-Ross (2001) interprets the results of her study from a different point of view from Povinelli's, emphasizing that the relatively poorer performance of the 3-year-olds in the delayed self-recognition test has less to do with the fact that a feeling for the association between oneself in the past and then in the present ("sense of an extended self-in-time") only just begins to develop at this age than with the general difficulties that children have at that age in recognizing causal relationships.

However well this difference in viewpoints may be resolved, autobiographical memory requires a self-concept that is located in space and time and can complete emotional markings for individual experiences. Or put more succinctly, autobiographical memory is finally at a functional level when a 3-year-old can report having fallen off a chair in kindergarten yesterday and that it hurt. At this age, children start to have their first success in using verb tenses and some understanding of time in the sense of temporal sequencing (temporality). A little later, they can form causal sentences or clauses (something has happened *because* . . .) for which temporality would have to be the logical basis.

Seen from the perspective of Nelson (1996, p. 114), speech acquisition in this phase can be viewed as establishing a system of shared meanings within a linguistic community. The fact that this is in fact successful, although children to a certain extent have to learn the basic meanings "from the very bottom up", is associated with the "experiential-social-communicative system" that was established between the parents and the child earlier, between the ages of 6 and 18 months: "The social world establishes activity contexts and the talk that takes place therein, which the individual child represents in terms of event representations. Parents, as social partners, guiders, and directors, focus the child's attention on specific aspects of the context of the activity, by the way of both verbal and nonverbal markers. Thereby, parents guide the child to extract aspects of the world that need to be given special status as concepts and categories of objects, people, scenes, actions, and events" (1996, p. 114).

It might be possible to say that Nelson emphasizes a kind of systematic intersubjectivity that is reserved for the social practice of everyday language. In addition to considering intersubjectivity, Dittmann (2002, pp. 43f.) also introduces intentionality as an essential factor in learning words and especially complex meanings: "The child has to recognize that their caregivers use words intentionally, that is, with the intention of designating something with these words. . . . An 18-month-old child accepts a word for a new object only when somebody utters this word, somebody whose attention is likewise directed at the object at the same moment. If the caregiver looks in a different direction or if the voice comes from a tape, the child will not construct a relationship between word and object" (Dittmann, 2002, p. 43; our translation).

According to Reese (2002, pp. 124f.), children start speaking about the past in the early phase of speech acquisition, around the eighteenth month of life. Their early oral reports on past events usually consist only of two-word sentences (or associations). Nelson and Fivush (2004), too, write that children start making reference to past events at the age of 18 months, and most often these events are ones just completed ("did it") or routine activities (such as breakfast in the morning). Here, too, the children's remarks are usually repeated by their parents in the form of "memory talk", corrected and commented on. Between the ages of 20 and 24 months, children start referring to events farther back in time, using multiple-word clauses or sentences (Nelson & Fivush, 2004); however, their remarks on such events are still rare and fragmentary.

Children's ability to talk about the past improves between the ages of 2 and 2½, when their remarks become more detailed, although even then they are usually first elicited by questions from their parents.

At the age of 3 years, finally (Nelson & Fivush, 2004), or at 3½ (Reese, 2002, p. 125), children are capable of relating more or less coherent stories of past events with some support from adults. These incipient narrative abilities will improve substantially in the following years.

The role that conversations on the past between parents and their young children play in the origin of autobiographical memory has been the subject of research on developmental psychology for over two decades now (Edwards & Middleton, 1988; Fivush & Fromhoff, 1988; Fivush, 1991, 1994; Nelson, 1993). In this research, the interest has been on the content of these conversations and even more so on the manner in which parents and children talk about the past.

Fivush and Fromhoff (1988), for example, distinguish between "elaborative" and "repetitive" mothers. The first group is rather more oriented toward narratives. They tell stories which invite their children to contribute their own memories. They arrange a story in a connected way and talk about the feelings of the children all the while. The so-called "repetitive" mothers provide less contextual information; instead, they use repeated questions to call on their children to talk about certain aspects of an event without detailing that event themselves. These mothers place more emphasis on the who and what than on the how and why. One long-term study based on these results (Reese, Haden, & Fivush, 1993) found a significant association between the structure of the mother–child dialogues and the later memories of the children. Children of "elaborative" mothers not only remember more details of events in the past, but their reports also contain more contextual information, and they are more complex in their narrative structure (see also Peterson, Jesso, & McCabe, 1999).

In addition, Tessler and Nelson (1994) found that the kind of memory depends significantly on the kind of conversations that took place during an event. In their study they recorded the conversations of mothers and their to 3–3½-year-old children during a visit to a museum. Some of the mothers were asked to answer all the questions of their children but not to initiate the conversations themselves. The other mothers were told that they should decide on their own just how and about what they would talk with their youngsters. One week later, the children were interviewed as to their memories, but without their mothers being present. One result of the study showed that the manner in which the children remembered the trip to the museum corresponded directly with the conversational style of their mothers, but that this was independent of whether the mothers had only given answers to the questions the children posed during the visit or had initiated the conversations actively themselves. Another result found was that the children only remembered objects that had been explicitly mentioned during their visit.

Another long-term study (Haden et al., 2001) confirmed these results by recording on video the conversations and activities of children and their mothers in different playing situations at different ages, and then comparing them with the later memories of the children. At the time of the first recording (mother and child in a tent), the children were 30 months old, 36 at the time of the second (mother and child observe birds), and 42 at the third (an ice-cream store is opened). The standardized interviews with the children, finally, took place 24 hours and 1 week later. Comparison of the video recordings and the remarks of the children made during the interviews revealed that, for all three of the playing situations, the objects and characteristics of these situations that were topics of discussion were better remembered than objects that were not talked about at all or only mentioned by the mothers. That is a further indication of the principal relevance of communication in memory and particularly of the importance of the communicative style in which the past is talked about.

As Reese (2002, pp. 133f.) summed it up, a good many studies already make it possible to conclude that, on the one hand, the motherly style of conducting conversations is a stable indicator of the manner in which children will later remember events. The conversational style of the father, on the other hand, seems to play only a subordinate role, which gives a further indication of how closely associated a child's discoveries of the material, social and symbolic world in the early phase of life are with deep emotional bonds.

The gender of the children, interestingly, plays an intriguingly important role in the manner in which mothers talk to their children about the past, at least in the predominantly white, middle-class population in the United States who make up the majority of the subjects participating in these studies. The mothers apparently used a more elaborative style when talking to their daughters and also emphasized the events more strongly than when talking to their sons (see Reese & Fivush, 1993; Reese, Haden, & Fivush, 1996). As a result, the quantity of memories in girls is correspondingly larger, something which can already be shown at the age of 3½. The differences are most striking for conversations on emotional topics. In talks about emotional events with their daughters, mothers put particular emphasis on having an elaborative style, far more so than with their sons, and this was especially the case when the talks were about sad events (Fivush et al., 2000).

By about the age of 2½, children can use verbal representations for (at least rudimentary) temporal and causal relationships (Nelson, 1996, p. 216). In the years following, they become more and more competent in storytelling and put in increasingly complex temporal references, more details, contextual information and evaluations. Their stories become longer, and more coherent and complex. At this time, the conversational style of the mothers still influences the narrative competence of their children. Haden, Haine, and Fivush (1997) have shown that 3-year-olds provide their listeners with more evaluations (on the subjective reactions and emotional states of persons) and more contextual information (concerning, for example, the when and where of an event) if their mothers included such information in their stories.

Importantly, however, none of these studies concludes that the influence of the mothers on their children's memories is one-sided, as if the mother's style of memory and telling stories were the only determinant in these conversations (Nelson & Fivush, 2004). The discovery of the world is a highly active process, which may be regulated, supported and shaped to a great extent by the mothers and other persons, but to understand it as purely a process of learning and adaptation would be to misinterpret it completely. It is not only the case that parents themselves in fact change over the course of time with their children (this is why the phrase "retroactive socialization" of parents through the influence of their own children has been coined), but it is also the case, and this is the decisive factor, that the unfolding of autobiographical memory in early childhood and the acquisition of language involve an active evaluation of a constantly available surplus supply of developmental potentialities. The medium of this evaluation is social practice, and, as the investigations on early imitation, protoconversations, musicality, etc. show, it is precisely this social practice that is continually shaped, from the moment of birth onward, through the social environment in which a human child develops. This holds true for the process of acquiring a language in which children start to maintain not only their own position in social reality but also their growing knowledge of the position that others have in that reality.

Theory of mind: psychological understanding

For over 20 years now, the concept of "theory of mind" has been a predominant theme in research on fully developed intersubjectivity, that is, on the question of at exactly which age children are capable of attributing wishes, ideas, feelings, intentions, purposes, etc., to themselves and others, as well. The problem in using this concept is, in our view, the fact that children of course do not develop a "theory" of the "mental status" of another person, nor a "theory of mind"; instead, they are able to "feel their way into the thoughts" of others spontaneously and as a result have some form of knowledge, on a practical level, of what is important for this person at the moment. We assume that, even in that case, this practical knowledge does not compare with a complex mental operation such as deduction, but rather that the child makes an analogy about what he or she would do in that situation, and in this way then draws a conclusion as to what the other person is thinking.

This manner of internalizing a perspective, or "psychological understanding" as we prefer to call it, does not develop spontaneously; instead, it is prepared for in a number of ways in ontogenesis: in turn-takings during the early mother–child interactions, in the large number of cases when imitation goes back and forth, and the many different times when shared attention is practiced, up to games and shared emotions in which, for example, feelings of sadness or happiness are communicated socially and to a certain extent are transmitted from one person to another. All of this would be unthinkable without considering the direct relationship to the activities of some other person. And psychological understanding expands this many-faceted relationship now with a decisive point: with the ability to abstract oneself so far removed from one's own view of things as to assume the position of some other person in order to see the world with his or her eyes.

Psychological understanding also logically encompasses the ability to recognize that one's own actions or those of somebody else may have been motivated by "false beliefs", that one may be convinced of knowing something (such as in which little box someone has placed some chocolate bars) and react accordingly (looking into one and only one of the boxes), only to discover that this knowing was erroneously only a belief (because someone has placed the chocolate in some other box). Since the first research by Wimmer and Perner (1983), certain tasks have become routine methods of testing the "theory of mind": For example, a child observes a boy placing chocolate in a closet and then leaving the room. While the boy is outside, another person moves the chocolate to another place. The question now is where the boy will look for it when he returns: in the place that he put it before, or where the other person put it? Three-year-old children who have been watching the experiment say he will look where the chocolate is actually at the moment, and not where he originally placed it, whereas 4-year-old children think he will look exactly where he put it first.

Box 7.1   Brain structures relevant to psychological understanding or the theory of mind: the orbitofrontal cortex and adjacent areas

When cognitive development reaches its final stage, with the ability to feel one's way into the thoughts of others, to have empathy for them, and to understand them as well, a corresponding level of maturity has also been reached, particularly in those brain structures that are important in social cognition and feeling, among which the orbitofrontal (or ventral prefrontal) cortex (see Figure 5.6, p. 134) is pivotal. Second in line are the cortical regions that interact strongly with the orbitofrontal area: the dorsolateral prefrontal and the temporopolar cortices. Even just a few decades ago, these areas were considered as "white spots" on the map of the brain, since it was thought that they were the only regions in the cortex with no or extremely few ascending afferents from the thalamus, meaning that they had connections only with the "highest" levels, that is, the cortical areas. But this view has since been rejected, although the truly unique role of these regions has also been confirmed, as documented by the fact that they lose their functions without the proper environmental stimuli and that they remain, even in adulthood, environmentally dependent on the quality of their activity. Studies have shown this even by functional imaging techniques, which have found differential activity in different forms of human love (for example, the love of a mother for her child, romantic love).

Maturing in the orbitofrontal cortex already starts at an early age – like other brain structures – nonetheless completion takes an unusually long time, apparently due to the fact that many long axon fibers have to be consolidated and that the synchronization of the corresponding networks requires frequent simultaneous activation, and because the appropriate stimuli are so complex and infrequent, activating the orbitofrontal cortex does not occur in rapid succession, but is parceled out rather slowly.

Another task involves showing children a package of Smarties (British candy, similar to M&M's) and then asking them what they think is in the package, whereby the answer "Smarties" would be expected, but in fact the children find pencils. When 3-year-olds are asked what some friends of theirs (not present at the task) will think is in the package, they say "pencils", whereas 4-year-olds give "Smarties" as an answer.

According to research on the "theory of mind" (see Perner, 2000), one essential prerequisite for autobiographical memory is awareness of the relationship between knowledge (for example, what the contents are of a package) and direct experience (having taken a direct look into it). There are, interestingly, studies that have already found an understanding of this relationship in 3-year-olds (Pillow, 1989).[2] Put in more general terms, children have to develop an understanding of the fact that memories represent earlier experiences and that the children themselves have a particular perspective on things, their own perspective, that they might share with others, but just as well might not. And that is something which, as we have already mentioned, they engage in over the course of parent–child conversations about the past (Nelson, 1996, pp. 303ff.; Nelson & Fivush, 2004).

With these considerations in mind, it does not come as a surprise that the ability to perceive and remember events in their complex temporal and causal relationships does not develop until around the fourth year of life. A study conducted by Pillemer (1992) aptly showed this. Two weeks after a fire alarm in a preschool facility, 28 children, aged either 3½ or 4½ years, were interviewed about the event. The two age groups were not differentiated according to the quantity of their memories, but in the nature of their memories. The younger children had difficulty in remembering causal and chronological relationships: 94 percent of the older children, but only 55 percent of the younger ones, remembered that they had been in the school during the alarm. The reason for the alarm was accurately remembered by only one of the younger children, but it was mentioned by almost half of the older ones. In a follow-up study done 7 years later (Pillemer et al., 1994), the authors showed that the memory of the event was significantly contingent on the age at the time when the memory was stored. A third of the children who belonged to the older group at the time of the event were able to report on it in a coherent way even after 7 years, while 57 percent had at least fragmentary memories of the occurrence. Only 18 percent of the younger could remember even only fragmentary details.

Having developed a "theory of mind" or "psychological understanding" is relevant in the development of autobiographical memory in at least two respects, according to Welch-Ross (1997), who does not maintain that autobiographical memories originate when children reach a certain cognitive level. In her view, "Research is needed to determine the skills that children bring to the activity of talking about the past that allow them to participate actively in these conversations and benefit from the narrative structure that parents provide" (Welch-Ross, 1997, p. 619). Communicative situations in

2 Everyday life can reveal amazing concept formations in children under 4 years that reflect causal associations between their own observations and information that was given to them. Considering the wealth of information gained in everyday scenes with the children, one of the authors of this book remembered a car trip with two 3-year-olds seated in the back of the car, in which he remarked about the wind turbines they were just passing, "Look at that, children, wind is made by those wind turbines!" The children burst out laughing, and one said, "No, no, that's nonsense. They make fresh air!" This is apparently a conclusion by analogy which combines direct experiences with fans with knowledge of what they are good for and then transfers this idea of their function to the turbines.

which the past is evoked convey the awareness that different persons have different degrees of knowledge of that past ("the ability to reason about conflicting mental representations"; p. 619), or even that they have different degrees of knowledge at different times in their own lives. In addition, and this brings us back to the topic of the connection between experience and knowledge (Perner & Ruffmann, 1995), during their third year children start to understand that only somebody who can actually look into a receptacle really knows what is inside it (Pillow, 1989). In the fourth year, they gradually understand that their knowledge is based on certain experiences or originates in certain sources (Taylor, 1988). This is an absolutely central aspect, inasmuch as a necessary characteristic of autobiographical memory is a direct reference to the person's identity. For this personal reference, there must be a degree of understanding of the source of a memory, that is, just what relation it has to *me*, personally. In the years before that time, the sources of a memory are rather unclear or interchangeable; for small children, memories belong to almost everybody, an idea which comes from their not having yet developed reliable differentiations between themselves and others. But now children can state that they know something because they have seen it. Here, too, we can see the close association between causal attributions, memories and the slowly developing autobiographical "I, me, myself".

"The ability to understand the relation between having an earlier informative experience with an object or event and knowing about it may enable children to represent their event knowledge as connected to an experience in their personal past. As a result, children can begin to link the events that they discussed in conversation with their own experiential history" (Welch-Ross, 1997, p. 619). In other words, autobiographical memories can come from long-term memories only when children are aware that they know something because they (for example) witnessed it before, and as soon as they know that somebody who has not seen the same thing that they did also does not have the same knowledge that they do. Such awareness, such consciousness, is absent before the third year of life at least.

Perner (2000) suggests that we can understand the phenomenon of infantile amnesia also from this background. Seen from the viewpoint of the "theory of mind", the problem "is infants' inability to encode personally experienced events as *personally experienced*" (p. 306). Therefore, adults cannot remember events before their third year of life because up to this age they have not had any experiences that they could refer to that entity that we would call continual self.

In her study, Welch-Ross (1997) tries to relate memory talk between mothers and their children and cognitive abilities in these children, finding a positive correlation: "Children with higher levels of representational understanding were more active participants in conversations about the past than children with lower levels of understanding" (p. 626). The interpretation of such results, however, poses considerable difficulties. Do better cognitive capabilities lead to greater conversational activity in the children, or is it just the other way around? Do children influence the conversational style of their mothers, or do the mothers influence the cognitive and interactive abilities of their children?

Recent studies also highlight the role that the kind of emotional bond between mother and child has on the development of autobiographical memories. A distinction is frequently made between "securely attached children" and "insecurely attached children or dyads" (see Reese, 2002, pp. 135f.). A study by Farrar, Fasig, and Welch-Ross (1997) revealed that negative emotions are more frequently talked about when the mother–daughter bond is classified as insecure, while in a secure mother–daughter bond, both emotional kinds, positive and negative, are the subject of talks (the daughters in the study were 4 years old).

Another study conducted by Farrant and Reese (see Reese, 2002) showed that in those cases in which the mother–child bond is seen as secure, the mothers speak to their children about the past more often in an elaborate form than in those cases with insecure mother–child bonds. "These findings suggest that memory socialization is taking place to a greater extent in dyads with securely attached children" (Reese, 2002, pp. 135f.) than in those with insecure bonding. Presumably, a close mutual relationship exists between the characteristics of the mother–child communication and the quality of their bond. That would imply that, in a deep bond, more intensive communication occurs, and this relation could be projected at the time of language acquisition onto the connection between bonding, communication style (elaborated or referential), the level of language acquisition, and the capacity for remembering.

8 Exploring autobiographical memory in young children

In an exploratory study (which we dedicated to Katherine Nelson), we examined the age at which children are capable of talking about past experiences in a coherent form and can position themselves in a context with concrete details as to place and time. We also looked for the age at which children first recognize themselves in photos, which would indicate that we could finally identify a "cognitive self" as having developed.

The subjects in the project were 28 children between the ages of 2 and 4 years:

- five girls and five boys aged 2
- four girls and four boys aged 3
- five girls and five boys aged 4.

All the children came from middle-class families and spoke German as their mother tongue. The assistant directing the work with the children, Silke Matura, first visited each child at his or her home, played a game (either dominos or beetles; US name "Cootie") with each child, and took a photo of each one. The actual experiment was performed two days later. First, the child was shown the photo that had been taken of him or her at the previous meeting, and was asked, "Do you know who that child is?", in order to judge recognition of the child in the picture. Then followed questions about that first meeting:

1 Do you still know what we did when I was here last time? (that is, a question as to whether the event was remembered at all. This is an open question, to evaluate the verbal abilities of the child)
2 Who else was there at the time? (an event-oriented question)
3 Where did we play the game? (a question as to whether the place could be identified)
4 How old were you then? (a question as to whether the event could be identified as to time)
5 Did you have fun playing the game? (did the memory have any emotional connotations?)

6   Would you like to play it again? (again, did the memory have emotional appeal for the child?)

The same series of questions was repeated but with two other photos, one that had been taken 6 months previously and another one taken 1 year before, both of which the parents had taken either on a trip, on vacation, or at a birthday party and had put at our disposal for the project. Table 8.1 shows the results.

Self-recognition

All the children recognized themselves in their photos, irrespective of the age of the photo (the recent one, the one taken 6 months before, or the year-old one): Strikingly, all the 2-year-old boys (*n* = 5) and almost all the girls (*n* = 4) gave their own names when asked about the person in the picture (irrespective of how old that photo was). The 3- and 4-year-olds, however, showed differences according to their sex. While half the 3-year-old boys used the personal pronoun ("it's me") when looking at the most recent picture of themselves, only one of the 4-year-old boys used the same pronoun when looking at the two older ones, and the other three boys gave their names. In the case of the girls, however, 75 percent of the 3-year-olds said "it's me" for the recent picture while all of them (100 percent) said that for the older pictures. Sixty percent of the 4-year-old boys used "me" when viewing the recent photo, and 80 percent did so for the older ones. Sixty percent of the 4-year-old girls made use of the personal pronoun for the recent picture and 100 percent for the older ones. The results show that a shift in cognitive development takes place in girls at the age of 3 years that enables them to associate their own photos with an internal representation of themselves ("me"), whereas the boys do not show this shift until the age of 4. Interestingly, according to the mothers, all the girls had started using the personal pronoun ("I" or "me") by the age of 2 in other contexts (such as "I want to go play", "I'm hungry"). This means that using one's own name, instead of the pronoun, to refer to oneself is probably not a sign of underdeveloped linguistic abilities but rather indicates that the children's concept of personal identity, of a "self", is only rudimentary.

Memory of events

If and how events were remembered and then reported on by the children was strongly dependent on the age of the child and on how much time had passed between the original event and the interview (Table 8.2). The recent event (the game with the assistant), which at the time of questioning had taken place 2 days previously, was remembered without exception by all the children in all the different age groups. However, only 40 percent of the 2-year-old girls and boys remembered an event from 6 months before, and only one of these

Table 8.1 Percentage of children demonstrating self-recognition from photos

	Boys, 2 years old	Girls, 2 years old	Boys, 3 years old	Girls, 3 years old	Boys, 4 years old	Girls, 4 years old
Most recent photo	100% (gave own name)	80% ($n = 4$) (gave own name) 20% ($n = 1$) (said "me")	50% ($n = 2$) (gave own name) 50% ($n = 2$) (said "me")	25% ($n = 1$) (gave own name) 75% ($n = 3$) (said "me")	40% ($n = 2$) (gave own name) 60% ($n = 3$) (said "me")	40% ($n = 2$) (gave own name) 60% ($n = 3$) (said "me")
6-month-old photo	100% (gave own name)	80% ($n = 4$) (gave own name) 20% ($n = 1$) (said "me")	75% ($n = 3$) (gave own name) 25% ($n = 1$) (said "me")	100% ($n = 4$) (said "me")	20% ($n = 1$) (gave own name) 80% ($n = 4$) (said "me")	100% ($n = 4$) (said "me")
year-old photo	100% (gave own name)	80% ($n = 4$) (gave own name) 20% ($n = 1$) (said "me")	75% ($n = 3$) (gave own name) 25% ($n = 1$) (said "me")	100% ($n = 4$) (said "me")	20% ($n = 1$) (gave own name) 80% ($n = 4$) (said "me")	100% ($n = 4$) (said "me")

children could remember an event that had taken place a whole year earlier. Of the 3-year-old children, half of the boys, but 75 percent of the girls remembered an event from 6 months before. Furthermore, half the 3-year-old boys but only 25 percent of the same aged girls remembered an event that was a whole year old. The memory performance of 4-year-old boys and girls was very good for events from 6 months before. All the 4-year-olds examined were capable of retelling their memories of such events. In long-term memory, too, the 4-year-olds had better performances than the younger children: 60 percent of the boys and 80 percent of the girls had memories of events that had taken place a year before.

 As we saw (in Chapter 1) from studies on childhood amnesia, children do not seem to have long-lasting memories of personally relevant events before the age of 3. The memories of 3-year-olds for events before that age are more likely to be fragmentary, and they depend largely on specific cues given by someone else taking part in the conversation. Narration of such events is more fluent and cohesive in 4-year-olds, and memories of events that are relatively old become much more frequent. At the age of 4, children begin developing narrative forms that enable them to share events in a linguistic form with their social environment. In this way, memories of events are continuously revived and increase in relevance, thus leading to long-lasting memories in time.

Locality as a context for events

When an event was successfully remembered in our study, the children of all the age groups were capable of remembering the place of that event. In the case of the recent event, 80 percent of the 2-year-old boys and girls and all of the 3- and 4-year-olds could tell where the event took place. For events farther back in time (6–12 months previously), details on the localization of the events were given in the majority of cases provided that the event was remembered at all. Localizing the event only rarely caused a problem for any of the children in any of the age groups. What did cause far more difficulty was the temporal sequencing of events, a topic which will be treated in more detail below.

Arranging events chronologically

The children were not capable of putting the events connected with our project into a correct sequence until the age of 4. None of the 2- and 3-year-olds succeeded in putting the recent event (the game) or the older ones into a proper temporal series.

We evaluated this ability of temporal seriation by asking the question, "How old were you then?" Most of the 2- and 3-year-olds already had difficulty in merely giving their age at the moment of the questioning. Asked how old they were at the time of the events farther back in time, most of their

Table 8.2 Remembering progressively earlier events

Time of event	Boys, 2 years old	Girls, 2 years old	Boys, 3 years old	Girls, 3 years old	Boys, 4 years old	Girls, 4 years old
2 days ago	100% ($n = 5$)	100% ($n = 5$)	100% ($n = 4$)	100% ($n = 4$)	100% ($n = 5$)	100% ($n = 5$)
½ year ago	40% ($n = 2$)	40% ($n = 2$)	50% ($n = 2$)	75% ($n = 3$)	100% ($n = 5$)	100% ($n = 5$)
1 year ago	0% ($n = 0$)	20% ($n = 1$)	50% ($n = 2$)	25% ($n = 1$)	60% ($n = 3$)	80% ($n = 4$)

answers were mere guesses. Those children, however, who did know their correct age regularly gave the same age for the earlier events or simply just said any age ("I was 7 then" or "I was 4"). At the age of 4, the children started giving some indication, if only a vague one, that they had a proper idea of temporal sequences. For the recent event, they gave their correct age. But confronted with the older events they could only answer "I was smaller then" or "I was 3 then". Two of the 4-year-olds (both girls) were able to give more exact temporal information, such as "That was last year".

Paying attention to the finer details of the interviews, we noticed that those children who already at an earlier age answered the question as to their age with a personal pronoun instead of using their name were also the ones who reported past events more elaborately.

All in all, in the exploratory interviews, the girls showed better memory performance than the boys did. This result confirms a number of studies that showed that autobiographical narratives by adult females are lengthier, are more detailed, and have more emotional content than those of adult males (Friedman & Pines, 1991; Ross & Holmberg, 1990). In addition, the earliest memories of adult females are on, average, 6 months earlier than those of adult men (Friedman & Pines, 1991). One possible explanation for this finding is that parents have a tendency to talk with their daughters about past events in more detail and with more emotional content, and this, through the medium of language, would allow autobiographical memories to form earlier and be richer in individual details. As an alternative explanation, it is also possible that the girls in our study had a greater degree of cognitive maturity.

In summary, the 2-year-old children in our investigation had very few and mainly only fragmentary memories of earlier events. This confirms our observation that autobiographical memory does not start developing until the age of 2–3 years and that earlier memories are usually lost. The 3-year-old children showed somewhat better recall of their earlier memories, although even here their reporting was only very fragmentary, requiring rather specific questions to release the memories. The 4-year-old children, however, were capable of reporting in considerable detail on memories that went back as far as a year. Only one of the 2-year-old children seemed to have a well-developed "cognitive self" and mentioned past events in considerably more detail than any of the other 2-year-olds. At the age of 3, the "cognitive self" seemed to have developed, especially in the girls. Their memories went farther back in time than those of the 2-year-olds, and had more content. With only one exception, all 4-year-olds had a "cognitive self" and talked about events from the distant past in considerable detail.

As can be seen, the development of autobiographical memory seems to be related, first, to the development of a "cognitive self" and, second, to the acquisition of speech. Those children who acquired a cognitive concept of "self" at an early age also were farther advanced in their linguistic abilities and could thus give more information on past events more frequently.

9 Autobiographical memory: a continuum in transformation

In summary of our views so far, the development of autobiographical memory is founded on the highly subtle coordination of biological, psychological, social and cultural processes. In the introduction, we already emphasized that it would be a basic mistake to consider autobiographical memory only as something individual, only as a personal ability. On the contrary, autobiographical memory is the functional element that guarantees both the synchronization of the individual with his or her social environment, and the confidence, for the individual and others, that in spite of all the time that has passed and all the physical and psychological changes across the entire life span, each person remains the same "I" and "me". In societies that are constantly increasing the degree of differentiation among their different parts and members, and that also demand patterns of behavior that are becoming longer and more complex, the level of the demands placed on us and our performance continually increases as well. The autobiographical subject is held responsible for fulfilling these requirements and keeping up the performance over time, because he or she is seen as a form of relay station for psychosocial synchronization. This explains why, throughout history, the phases allowed for education, training and development have been growing in duration. At the same time, however, as anyone can see in the numbers of stress-related disorders and diseases today, the vulnerability of individual persons increases just as well, in face of the many and varied expectations that their own autobiographies have to keep up with and also integrate successfully into their lives. There are myriads of demands for living up to different social roles in life such as in one's occupation or in several occupations over time, in relationships with others, or even in different relationships one after the other in a sequence as parent, amateur athlete, friend, a patient, etc., and when the roles become all the more varied and complicated, the autobiographical self becomes all the more fragile at the same time that it is expected to integrate all these different roles more and more efficiently, across the whole life span.

Of course, the autobiographical self is constantly adapting itself, but usually with the help of slow, fine calibrations that keep one from abruptly losing control of either the situation or the ability to fit into the relevant social environment.[1] But social reality is usually highly variable as well. Some persons, such as our parents, or brothers and sisters, accompany us over a considerable portion of our life span, while others, such as our friends from school days or at the university, are with us usually only for a shorter time, even though they might play an important role. And then there are those, such as our partners or spouses, who enter the picture at a relatively late point but accompany us on our way more or less continuously. In addition, there are mere acquaintances, colleagues, people we only get to know on vacation, doctors, hairdressers, friends, etc., and these persons appear in our auto-biographies in very different functions, at different times, to accompany us for equally different lengths of time and in various degrees of intensity. The autobiographical self has the ability to give us the feeling that we are one and the same person through all contacts and that our own introspection is correct in saying that we are always (or at least usually) identical with that one person. But however much we take this ability for granted day by day, it is actually astonishing, when we consider the fact that this ability involves considerable morphological, physical changes. In addition, the culture in which people grow up has precise behavioral codes for each person in every phase of life, and expects them to be fulfilled. What is more, if we take into consideration that socially acceptable, "proper" emotional reactions are expected of us at times of loss, difficulty, joy, etc. – expectations that may even change, however, in later phases in life – then we may justifiably ask whether all these different things can really be fulfilled by one person who somehow remains the same person all through the different phases he or she experiences. Would it possibly be more realistic to assume that not a single, unified person, but actually a rather multiple one is navigating effectively through all these roles and phases in life? Is it possible that only because all the others change at the same time, each multiple personality only seems to be some-thing that remains the same, keeping some form of personal, lasting identity?

This, then, is what autobiographical memory guarantees: it integrates the multiple "I" and the multiple "me" by performing the "miracle" of enabling the self to see itself as always being the same because it is constantly chan-ging. Granted, such an explanation is quite complicated, but it helps us to remember how those of us living in Western societies like to criticize someone for not "moving on", "not keeping up with progress", or failing "to go with the times". When using such expressions, we want to emphasize that such persons do not conform to the demands for change that we take for granted. Put somewhat more extremely, if a man at 50 has seemed "normal" up to

---

1 For the sake of simplicity, we will exclude for the moment the discussion of critical life events (serious accidents, debilitating diseases, etc.) and changes in social status (adolescence, adulthood, old age, etc.), which typically occur when the individual and the social environment no longer seem to fit each other adequately and both show a considerable lack of coping mechanisms.

now, but suddenly starts making sand castles while on vacation, and decorating them with shells he has collected himself, we typically describe him as childish, whereas if his behavior has been that of an 11-year-old for years and years, we would probably consider him mentally handicapped. The two judgments are the result of observing behavior that we do not consider normal for a particular age group. This shows how much our autobiographical identity is related to social standards that define quite specifically how someone should behave at whichever part of life he is in. We can also put it this way: The autobiographical self is a social institution that produces the proper match between the individual and others. From the perspective of evolutionary theory, such a proper fit only becomes necessary when an organism acquires a consciousness of itself and experiences itself as different from other organisms.

We will not be treating the close relationship between consciousness, memory identity and alterity here; the philosophical questions associated with these concepts go far beyond the subject of this book; instead, we will return to the topic of the ontogenesis of human memory and go on to the question of how the development of consciousness of oneself and social synchronization are related to each other. Our observations up to this point have shown that the social existence of a child begins at the age of approximately 9 months with the ability to share attention, at the age when intersubjectivity develops, that is, the ability to understand the "other" person as an intentional being whose attention to and interest in the child can be harmonized with the child's own being. In that case, certain feelings concur between the child and the "other" such as joint happiness, joint surprise and the ability of sympathy and empathy.

The ability to "feel oneself" into and understand the perspective of another person, to see the world with his or her eyes, originates, as we have already pointed out, quite some time later, and is finally fully acquired in the stage of the "theory of mind", some time between the ages of 3 and 4 years. That is the age at which children possess a considerable vocabulary (that is, an impressive amount of symbolic connecting points with other persons) and at which they feel confident in the use of personal pronouns. Not by accident, this is also the age at which children in Western countries are first introduced to extrafamilial social interaction, entering kindergarten at the age of 3; this means that they can stay for a longer period of time without their mother and are instead confronted with other children and a different hourly schedule from the one at home, as well as new responsibilities, a new person of authority, new games, etc.

Life after that experience is a long sequence of similar passages into new communities and their rules of socialization. Even if autobiographical memory slowly evolves over a rather long period of time, it does not finally appear, in successive stages, until kindergarten age, that is, when the child enters the first extrafamilial field of socialization. Western societies seem to feel that children must have reached a certain level of autobiographical self-confidence before going on to the next step, and this corroborates the idea that auto-biographical memory has a fundamental social dimension and function. But what kind of memory, consciousness and self-understanding does a child have before then? How can we describe the self-identity of children in the months and years before? Very probably, the first months of life can best be seen as a phase in which some form of experiential consciousness exists that does not yet have anything to do with a consciousness of self. The child communicates, feels and expresses things, has good and bad experiences, learns, and develops any number of abilities, but does not "experience" dir-ectly all these happenings. We can say the child "lives life" simply, in one particular material and social environment of which the child is a part. In this phase, there is still no "self-identity" that somehow "processes" whatever experiences it "has", or that "interacts" with others; instead, there is only a being that learns procedurally, habitually, cognitively and emotionally, and is capable of truly astonishing things. This being does not yet have the slightest idea that there is something else (a personal self, an "I" or "me") that he or she could relate these experiences to, and there is still no idea that what the parents or other caregivers keep identifying with a name and talking to is a reality in itself.

Katherine Nelson reconstructed the development of the ability of self-understanding, as given in Table 9.1.

The first phase of self-understanding or self-experiencing – self-feeling – is mainly one of physical experience. The baby experiences a boundary between its own body and other persons to whom an emotional relationship has been established through their practical, everyday caring. But we rather doubt that the child at this early stage in fact already has an "idea" that the others are just like he or she is, as Meltzoff (1999) has suggested, and we base this doubt on the assumption that the baby most probably does not yet have anything similar to an "idea". Meltzoff assumed that the ability to represent something mentally is already functioning in the child, while we find no arguments to support the existence of such an ability at this stage of development. But the child can do something different: it can communicate. And even though this ability may be rather one-sided for the time being, we can assume an "aware-ness of aspects of the world that are outside the self and that provide opportunities for interaction, initially with caretakers and other social beings, then with inanimate objects as well" (Nelson, 2003, p. 5).

Later, at approximately the time of the decisive 9 months' phase, the child gradually "makes relational contrasts, understanding the roles that the other and self play in routines such as feeding, dressing, and play, and understand-ing the relational differences between people – for example, mother and stranger" (Nelson, 2003, p. 5). This phase can be called one of "social self-understanding" and correlates highly with memory development because it is based, first, on the ability to distinguish between other persons and between others and oneself, and, second, on knowledge of recurring chains of events (script knowledge), which enables the child to have systematic expectations of

Table 9.1 Levels of self-understanding (modified from Nelson, 2003)

	Level of understanding	Age	Mental ability	Difference between self and others	Difference between self and world	Memory
1	Physical	Postnatal, 0–9 months	Emotional ties	Physical border	Physical border	Experiential
2	Social	6–18 months	Social exchange	Attentiveness, intention, communication	Routine, objects, words	Semantic
3	Cognitive	16–36 months	I–you perspective	Object vs. other perspective	Self vs. objects perspective	Episodic
4	Representational	2–4 years	Continuous experience of self	My mind vs. your mind	Mental vs. physical	Episodic vs. autobiographical
5	Narrative	3–6 years	My history	Stories about me vs. stories about others	Past vs. future, worlds outside my own	Autobiographical
6	Cultural	5–7 years	Our history	Cultural roles	Cultural knowledge, institutions	Autobiographical

events yet to occur (such as knowing that someone will feed him, or that clothing or being close to someone else can keep him warm). And the social agents, which now take the form of genuine interaction, are attentiveness, intention and multimodal communication.

Cognitive self-understanding is finally acquired when children begin to refer to themselves with the help of elements of language, such as using personal pronouns or their own proper names. This is also the phase in which children recognize themselves in the mirror, and in addition learn to compare their own perspectives with those of others. For example, they constantly check on whether another person is really looking at the same page in a picture book by watching the other person's eyes or by making comments on the contents of the picture, that is, by checking on whether attentiveness is really being shared. What is even more important, children start to perceive themselves as an object from the perspective of others, and as Nelson emphasized, that is a decisive step in the development of a consciousness of oneself. By this time, children are no longer simply a part of a social network of relationships; rather, they sense that this is so and perceive themselves with the eyes of the others. This explains why feelings of embarrassment and shame first occur at this age, that is, feelings that somehow reveal the children are not fulfilling social expectations.

Children also start to interrupt activities when they fear negative reactions from their mother. But, importantly, this ability to adopt the perspective of others does not mean that the child has now reached a representation of his or her own self. "The 2-year-old may view the self as an object in the ongoing activity, but does not represent the self outside the context of present experience. The representational self has a continuing mental reality that can be decontexted from the present; it is not just the experiencing self, or the self in action, but a contemplated conceptual object" (Nelson, 2003, p. 6).

In this context it is possible to explain findings which show that 3-year-olds still have difficulty in recognizing themselves in photos or videos (DeLoache, 2000; Povinelli et al., 1996). Interestingly, this is the phase in which "memory talk" starts: the time in which parents talk to their children a good deal about past events in which the children played a role.[2] Such talk could evoke the

---

2 An example of a dialogue between a 2-year-old girl and her mother:

Mother: Did you like our vacation apartment at the beach?
Daughter: Yeah, and in, in, in the water, I liked the water too.
M.:   You liked the water?
D.:   I got to the ocean.
M.:   You got to the ocean?
D.:   Yeah.
M.:   Did you play in the water?
D.:   And took off my sandals.
M.:   You took your sandals off?
D.:   And my pajamas too.

impression that the parents are deliberately helping their children to develop a representation of their own selves that would survive through completely different situations and phases in time. Children learn not only that there is a past in which they did this or that, but also that it is apparently of considerable importance to make this past a theme for discussion, meaning that in this phase something like a retrospective dimension of perception is being developed, and because references to the past are directly related to an orientation to the future, we can conclude that here is the first station for those mental time travels that Tulving considers the central characteristic of autobiographical memory.

Nelson concluded that self-understanding in 3- and 4-year-olds is based on the children sensing a new contrast between their view of themselves as an object in the present and seeing themselves as a supratemporal, permanent self. She accounted for the difficulty younger children have to form a representation of themselves by their lack of confidence in distinguishing the sources from which they derive their memories and by their lack of a "theory of mind", that is, the ability to sense what the background is behind the decisions of another person (Nelson, 2002, p. 244).

According to Nelson, the end of the preschool age coincides with the development of "narrative self-understanding", with children experiencing themselves as a self that has a history different from those of other persons.[3] This self-hood of a child possesses a past and a future, and the ability to tell that story creates a new level of integration in relation to the social environment of the child. By acquiring this self, which looks both back into a past and forward into a future, a child is recognized socially more and more as a person who has a unique role within social relationships, which become ever more differentiated: in the family, circle of friends, sport clubs, etc.

Finally, the child reaches a level that Nelson called "cultural self-understanding": "The child's self history comes to be set into a cultural framework that differentiates it in terms of cultural settings and time frames, babyhood, adulthood, school, home, playground, each with its own rules and

---

M.:	So, you took off your pajamas. Then what were you wearing on the beach?
D.:	My hot chocolate T-shirt.
M.:	Oh, your hot chocolate T-shirt, right. And your swimsuit.
D.:	Yeah. And my hot chocolate T-shirt.
M.:	Did we go to the beach on foot?
D.:	Yeah.

(Hudson, 1990; quoted and translated from Miller, 1993, p. 345)

3 As Piaget demonstrated in a classic investigation, this is not in any way synonymous with the child's actually having a concept of age in life. For example, children often say at this age that one's age in life can be measured by size and that for this reason adults no longer grow older (Piaget, 1974, pp. 283ff.).

participant roles. Henceforth, typically at the school level, an autobiograph-ical memory can come into existence, culturally framed, full of incidents and meanings for the self. The self then may make contrasts between the ideal self portrayed by the culture and the actual self as understood, and then may strive to achieve a more ideal self" (Nelson, 2003, p. 7). In an abstract sense, the child navigates in a world of multiple relations and experiences himself or herself in terms of different modes of activities, relationships and situations as a self that lives on continuously and learns to react flexibly to completely different demands in social roles. Nelson emphasized, however, that the schematic levels blend together and cannot be distinguished from each other in any strict sense of the word.

These considerations bring us back once again to the question of which changes memory goes through in the different levels of self-understanding. In the early phase, memory enables the child to learn things by habituation, storing bodily experiences and remembering recurrent activities and events in their sequence; none of this is tantamount to conscious memory, but is, rather, noetic and experiential. When the child reaches the stage of social self-understanding, memory takes on a new quality: persons and objects can now be understood as constants. Semantic memory arises that contains things for the child even when they are not physically present. With the development of cognitive self-understanding, episodic memory starts to form. When children experience themselves in relation to other persons as well as, for example, common moments of pleasure, or, just the opposite, when they feel disap-pointment because something has been postponed for the moment, then their memories have an emotional index: one of the central prerequisites for episodic and, later, autobiographical memories. Once a representational self has developed, this still rather rudimentary form of episodic memory acquires a further central characteristic: an "I-reference", a reference to the self that is then a further prerequisite for remembering personally relevant experiences at the same time as somebody else.

This short review already reveals how closely related the development of memory is to the growing social bond or the synchronization of the child with persons in the environment, which itself expands more and more over the years. When autobiographical memory starts to develop, the child expands his or her circle of group membership, and that becomes possible at this time because the child experiences that degree of self-continuity that, in the face of fluctuating contacts and situations, guarantees a feeling of con-fidence in being a unique, unmistakable, and at the same time coherent self. And once again, the correlation with the successively expanding environment becomes all the more subtle, and the pervading social character of auto-biographical memory becomes undeniable. Surveying the development of memory can reveal how a child becomes an active and responsible member of a social and cultural community.

George Herbert Mead, in his classic theory of development, already described the different phases a child goes through on the way to social bonding, phases which go from an experiential phase (play), to a world with social rules (game), in order to learn to accept the perspectives of significant others and finally to share the ethical and moral norms, behavioral codes, and attitudes of the culture (generalized other). With this theory, Mead hoped to show that all these events take place only within the frame of sociality. Childhood development, the successive steps in making children more and more fully autobiographical persons, and their emerging ability of intersubjectivity can only be understood when we view them, with Daniel Stern, as a co-development (Stern, 1998; Welzer, 2002). Children do not come as individuals into the world, which then socializes them. Instead, from the very start, they are part of a network of relationships in which they grow up. They acquire in time more and more social competence and finally reach a stage in development at which the social and cultural community that they belong to places clear demands on their qualities of responsibility, self-control, cognitive, social, and emotional behavior, etc. The stage that we usually call adulthood is far from something that is once and forever successfully attained, a level which, by this age, is no longer adaptable. Adulthood, on the contrary, has been shown by research on aging, adult socialization, and, not least, brain development, to be a constant readjustment, a recalibration within the autobiographical subject, whose memory then rewrites its own life history according to the current demands placed on the person.

10 The age at which memory appears: results of an interdisciplinary research project on remembering and memory

Our interdisciplinary approach allows us to examine the contents of auto-biographical memories according to their origins, their age-specific process-ing, and their emotional coding. In addition to the empirical examination of subjects from different age groups, an interdisciplinary developmental model of autobiographical memory was derived from a secondary analysis that can take into account the processes of brain maturity and connectivity as well as the evolving competence in memory and the age-related possible social interactions (see Figure 10.1, p. 199).

Such a model can reveal an interesting direction for systematically investi-gating the interrelated nature of sociocultural, psychological and organic functions in development, especially when critical developmental jumps are also taken into consideration. At the same time, the model has to be supplied with sufficient background information on brain maturation, developmental psychology, and the social developmental context from specific phases, so that for each of the different developmental phases a synopsis of the ontogenetic events can result.

Throughout a review of the secondary analysis of the results on the onto-genetic development, phases with high-density events take place in which a good deal happens at all four levels of observation, as well as phases of relatively constant event density, indicating that phases with a high number of changes mark developmental jumps, while the somewhat more "quiet" periods mainly serve to consolidate the new experiences and competencies. Based on this model, an examination was done on age-specific memory pro-cessing, and pilot studies were performed on autobiographical memory both in small children and from a longitudinal perspective. The results demon-strated how important the phase of young adulthood is for older age groups as to subjective representation, neuronal activity patterns, and the develop-ment of evaluative components of autobiographical memory over the stages of life. In addition, we found a relatively slight activity level for memories from early childhood, even though these memories were clearly represented in the accompanying narratives of the subjects. This last finding would sug-gest the influence of an increasing semantification of old memories in the course of one's life. Finally, it was intriguing to find a specific activity pattern for memories from early childhood in the sample of the younger adults, revealing a neural correspondence to what is called the constitutional phase of autobiographical memory postulated in developmental psychology for the ages of from 3 to 6 years.

The results clearly show that memories formed in early childhood are processed differently from those formed in later childhood, in adolescence, and particularly in adulthood.

Our examination of the development of and the changes in autobiographical memory across the life span are derived from a plan of sampling that varies according to age (Table 10.1).

Figure 10.1 shows a detail from the model we developed on autobiographical memory, and using this model, we conducted multimethod examinations in older and younger adults, in adolescents, and in children, and we combined social scientific approaches, such as biographical interviews, with psychological tests as well as with imaging techniques. We also interviewed the subjects in different age groups and were thus able to reconstruct the subjective meaning of individual autobiographical memories and then to correlate them with activity at the level of the brain. Furthermore, we showed how the neuroanatomical activity of autobiographical memories varies over the course of life and which brain areas are involved in remembering such events.

For technical reasons, autobiographical interviews cannot be conducted during fMRI (functional magnetic resonance imaging) investigation work. So the events narrated and evaluated by our female subjects themselves in previous interviews were presented to them over headphones as a trigger for evoking reactions: They heard their own stories in the form of short descriptions and were requested to remember the events and experiences as vividly as possible. For the acoustic presentation, we paid particular attention to the exact age when the events originally took place, and related biographically neutral events from the same period so as to distinguish between processing either episodic or semantic memories. The combination of methods from

Table 10.1 Samples from the research project "Remembering and Memory"

Group	Age of adults	Age of adolescents
1: $n = 14$	62–74 years	
2: $n = 14$	38–42 years	
3: $n = 14$		20–21 years
4: $n = 14$		16–17 years
Total $n = 56$		

Time Axis	Month 7	Month 8	Month 9
Neurological Development	*Month 7*: synaptic contacts between granular cells and pyramidal cells in the CA3 region of the hippocampus are formed. Intrahippocampal projections, which are important for LTP, develop. This development may be a determining factor in the learning and memory functions localized in the hippocampus.	*Month 8*: strong increase in synaptic density in the frontal cortex. Highest density in synapses at the age of 2 years.	*Months 8–12*: strong increase in glucose metabolism in the dorsolateral prefrontal cortex (plays a significant role in spatial working memory).
Memory	*Months 7–10*: development of working memory. The child can maintain the representation of a past event in working memory and make use of it at the proper moment. At the same time, object permanence develops.	*By Month 8*: development of the system of knowledge: the child starts thinking about things that are not physically present, and builds up a fundament of knowledge. Origin of concept formation: global categories (e.g., animals, vehicles) are distinguished. Memory of past events is organized mainly in scripts and constitutes a part of the semantic memory system.	
Social Communication	*Months 7–8*: startle reaction begins, possibly a result of the development of working memory and the myelinization of the capsula interna, which connects the amygdala with the cortex.		*By Month 9*: children start to understand the meaning of words. They now communicate by a joint manipulation of objects with their caregivers. Children who point at things in their environment at an early age so as to communicate usually learn to speak early as well. *Months 9–10*: "secondary intersubjectivity" – beginning of anticipatory view of interaction with others in acts of cooperation.

Figure 10.1 Partial view of the developmental model of autobiographical memory. LTP: long-term potentiation.

biography research[1] in the fields of both social science and psychology proved to be very effective, for the following reasons:

- The biographical interviews and the inventory of events made it possible to correlate the measurements of activity patterns with the life-history memories, which were narrated as clearly important from the subjective point of view, and then to differentiate them from semantic information.
- With the help of the autobiographical interview material, the subjective presentation and personal evaluation of memories were correlated with the corresponding activity patterns, as is essential to study the association between age, emotion and memory.
- This procedure avoids measuring subjectively unimportant activity from memories, guaranteeing the multimethod approach a high degree of ecological validity, compared to other studies with imaging techniques.

Results

Comparing the sample according to age groups is highly interesting because the experimental design chosen allows both vertical and horizontal comparisons. A vertical comparison between the different age groups permits measuring the age-specific processing of autobiographical memory contents, while the horizontal comparison of autobiographical retrospection examines the character of the various age-specific memories, differentiated according to static vs flexible, neutral vs personally relevant, or fact-oriented vs evaluative. The results on age-specific memory processing have uncovered associations that explain some of the phenomena discussed in developmental psychology, the social sciences, and related fields. For example, we can now demonstrate that adolescents' memories from the time when they were 3–6 years of age (that is, from their childhood phase) are processed differently from those from a later phase, such as a year before they took part in our project (see Figures 10.2 and 10.3).

This supports the concept that autobiographical memory in fact does not

1 Relying on parameters for comparing age, emotion and biographical transitions, we extracted life-history experiences of the subjects from their interviews, by the method of qualitative content analysis, and then classified them according to intersubjective categories. The main categories were generated inductively within the frame of "open coding" according to grounded theory (Glaser & Strauss, 1998) from the interview material, so that the emphasis of explorative analysis could be placed on the topics made relevant by the subjects themselves. The result is a highly differentiated scheme of categories that, first, captures the full inventory of autobiographical stories and, second, also keeps the attention on the cognitive level where self-reflective statements with relevance to a theory of daily life can be coded. The affective dimensions of the experiences and events were derived with the help of dichotomous classifications (positive vs negative, "I" vs the group). In addition, the richness of details and information on whether or not the related episodes are systematic were also considered in the analysis.

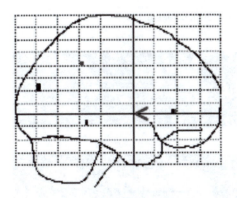
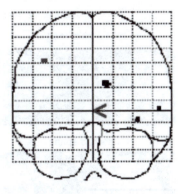

Figure 10.2 Functional magnetic resonance imaging activity projections onto representative "glass-brain" pictures: remembrances from childhood in adolescents.

originate until after the first 3 years of life, and that it only attains a relatively stable form of processing after the sixth year. It also supports an approach to explaining the well-known phenomenon of "childhood amnesia" that prevents us from accessing our memories of events before the age of the third or fourth year. A system of memory that relates experience to a continuous feeling of being an "I", and that allows "mental time travel" between a yesterday, a today and a tomorrow, is not yet available in early childhood.

In older persons, events from a more distant past (see Figure 10.4, group 1, childhood, middle adulthood) seem to be remembered in a more stable and more intense fashion than events from the more recent past (Figure 10.4, group 1). It would appear that more recent events become less important with increasing age, and that the evaluative dimensions of memory increase all the more. In adolescent subjects, on the other hand, more recent events

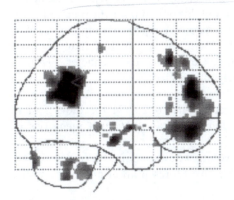
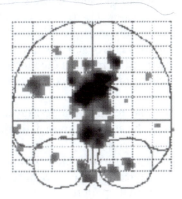

Figure 10.3 Functional magnetic resonance imaging activity projections onto representative "glass-brain" pictures: remembrances from the previous year of life in adolescents.

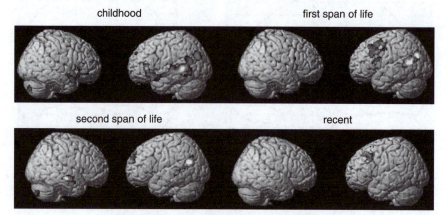

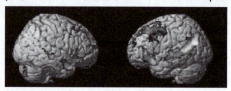

Figure 10.4 Functional magnetic resonance imaging pictures: group 1 (62–74 years). (A color version of this figure is on www.cognitiveneuroscience.com/ brain-scans)

(Figure 10.5, group 2, previous year) are remembered more intensively (and more emotionally; see the increased activity in the right hemisphere) than those from farther back in time (Figure 10.5, group 2, later adolescence). In the group of older subjects (Figure 10.4, group 1, 62–74 years of age), the high level of activity is quite obvious for childhood and for the phase of early adulthood, and this is the case for both narrative representation and activity pattern. This result fits quite well the "reminiscence bump" that has been discussed so much in the literature on this age group (e.g., Schacter, 1996).

Some of our results were particularly unexpected:

1   The relative unimportance of "recent memories" in the older female subjects, as opposed to the greater importance of such memories in adolescents.

2   The considerable relevance of young adulthood in the older female subjects at the level both of subjective representation and of neuronal activity pattern.

3   The increase of the role of evaluative components of autobiographical memories, at the level both of subjective representation and of neuronal activity pattern.

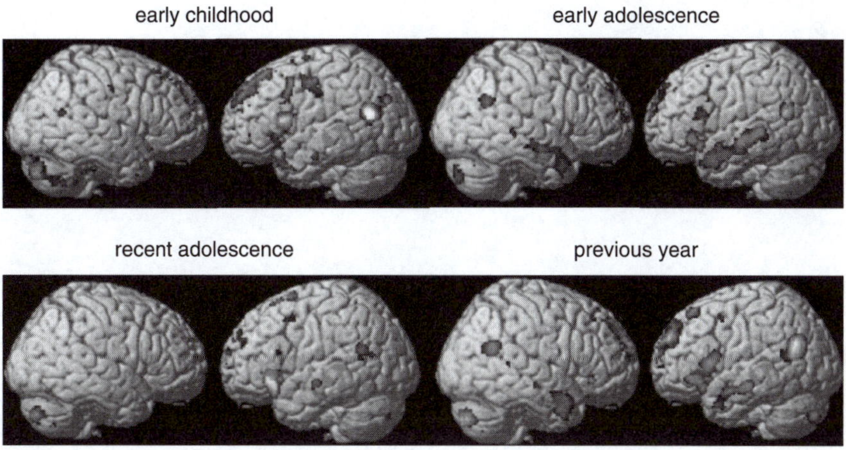

early childhood   early adolescence

recent adolescence   previous year

Figure 10.5 Functional magnetic resonance imaging pictures: group 2 (20–21 years). (A color version of this figure is on www.cognitiveneuroscience.com/brain-scans)

4 The minor activity level for memories from early childhood in the sample of older female subjects, although the memories are clearly represented in their narrations. This finding implicates an increasing role of semantification of older memories in the course of life.

5 The specific activity pattern for memories from early childhood in the sample of younger adults. We consider this result especially unique in that a neuronal correspondence can be identified for the constitutional phase of autobiographical memory postulated in developmental psychology for the ages from 3 to 6 years.

Our project thus allowed us to prove the age-specific nature of autobiographical memory within a neuroscientific context and to describe it in social scientific-phenomenological terms, and this especially can stimulate further research, as it furthers systematic, neuroscientific classifications of memory and also supplies basic information for research on biography.

11 A formative theory of memory development

The chapters up to now have treated in some detail the ontogenetic origin and differentiation of memory systems based on their content and relevant brain structures. The subject of this chapter is how memory and other related cognitive functions change over the life span once the first years of childhood are completed.

At the age of 4 years, episodic memory is fully functional and autobiographical memory begins to differentiate. The child perceives itself as a "self", existing as opposed to "the others". A prerequisite for this process is the full development of episodic memory (see Box 11.1 for Tulving's (2002, 2005) definition).

This is the age at which the ideas of self, autonoetic consciousness and subjective purpose arise, among a series of further mental abilities. The functionality of the left hemisphere develops through the use of language, and the right hemisphere matures through practicing empathy, sympathy and other social-emotional dispositions. Axons connecting the two hemispheres – the corpus callosum and the anterior commissure – make it possible to integrate these different social-emotional and cognitive processes, and thus to contribute to a mature, unified personality. In the first 2 years of life, the surface of the corpus callosum doubles in size, and by adolescence it has further increased by over 100 percent (Rakic & Yakovlev, 1968). In fact, it is complete only at early adulthood (Yakovlev & Lecours, 1967).

Improvements in both the size and differentiation of vocabulary and the use of grammar are necessary for mental time travel. The different forms of the past and future tenses, and the indicative and subjunctive moods are highly mature cognitive achievements, expanding the mental horizons of an individual. It thus gradually becomes possible to think and speak on a meta-level. Mathematical skills are of course similarly expedient for these acts of thinking, as they allow us a further integration of space and time levels.

The ability to compare different packets of information, and, just casually or deliberately, to reflect on what takes place while thinking about oneself or others, arises only after the first 10 years of life. While it is obvious that children participate in role-playing rather early in life and develop an avid interest in playing "theater", they "disappear" into their roles rather than

Box 11.1   Episodic memory in the definition of Endel Tulving

Episodic memory is a recently evolved, late-developing, and early-deteriorating brain/mind ("neurocognitive") memory system. It is oriented to the past, more vulnerable than other memory systems to neuronal dysfunction, and probably unique to humans. It makes possible mental time travel through subjective time – past, present, and future. This mental time travel allows the "owner" of episodic memory ("self"), through the medium of autonoetic awareness, to remember his own previous "thought-about" experiences, as well as to "think about" his own possible future experiences. The operations of episodic memory require, but go beyond, the semantic memory system. Retrieving information from episodic memory ("remembering") requires the establishment and maintenance of a special mental set, dubbed episodic "retrieval mode". The neural components of episodic memory comprise a widely distributed network of cortical and subcortical brain regions that overlap with and extend beyond the networks subserving other memory systems. The essence of episodic memory lies in the conjunction of three concepts – self, autonoetic awareness, and subjective time.

reflect on what their real self is compared to the superficial stage role. Unfortunately, there has been very little research done on how much the development of another field of learning, logical thinking and practice in mathematical tasks, helps in this respect.

Mental horizons expand by our learning to think in terms of numbers, to grasp different kinds of dimensions, and to integrate aspects of time and space. Changing from a spatial dimension to the time dimension is certainly a milestone, from both a phylogenetic (Tulving & Markowitsch, 1994) and an ontogenetic point of view, for the development of autobiographical memory (see also Singer, 1999). On the level of the brain and in particular within the neocortex, this especially requires activation of parts of the lateral temporal lobe, a region that gained unexpected attention by the discovery that precisely this area showed special development in the brain of Albert Einstein.

The lateral temporal lobe has a role in the integration of space-time aspects and in the perception and comprehension of chronological processes, which are essential for the development of intellectual functions. This role can be particularly well seen in pathological cases, when this area fails to function correctly after a traumatic accident or an infarction. Typically in such traumas to the temporal lobe, the patients experience time as compressed or expanded. They fail to perceive the normal progression of time, instead reporting, for example, that a minute seems to last as long as an hour or, vice versa, a day seems to last only 10 minutes. The ability to perceive units of time, such as months or years, is warped in both directions so that they are either notably shorter or longer than usual.

It is not surprising, then, that so much research has stressed the relation between time, consciousness and memory (e.g., Engel, Fries, König, Brecht, & Singer, 1999; Markowitsch, 2004a, 2004b, 2004c). Quite early, Krauss (1930) considered "time consciousness" a key word to characterize the cognitive deficits of amnestic patients (i.e., Korsakov patients[1]), and van der Horst (1928, 1932) held time perception to be precisely the basic deficit of these patients. Grünthal (1932, 1939) and Becker and Sternbach (1953) described severely amnestic patients who had lost all feeling for time or who experienced a major change in their perception of time. Becker and Sternbach's first patient felt that time was shrinking, while their second patient reported the opposite, time expanding toward infinity so that a single day never seemed to come to an end. Williams and Zangwill (1950) described Korsakov patients who felt that a minute lasted as long as a quarter of an hour and at the same time dated events of the immediate past as having taken place considerably earlier. Interestingly, time shrinkage and similar phenomena occur in other abnormal mental states such as mescaline intoxication (e.g., Beringer, 1927; Fischer, 1946) as well as in lesions in the area of the temporal lobe (Hoff & Pötzl, 1938). (Changed perceptions of time occur of course under normal conditions also – dreams are a case in point; see Palombo, 1978; Zulley & Geisler, 2004.)

Along this line of thinking, van der Horst (1928, 1932) argued that the memory deficits typical of Korsakov patients are mainly caused by the fact that chronological continuity is lacking at the moment of memory storage, so that whatever they undertook was performed in "pieces of time" and "points of time" (p. 74). The direct comprehension of and feeling for time as a principle of orientation are disturbed (p. 83). The ability to evaluate and measure time, to arrange episodes in one's life according to what occurred earlier or later, to anticipate future events in thought – these are decisive prerequisites for autobiographical memory. Ewald Hering, working at a very early time (1870) on sensory perception, wrote: "Memory unites the uncounted individual phenomena into a whole; and just as our bodies would dissipate into countless atoms if the power of attraction in matter did not hold them together, our consciousness would break up into as many different

---

1 Korsakov patients lose the ability of recent memory usually through long-term and intensive alcohol abuse. The loss most often includes the ability to recall old biographical episodes. The direct pathological cause is damage (in the form of degeneration) to structures in the vicinity of the diencephalon (the medial thalamus region and the mammillary bodies; compare Figure 4.4). Earlier, this condition was seen far more frequently (e.g., Bonhoeffer, 1901), but today it is still surprisingly frequent (Brand et al., 2003; Fujiwara, Brand, & Markowitsch, 2002; Kessler, Irle, & Markowitsch, 1986; Kessler, Markowitsch, & Bast-Kessler, 1987). The underlying pathological mechanism of the damage is most probably a metabolic disturbance that makes it impossible for the patients to co-opt vitamin B_1 (thiamine) in sufficient quantities.

splinters as there are moments, without the power of memory" (Hering, 1870, p. 12, our translation). Consciousness, memory and the feeling of time constitute a triad which forms a core part of one's personality and at the same time creates the essential aspect of cultural memory (Fried, 2004; Markowitsch, 2001b, 2002b).

As we have already pointed out, an integrative model of memory processing and representation over the life span has to take into consideration several levels: maturing processes within the brain, the social and cultural environment, personal experiences with special relevance to the perspective of the individual, and any unique styles of processing these experiences. Ontogeny does not proceed in a linear fashion; instead, there are phases of increased activity in which essential events take place on all these levels, and then phases of relative inactivity. Phases with a high density of change and growth mark developmental transitions, while more stable phases rather serve to consolidate the new experiences and skills. The relevant phases can be shown schematically (Table 11.1).

The integrative approach to memory development that we are proposing here offers, we believe, a better and more fruitful understanding of the interactions between physical and social factors in ontogeny. In the end, it may also help to reduce the mystification that has arisen about the actual abilities of early childhood as well as some of the very sterile academic and philosophical discussions about them. To expand on this point briefly, when developmental psychologists improved their methods of observing with the help of film and video techniques, and applied elements of microanalysis to mother–child interactions, their appraisal of just how much infants are capable of improved substantially. Well into the middle of the last century, children under the age of 1 year were usually considered as interesting but small "packages of biological needs", and a well-known remark by William James aptly captured just this view, portraying children as more or less stumbling through development in "blooming, buzzing confusion" (1890). More recent work in developmental psychology, such as from the Edinburgh school, has also found convincing evidence of the cognitive and communication skills of children. In case studies, some of these skills have been shown to precede the infant stage, going back to the fetal stage. Similarly, concepts such as "primary intersubjectivity" (Rochat, 2001; Trevarthen, 1998, p. 203), assumed to function already at birth, suggest that infants are certainly quite capable of social exchanges with others. However, this may appear to be the case only superficially. Without doubt, infants do have surprising communicative abilities from the moment of their birth, and they improve on them essentially over the first months of life, but it would be erroneous to assume that they do in fact interact with or even gradually feel their way into another person's mind, which would fulfill the basic meaning of intersubjectivity. This erroneous impression is probably due to the facts that infants are capable of far more than what was previously assumed, and that mothers and other caregivers treat their infants as if they were interactive partners – by talking

Table 11.1 Phases of development

Age	Brain maturation	Cognitive and emotional development	Social environment
1. Prenatal memory development			
18–24 days	Neural plate develops		
24–40 days	Neural tube develops		
5th month	Axonal arborization begins		
8th month	Brainstem, cerebellum	Habituation and stimulus association	
2. Postnatal development to the age of 8 months			
Month 1	Amygdala Colliculus superior (brainstem)	Perceptual priming Recognizes voice of the mother Interest in social objects Imitation behavior	Attention giving, skin contact, looking at, speaking with, nursing, cleaning, etc.
Month 2	Cerebellum Basal ganglia	Trial and error learning (operant conditioning) Social smiling Protoconversation, cooing	The same
Month 5	Hippocampus Visual cortex	Perceptual memory Expressions of joy	The same
Month 8	Dorsolateral prefrontal cortex	Working memory Object permanence Impulse control Stranger anxiety	Shared attention
3. The 9 months' revolution			
	Orbitofrontal cortex	Genuine binding behavior Pointing, showing Divided attention Subjective feelings Intersubjectivity	Intersubjectivity Affect reinforcement
	Prefrontal cortex		

(Continued Overleaf)

Table 11.1 Continued

Age	Brain maturation	Cognitive and emotional development	Social environment
4. Second year of life			
Month 15	Medial prefrontal cortex	Intentions of others recognized	Scaffolding
Months 18–24	Wernicke's area Broca's area Orbitofrontal cortex (completed)	Vocabulary expansion Self-related feelings (embarrassment, jealousy) Use of personal pronouns Self-recognition in mirror	Memory talk
5. Third year of life			
Month 24–year 3	High density of synapses in medial frontal lobe Right hemisphere loses dominancy	Self-concept develops in which knowledge of one's own personal characteristics is integrated Origin of autobiographical memory Self-evaluating feelings: pride, shame, feelings of guilt	Increased demands for independent behaviors, "being reasonable" and control of behavior
6. Fifth year of life			
	Frontal lobe	Source memory Theory of mind Causal comprehension of permanent self Narrative structure develops	Increased demands for understanding motivation, ability of insight, causal understanding

to them constantly, giving them attention, and interpreting and then satisfying their supposed needs; in short by treating them as if, but still counterfactually, they were beings who already understand their caregivers. This is certainly highly advantageous for infants' development, since they learn a great deal through social communication, but successful learning here does not demonstrate that intersubjectivity, sharing the views of another, is already at work. In this phase, a child has an existential selfhood, but not a subjective or even self-reflective self, and probably exists in a permanent present that does not require any form of self as a final resort for social exchange (compare Nelson, 1996, pp. 204ff.).

There have been some sterile academic discussions concerning the questions of (1) whether development of a self-concept is the decisive condition for unfolding an autobiographical memory system, as Howe and coworkers (2003) postulated, and (2) whether an elaborate level of language comprehension is necessary, as Katherine Nelson (1993, 1996) argued. We are convinced that both conditions (having not just self-reference but also the use of a symbolic medium) are essentially important. This medium itself then makes possible, for the first time, an objective positioning of the self in time and space and "mental time travel", which are indispensable for the unfolding of autobiographical memory. In addition, even performing simple protonarrative sequences in the early phases of childhood is an essential prerequisite of this memory because, without such sequenced communication habits and experiences, neither the later, genuine interaction nor the exchange of linguistic symbols could be possible.

We assume that ontogeny can best be understood by viewing it as a cumulative process of acquiring skills that improve systematically when the original or basal formats of these skills are overwritten by relatively more complicated ones. One such basal format in ontogeny is, for example, the ability to take part in communication, already functioning at birth (format I), which is increasingly elaborated on (format II) through constant communicative sequences in feeding, bathing, playing, etc., so that by the age of 8 or 9 months the first moments of intersubjectivity are possible through shared attention between the mother and her infant. This advances to a level of genuine interaction (format III). Speech acquisition gives a completely new frame to such interactions in the following months of life, in which the child evolves into a more and more compatible, interactive partner and, for that reason, a more and more active participant in social intercourse (format IV). Finally, continuous intersubjectivity is developed and starts to function when both a personal theory of mind and the use of symbolic language (format V) are available, and these are basic prerequisites for all further developmental steps to adulthood.

While viewing such schematic tables on the development of individual human abilities, it is always wise to remember that reaching one particular and more advanced stage never entails complete detachment from the previous stages. The old format establishes a new frame of experience and level of

Table 11.2 Ontogeny of intersubjectivity

Format I	Basic communication	Birth – month 2
Format II	Communication Protonarrative sequences Mental event representaions	Month 3
Format III	Shared attention	Month 9
Format IV	Verbal communication Interaction	Month 12
Format V	Intersubjectivity	Month 36

world knowledge and competence, from the perspective of the particular child passing through development. For this reason, once the ability to represent one's own existence and self in symbolic language reaches a functional level, no deliberately intended return to the subjective universe of earlier childhood can ever be possible. Put in mythological terms, whoever has "eaten of the tree of knowledge" is forever banished from the Garden of Eden. Nonetheless, what is learned and mastered earlier remains, either below or parallel to the present, newly won abilities. We can see that happening when a child communicates with others constantly, such as in the very first months of life, even though he or she is not in the least aware of communicating. We see this happening again when communications take place through very different channels at one and the same time, although only one is actually paid attention to: Usually, it is the contextual or symbolic level that we directly, immediately become aware of, but there are other channels of communication such as prosody, gesticulation and facial expressions that we do not consciously watch for but which attach considerable connotations to the actual conscious part of the message. These are the channels that give structure to the content level of the communication as it takes place, although we are in general not aware of this.

On the level of the brain, this concept of formative ontogeny seems to us to supply the most adequate descriptions. Even if memory systems evolve ontogenetically one after the other, in sequence, the earlier systems do not cease to function when, later, more comprehensive ones emerge and take over their own functions. In addition, a formative view of ontogeny seems very fruitful in other respects as well. First, we can gradually understand the importance of time windows in development (before the second format is operating adequately, the third either cannot evolve at all or only under severe limitations). Second, we gain an appreciation of the concept of potentiality within individual developmental phases, that is, of just how much each phase contributes to the next one. And finally, a formative perspective makes it possible to describe individual formative steps on different levels all in direct relation to each other, for example, the relation between maturation in the hippocampus, the development of working memory, and the ability to share attention.

In this way, human memory can be seen as a continuum of changes that advances by spelling out the potentials available at the moment in the ontogenetic formats. This continuum helps us understand the paradox of everyday life that we remain the same all through our lives precisely by changing constantly.

12 Memory at advanced ages

Memory is a dynamic process. We store information in a manner dependent on our momentary condition and, likewise, we recall it in a state-dependent manner. For example, whenever a person is in a depressed state, he or she will recall more material that has a far stronger negative loading than someone who has perhaps just won a large sum of money in the lottery or who has only recently fallen in love. This state-dependent nature of memory thus hints at the idea that our memory will also change dependent on the factor of age – first, because we acquire more and more information the older we get and, second, because our brain is less and less capable of acquiring this information with the same degree of precision and "youthful energy" as was the case years before. Of course, our memory also changes in another undeniable respect. With advancing age, we are again and again occupied with reassociating the contents of memory and with integrating them anew, so that every recall results in a new storage (and thus a reencoding) of the original material, which is subsequently processed in the momentary mood predominant every time the process is repeated (Markowitsch, 2002a).

Just as in other functions, such as intelligence as a case in point, our memory goes through changes over the course of aging, although we still consider ourselves to be basically the same persons, identical with our earlier selves. We can distinguish changes that are of a dynamic nature from those that are rather stable over time or essentially constant. It is easy here to see obvious parallels to the physical condition of a person. Up to early adulthood, the body is involved in growth and accretion, and then it reaches a plateau after which decline sets in. Muscle mass, body size and brain volume are all examples of areas which demonstrate clear periods of growth until well into the third decade. The somatic developments are directly reflected in the concomitant performance curves of different intellectual-cognitive functions, so that during the phase of physical growth a general increase can be observed in knowledge, mental flexibility, social competence and maturity, emotional empathy, and the motivation to learn more. So much for the phase of growth. The subsequent plateau phase is, however, defined and evaluated far differently, and general descriptions of the physical-mental status at this stage in life have usually relied on two models (see Figure 12.1). The first model

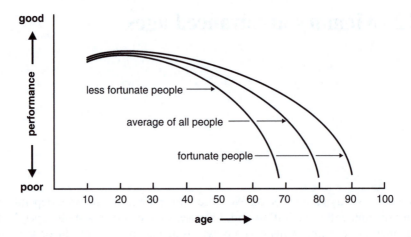

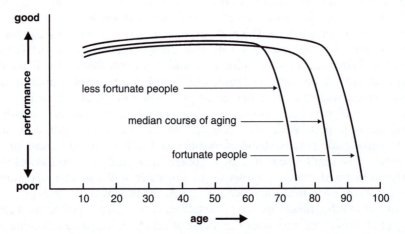

Figure 12.1 Models of age-correlated decrease in performance ability (generally defined as a combination of physical and mental performance) in less gifted, average and gifted persons.

maintains that performance decreases as of the third decade more or less rapidly for all three groups, irrespective of whether the subjects are more or less gifted. The second model, and the more optimistic one, maintains that performance ability is generally preserved into a higher age group, decreasing in less gifted persons by 60 years of age, and in the more "fortunate" group of gifted persons not until 90, although the decline then is rapidly apparent.

It is generally assumed that there is a direct association between intelligence and memory, so that a person with an above-average ability to store and remember things, will also have a similarly above-average intelligence. Researchers in the field of personality have suggested that intelligence can be measured by, for example, the speed of eye movement, a suggestion that would avoid confusing intellect with a person's command of cultural know-ledge. There are "culture-free" intelligence tests in which geometric patterns have to be compared with each other and then later recognized. But because intelligence, in conventional usage, includes considerably more than nonverbal abilities and skills (so that psychologists often define intelligence ironically as "what is measured by intelligence tests"), intelligence is usually divided into a static-pragmatic element and a dynamic speed-related one (see Figure 12.2).

Because this view of intelligence as a multidimensional construct fits the Cattell–Horn model (Cattell, 1963, 1987; Horn, 1982), age-related changes and their neural correlates were frequently investigated selectively (Horn, 1982; Woodruff-Pak, 1997). Work along these lines designates fluid intelligence as "the intellectual potential that plays a particular role in the acquisition of knowledge and in solving new problems", whereas crystalline intelligence means "the ability to apply knowledge already acquired to a problem of the moment" (Zimprich, 1998, p. 80).

The structural characteristics of intelligence in middle and old age have been investigated by concentrating on different psychometric abilities. Five general dimensions have thus been identified: logical thinking, memory and the speed of perceptual processing (belonging to the mechanical domain or fluid intelligence) and knowledge and divergent thinking (belonging to the pragmatic domain or crystalline intelligence) (Lindenberger, Mayr, & Kliegl, 1993). Since that work was published, several cross-sectional and longitudinal studies (for example, the Bonn Longitudinal Study of Ageing, the Berlin Study of Ageing) have found numerous indications of a divergence in the further development of intelligence in higher age brackets, involving, first of all, a significant decline in fluid performance and, second, a relative stabilization or even improvement in crystalline knowledge based on experience (Ackerman,

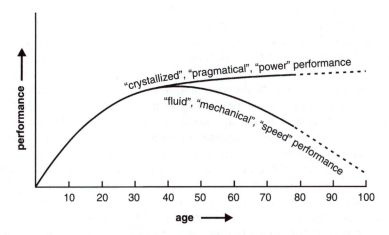

Figure 12.2 The course of intellectual abilities throughout life, distinguishing abilities that remain rather constant or even improve over time from abilities that have already decreased shortly after adulthood is attained.

2000; Meyer & Baltes, 1996; Rudinger & Rietz, 1995). The extensive data accumulating in the Berlin Study of Ageing show that crystalline abilities, however, do undergo a decline beyond the seventh decade, but this is not seen so strongly as in fluid abilities (Lindenberger & Baltes, 1997). Altogether, the age-related growth or decline in intellectual performance ability demonstrates a high degree of inter- and intrasubjective variability (Baltes, 1998; Salthouse, 1996a).

Memory, which is at least every bit as complex as intelligence, is composed of subordinate systems (due to temporal and contextual diversification; see Figures 4.10 and 4.11, pp. 67, 69), and because of this it should not be surprising that the functions of this memory change over time, that some skills, such as quick comprehension, or short-term memory under conditions of high interference ("divided attention"), undergo considerable degrees of decline, while yet others, such as the passive acquisition of knowledge (for example, one's vocabulary) continue to expand even into old age. It cannot be emphasized too often or too strongly that our memory is state-dependent and functions in a reciprocal way with many other cognitive, attentive and personality-related dimensions. And quite obviously our personalities change over time: The person who votes for a radical party at the age of 18, does not necessarily do so at 58, or the person who becomes emotional about a tender kiss at 16, will probably react far less romantically at 46. Considering such changes in personality throughout the years, changes in information processing should also be expected. We are nonetheless rather astonished when at special, unique moments in life we are in fact "moved back in time" in our memory to a particular mood that occurred a long time ago, but that we have not experienced at all since then (see Figure 12.3). We possess more or less consciously a highly emotionally charged structure of thoughts within us which, on the one hand, makes up our basic definition of ourselves as a person, but which can be "painted over" (affectively colored), on the other hand, from moment to moment, at any time, so that, when our mood is on the downside, certain contents are specifically blended out and others are likewise specifically highlighted. And so, depending on what "life brings us", or what kind of emotions have been predominant in our experiences, our ability to remember will vary over the life span, and so the longer one particular mood holds up, the greater is the probability that our memory will selectively support only certain of its contents to the exclusion of some others.

Box 4.6 mentioned several extreme examples of the relevancy of particular life situations to autobiographical memory, most of them relating to patients who had to face psychological stress or even traumatic experiences, did not succeed in coping particularly well with these challenges, and had thus experienced psychological disorders for the rest of their lives. For example, a mother has forgotten the last 13 years of her life and as a result does not recognize two of her three children; in an accident, a soldier stationed in Arabia is trapped in a car, from which he can only be freed after many hours, and loses all memory of his wife, child and previous personal experiences (see

Dear Professor Markowitsch,

An article in the news magazine *Der Spiegel* on the "Corporal without a Past" drew my attention to your work. I was an economics correspondent, and now that I've retired I am busy putting experiences from out of my generation's past into some sort of historical and political perspective. To check the accuracy of my own memories and to document them correctly, I spend a good deal of my time in archives and libraries. In this glance backward, I had the following experience.

One day I was standing alone in my room, next to my desk, and took a look outside into a beautifully clear and bright summer day; the constant hum of the city streets came in through the open door to the balcony. Suddenly, both the street sounds and the summer day disappeared – and I had the impression that I was in the relaxed atmosphere of a room somewhere indoors, with the light turned down, standing next to a long table as in a clubroom, but filled with American military officers. One officer at the head of the table spoke to me, and then I was standing next to this officer, but somewhere outside the clubhouse, under an absolutely clear summer sky filled with stars. He asked me something and I answered him.

The two scenes had in fact taken place the way I recalled them, spontaneously, without any deliberate effort on the part of my conscious mind, but 56 years before! (At the time when I was a young girl, a refugee, fortunate enough to get a job that gave me at least food to stay alive on.)

Then I was next to my desk again, listening to the hum of the streets and looking out at the beautiful summer day. I had the distinct feeling that I had made a journey through time. I recovered from being absolutely amazed at this eruption from out of my memory, but it struck me that I had just relived the very moments when I had decided on the path that eventually led to my present task of documenting events in recent history.

You can surely understand that this experience of remembering something long, long past has been occupying my thoughts again and again. I would be very grateful if you could tell me what term or concept I could look up in scientific literature to find out more on how elements of memory can suddenly suppress or extinguish the perception of reality of the moment.

Thank you in advance for your efforts.

Sincerely yours,

Figure 12.3 Affective memory.

Fujiwara et al., 2008). The memories lost in such cases are usually not recovered even years later; at best, they can only be relearned after some time but only as dry facts, without any special personal feelings (see details about the knowledge system, in Figure 4.11, p. 69).

In addition to these extreme cases, recent research has demonstrated that, in areas of normal memory functioning, we show more variable as well as increasingly poorer performance with advancing age than we are aware of. Denise Park, in particular, has done a series of projects on this theme, and the results are summarized in Figure 12.4. With the exception of one aspect of our verbal knowledge – our passive vocabulary, which continues to expand even in high-age groups – almost all other areas of memory performance

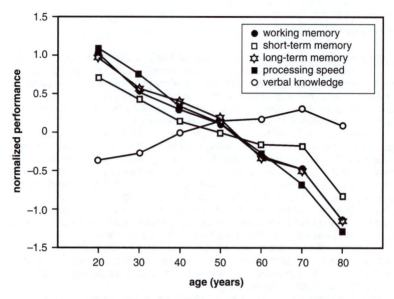

Figure 12.4 Changes in cognitive performance in increasing age brackets (from Denise Park; compare Park & Gutchess, 2002).

decrease after the age of 20. It is thus not surprising when 50-year-olds frequently complain about not being able to remember people's names, or that the major indication of a newly defined disturbance ("mild cognitive impairment") is precisely the decrease in memory performance. This symptom of mild cognitive impairment can reflect an early stage of developing dementia in a geriatric population, but it does not in any way have to be so (Bozoki, Giordani, Heidebrink, Berent, & Foster, 2001; Braak, del Tredici, & Braak, 2003; Busse, Bischkopf, Riedel-Heller, & Angermeyer, 2003; Galvin, Palmer, & Morris, 2003; Hogan & McKeith, 2001; Morris et al., 2001). To confirm the diagnosis, the impairment is required to extend clearly beyond the "benign forgetfulness in old age", which has long been viewed as the nonpathological, normal decrease in memory in older age groups.

Working memory, executive functions and long-term memory

Working memory involves the short-term activation and manipulation of information (D'Esposito & Grossmann, 1998). *Executive functions*, on the other hand, entail mental processes on a higher level for regulating and optimizing activity and behavior in situations that are not routine (Matthes-von Cramon & von Cramon, 2000). Research on these topics is rooted to a large extent in neuropsychology and studies of different age groups using both imaging techniques and comparative clinical methods (Markowitsch & Kessler, 2000; Rabbitt, 1997). Working memory and executive functions are viewed as metacognitive processes and constitute the foundation for, or have decisive effects on, the other cognitive abilities (such as memory and language). From a neuropsychological viewpoint, their overlap is seen in the control over components of processing by the frontal lobes and in particular by the prefrontal cortex (Rabbitt, 1997). The systems of *long-term memory* are subject to varying degrees of age-related changes.

There is considerable controversy in the research to date as to whether the functions of our working memory decline with age. On the one hand, a good number of findings support the view that short-term memory (the "memory span") is intact even at higher ages or is at most only slightly weakened (Corey-Bloom et al., 1996; Grégoire & van der Linden, 1997; Howieson, Holm, Kaye, Oken, & Howieson, 1993). On the other hand, numerous other studies document distinct, age-correlated detriments in working memory. When working memory is further differentiated into various subfunctions, clearly age-associated deficits are also found in the different tests used to measure performance in working memory (for example, Brébion, Ehrlich, & Tardieu, 1995; Gilinsky & Judd, 1994), but not all subsystems in working memory are involved to the same degree (Dolman, Roy, Dimeck, & Hall, 2000). The differences observed in performance due to aging appear to depend on the degree of complexity in the tasks required. When additional cognitive resources are required, more deficits will result in working memory (Salthouse, 1994a, 1994b).

The functions of working memory also depend on the basic quality of sensory perception and the speed of cognitive processing, as well as the degree to which a person is susceptible to interference, and these aspects in turn influence other cognitive functions such as speech reception and speech production. Making any kind of clear distinction between cognitive deficits and deficits in working memory is thus every bit as difficult as distinguishing the speed of processing from performance in working memory. And it becomes all the more complex when considering age-dependent deficits in executive functions, which always involve performance in attention and working memory.

Distinguishing attention, working memory and executive functions leads to nonuniform concepts because attentive and executive processes necessarily enter into working memory, and because functions of working memory and resources of attention are prerequisites for executive tasks. In the following discussion, we will describe the age-related changes of those executive functions that were not discussed under age-induced changes in attention and working memory.

Executive functions enable a person to act in a purposeful and systematic way, but at the same time in a flexible and efficient way, and these functions undergo evident decrements in the course of aging. This can be seen in, among other factors, the increase in cognitive inflexibility in older persons who regulate their everyday living with the help of strongly habitual behaviors. Neuropsychologically, executive functions are measured by tests in which cards are sorted according to various categories, which are shifted sometime during the course of the test (so that the old category, which was considered correct up until then, is now false, and another category now has to be found). With such tests and other, similar ones, age-related effects become clearly evident (see, for example, Brennan, Welsh, & Fischer, 1997). Two aspects seem to play a major role here: the correct processing of feedback and a slight increase in the tendency to perseveration. Levine, Stuss, and Milberg (1995) examined 60 subjects between the ages of 18 and 79 with a test for concept generation and found clearly age-related deficits in self-initiated concept formation, in "set shifting" (changing category), "answer monitoring" and a measure for perseveration tendency. In susceptibility to interference, as in tasks for color-word-interference, age-related differences have also been demonstrated (e.g., West & Baylis, 1998).

Performance deficits clearly appear in older age groups in the areas of sensation, attention, working memory and executive functioning, but they appear even more so in long-term memory. And although research on age-related changes is relatively new (Anderson & Craik, 2000; Small, 2001) and functional imagery has only been applied in rather recent studies (see Prull, Gabrieli, & Bunge, 2000), some of the results of this research have been well established. For example, there are clear decrements in different regions of memory, including priming (Cherry & Pierre, 1998), prospective memory (West, Jakubeb, & Wymbs, 2002), and the recall of information already stored (Cabeza, McIntosh, Tulving, Nyberg, & Grady, 1997), and these decrements have been referred to decreases in the volume of the frontal and temporal lobes (Bartzokis et al., 2001; Parkin, 1997; Schretlen et al., 2000), or, more particularly, in the area of the hippocampus (Heinsen et al., 1994; Ylikoski et al., 2000) and in the white matter (Bartzokis et al., 2003; Garde, Mortensen, Krabbe, Rostrup, & Larsson, 2000). In addition, the distribution of activity patterns in the two hemispheres is increasingly reduced more on the right side (Dolcos, Rice, & Cabeza, 2002) (compare in Chapter 4 the hemispheric-encoding-retrieval-asymmetry (HERA) model of the course of development, p. 70).

While early work failed to demonstrate any age-related deficits in priming (e.g., Light & Albertson, 1989), a meta-analysis published by La Voie and Light (1994) did find decreases in priming performance in later age. Nonetheless, the results of recent research are still contradictory. The extent of any age-related deficits in priming appears to be determined by the specific requirements for recall. For example, Gabrieli and coworkers (1999) assume that differences in recall (active reproduction as opposed to passive identification) can explain the contradictory results on age-related changes in priming. As to the neuronal correlates of priming, studies using functional imaging were able to demonstrate the same pattern of neuronal activity (that is, a deactivation in posterior cortical areas) in both young and older subjects during tasks of priming (e.g., Bäckman et al., 1997).

To date, little is known on age-related changes in procedural memory, and once again the results are partly contradictory. While, for example, Schugens,

Daum, Spindler, and Birbaumer (1997) found no correlations between age and impairments in performance in tasks for procedural memory (in reading mirror writing), other results show just the opposite, namely definite decrements at higher ages. Age differences were found for learning motor as well as nonmotor skills, such as pursuing a series of rotating stimuli, reading sentences where the word order has been inverted, or identifying incomplete words (Hashtroudi, Parker, Luis, & Reisen, 1989; Johnson, Hashtroudi, & Lindsay, 1993; Moscovitch, Winocur, & McLachlan, 1986). The authors argue that deficits in tasks of procedural memory at higher ages are related to decrements in perceptual organization. Similarly, these partly contradictory results might be explained by referring to differences in the strategies that are required to perform the different procedural tasks. We can assume, for example, that deficits appear in older subjects when the performance depends on the efficient use of various strategies (for structuring) and other cognitive functions, such as working memory.

We assume today that information within semantic memory is organized according to conceptual and hierarchical aspects, with an "internal lexicon" located in a neuronal network that represents the meaning of words and concepts as well as their associations. Its organization seems to have a top-down structure in which hierarchically superordinate concepts (such as "animal") are characterized with the help of general attributes while subordinate categories (such as "birds") have more specific attributes (Anderson, 1976).

A number of publications indicate that the organization and structure of the internal lexicon is rather stable throughout the life span and is well preserved in higher age groups (e.g., Laver & Burke, 1993). Likewise, vocabulary seems to remain stable over this same period or in fact to expand (Bäckman & Nilsson, 1996). Summarizing, we can assume that semantic knowledge is basically quite intact at higher ages although access to this knowledge is slower than in younger age groups. Such differences, however, might be due to yet other causes affecting semantic memory indirectly such as deficits in working memory, the speed of information processing, and decrements in executive functions (such as "monitoring").

Autobiographical memories of recent episodes and events are usually at the fore when older persons describe problems in their memory. In a neuro-psychological setting, such deficits are usually examined with the help of the free recall of words, sentences, stories and pictures that had to be learned by the subjects a short time before testing. In such situations, clear differences can be demonstrated between the performance of young adults and older persons (for a review, see Bäckman, Small, & Wahlin, 2001).

The decrease in performance in the episodic-autobiographical memory begins at a rather early age and progresses slowly but continuously over the life span (Nilsson et al., 1997; Salthouse, 1998). It is precisely this slow-setting increment in deficits that might offer an explanation of the results from studies performed over relatively short-term periods that found no indication of age-related deficits, thus inducing Zelinski and Burnight (1997) to recommend an interval of at least 6 years between the primary investigation and its follow-up so that any possible age differences are examined reliably.

Age differences in episodic memory appear to be dependent on the extent of recall aids (free recall versus recall with stimulus aids versus recognition). There are indications that such differences in memory performance increase all the more when fewer recall aids are given (e.g., Bäckman & Larsson, 1992), although, admittedly, other studies could not confirm this (for a review, see Bäckman, Mäntylä, & Herlitz, 1990).

One significant aspect of episodic memory is being able to remember the source of the information (the "source memory"), meaning the precise conditions in which the information was experienced, that is, the temporal, spatial and social context of the event as well as the modality (in most cases either visual or auditory) in which this event or information was perceived. Johnson, Hashtroudi, and Lindsay (1993) distinguished three different kinds of source memory: first, the process of distinguishing between internally generated and externally perceived information (for example, between imagined and actually experienced events), which is also called "reality monitoring". Second, "internal source monitoring" was described as the process of distinguishing between different kinds of purely internally generated information. Finally, "external source monitoring" discriminated between different external sources, for example, between the statements of various people on the same topic.

Research on aging and source memory has focused strongly on external "source monitoring". A number of publications reported on age-related deficits in remembering the context of stimuli given to the subjects, such as the modality involved (Larsson & Bäckman, 1998), the color (Park & Puglisi, 1985), or details of handwriting (Naveh-Benjamin & Craik, 1995). One critical factor that has been cited as a possible explanation of such differences in source memory is the degree of differentiability in the source stimuli themselves. For example, Ferguson, Hashtroudi, and Johnson (1992) demonstrated that older subjects were disadvantaged in tasks of external source monitoring only when the sources, that is, the original events of exposure, were essentially similar, and not when they were very clearly different. Interestingly, no age-related differences have been reported to date for reality monitoring. Arguably, distinguishing whether an event was generated internally or by external perception makes use of more unequivocal discriminatory factors than are available to distinguish between internal and external sources. In summary, there are clearly age-related increments for source memory, but these essentially depend on the extent of the accompanying stimuli.

Chapters 2 and 8 have already referred to the existence and relevance of false memories. Work on this topic frequently applies "Deese lists" (Deese, 1959; Roediger & McDermont, 1995), which present the subjects with semantically associated words (such as *night, bed, snoring*), but then, at recall, a word is introduced that is still related along semantic lines, but was not given at the initial presentation (such as *sleeping*).

The results of working with both younger and older subjects revealed that the older persons repeated fewer of the original words, but in producing the semantically related intrusions they were not essentially different from the younger persons. But this meant that considering the ratio of false memories to the sum of correctly repeated stimulus words, the older subjects had a relatively larger percentage of false memories (Balota et al., 1999). The authors discussed the possibility that older persons focus more strongly on the more general characteristics or information of an object, topic or person, thus explaining the greater percentage of false memories. Similarly, Koutstaal, Schacter, Galluccio, and Stofer (1999) performed a study explicitly requiring the subjects to scrutinize the objects they remembered carefully, that is, in relation to specific characteristics, and the results showed that (falsely) remembering objects, topics, or individual persons that had not been presented was reduced under such conditions in both the young and the old subjects, but the effect of age-related increase in false memories was nonetheless still observed.

In the search for a neuronal correlate for age-associated memory changes, degeneration in the regions of the prefrontal cortex and the medial temporal lobe have been frequently described and are thus the most likely candidates. Recent studies using imaging techniques indicate that the prefrontal cortex is especially implicated in the recall of memories, but is also activated in the process of encoding information (Cabeza & Nyberg, 2000; Habib, Nyberg, & Tulving, 2003). Likewise, it has been shown that regions of the hippocampal formation, which are now viewed as critical structures for encoding information (see reviews in Markowitsch, 2000, 2005; Markowitsch & Borsutzky, 2004), may be involved in the recall as well. For these reasons, the deficits described in episodic memory in older age could be caused by changes in the prefrontal cortex as well as in the medial temporal lobe, whereas deficits reported for procedural memory may rather be due to changes in the area of the basal ganglia and the cerebellum. Lastly, deficits in priming and perceptual memory in older age appear related to neocortical changes (most particularly in the association cortex).

Deficits in other cognitive and emotional functions

As we described in Chapter 4, the development of memory goes hand in hand with other functional areas. Frequently mentioned in this relation, speech is an example of a functional complex that can be influenced negatively by changes in both the peripheral and the central nervous system typically found in aging persons (for a review, see Wingfield & Stine-Morrow, 2000). In particular, difficulty in finding the appropriate words or names is frequently reported in older subjects (Hodges, Patterson, Graham, & Dawson, 1996; Nicholas, Obler, Au, & Albert, 1996), but deficits are also found in correctly naming objects and activities (Cappa et al., 1998), as well as living and nonliving things and individual persons (Montanes, Goldblum, & Boller, 1995).

The most apparent loss is in recalling words, or naming something. Precisely in older persons in contrast to younger ones, we find the "tip of the tongue" phenomenon (see Box 2.1, pp. 17ff.) far more frequently, that is, a person has the feeling that he or she very well knows the name of an object or person, but just cannot find it at the moment. Experimental studies have also shown that older subjects are slower and have less success in recalling words, especially when these words are less frequent in everyday use (e.g., Bowles & Poon, 1985), whereas lexical knowledge remains basically unchanged even in higher age groups. Longitudinal as well as cross-sectional studies have demonstrated that the knowledge of the meanings of words, as measured in the ability to define the words, remains constant and can even increase with advancing age (Botwinick, 1977; Bowles & Poon, 1985; compare Figure 12.2, p. 217, on crystallized intelligence).

A summary of the most distinct changes in cognitive-emotional abilities with age is given in Table 12.1

Table 12.1 Neuropsychological functions in older age

Neuropsychological functions	*Kind of change*
Perception	
Higher perceptual functions	Decrease
Intelligence	
Fluid intelligence	Decrease
Crystallized intelligence	No change (or even an increase) ≥70 years: discrete decrease possible
Attention	
Focused attention	No change
Selective attention	Decrease
Shared attention	Decrease
Shifting attention	Decrease
Vigilance/sustained attention	Decrease
Working memory	Decrease
Executive functions	Decrease (less flexibility, increased perseveration tendencies)
Memory	
Episodic memory	Decrease
Semantic memory	No change
Procedural memory	At most only a slight decrease
Priming	At most only a slight decrease
Speech	
Naming	Decrease
Syntax	Decrease
Emotions	Decrease/increase

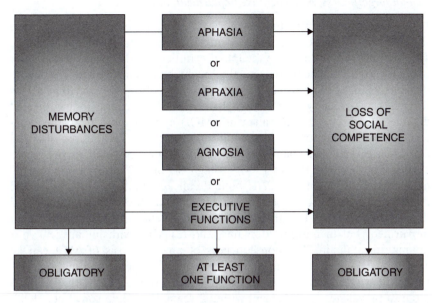

Figure 12.5 Schematic representation of the combination of disturbances required for the diagnosis of dementia.

level 7 very severe	loss of language, motor behavior, consciousness, death
level 6 severe	in need of full support, institutionalized
level 6 severe	unable to live by him- or herself, incontinent, depressive
level 5 moderate-to-severe	unable to live without the help of others, agitated, in need of support
level 4 moderate	friends and family realize deficits
level 3 minor	minor deficits, "forgetful"
level 2 very minor	no cognitive reduction perceivable
level 1 appears normal	normal

Figure 12.6 Cognitive and behavioral changes in dementia in old age (in particular Alzheimer's disease), according to the stages of the Global Deterioration Scale of Barry Reisberg.

Benign forgetfulness, mild cognitive impairment, and dementia

It is generally recognized that memory functions become weaker with age. But precisely because deficits in memory are the main ones among the symptoms of dementia many people are rather worried that, if ever their memory for names does weaken, this might be a sign of their developing dementia. An additional reason for worry arises from the fact that a new diagnosis has recently been accepted into the classification for age-related disorders: "mild cognitive impairment" (MCI) (compare pp. 220ff. in this chapter). While the diagnosis of dementia in old age requires the loss of social competence, and disturbance in the realm of memory and in one other cognitive ability (see Figure 12.5), a diagnosis of MCI only needs impairment in memory. However, Petersen and colleagues (1999, 2001), who have done extensive research especially on MCI, make three further, finer-tuned distinctions: (1) MCI with memory impairment, (2) MCI with slight impairment but in multiple domains, and (3) MCI with impairment in a nonmnestic domain. The consequences of any diagnosis of MCI can be seen in the fact that approximately 10 percent of persons found to have MCI will be given the diagnosis of dementia within a year. Other authors report a prevalence of 40 percent within 2 years' time (Johnson et al., 1998), and prevalences of 20 percent (Wolf et al., 1998), 30 percent (Black, 1999), and even 53 percent within 3 years (McKelvey et al., 1999). Finally, Krasuski et al. (1998) report 100 percent conversion of MCI into dementia within 4–5 years.

At present, we have a series of simpler neuropsychological test instruments (Kessler, Denzler, & Markowitsch, 1999), as well as more complex ones (Kessler, Markowitsch, & Denzler, 1990), to clarify age-related cognitive changes. And, of course, more and more significance is being given to imaging techniques, in particular functional imaging. But for a completely valid diagnosis, postmortem examination and dissection are necessary.

At postmortem examination, the typical findings are a decrease in general volume and weight of the brain, which, however, may be related partly to loss of fluids in the tissue before death (for a review, see Kemper, 1994). The ventricles within the brain are seen to have expanded over time, and the typical number of dendritic, axonal and synaptic branches has decreased substantially (though in different proportions depending on the region in the brain) (compare Figure 4.17, p. 78). Cerebral metabolism and circulation of the blood are decreased, while molecules of heterologous proteins increase within and around nerve cells (neurofibrillary tangles, amyloid plaques). Moreover, cases of Alzheimer's disease in particular follow a distinct and predictable pattern in development over time, whereby regions in the temporal lobes, surrounding the hippocampus, are the first to perish, followed by the hippocampus itself, and then cortical areas in the temporal and parietal lobes are affected, followed by those in the prefrontal cortex (see Figure 4.1, p. 53, and Figure 4.27, p. 99) (Braak & Braak, 1996, 1997). The (primary) sensory and motor cortical regions, on the other hand, remain intact until well into the later stages of the disease (these are the dark gray regions in Figure 4.18, p. 81, which are fully functional already at the time of birth). Thus, as at the behavioral level, where stages of regression can be described (see Figure 12.6), corresponding stages can be seen at the level of brain anatomy. It is possible to conceptualize a reverse development in individual humans, regressing from the adult level, in full possession of their powers, back to the stage of the embryo.

This also means that those structures in particular that are involved in attention, memory and emotions will degenerate most strongly. In that situation, the brain requires more and more resources in order to keep up the level of performance that it previously attained with less energy and with fewer structures being recruited. Both hemispheres thus now become activated whereas, earlier, only one was essentially involved, neural networks have to expand so as to include more and more cells, and information processing becomes less precise and more defective and the performance is only short-lived.

And still, the neuropsychological data show that the process of aging has a surprising array of facets that include, of course, a series of well-known deficits, but also well-preserved abilities and in fact some cognitive-mnestic

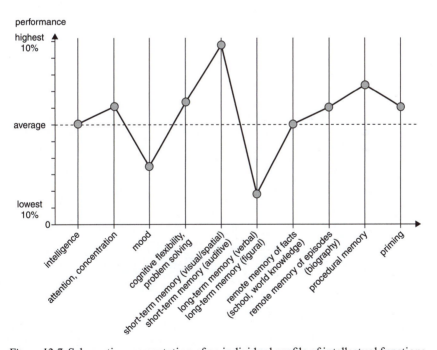

Figure 12.7 Schematic representation of an individual profile of intellectual functions, showing some which lie either above or below the average performance level.

abilities that improve over time. Only by creating the kind of cognitive profile that we proposed for the routine examination of brain-damaged patients (Markowitsch, 2003b; Thöne-Otto & Markowitsch, 2004), can the intellectual changes of an older person be made apparent over a very broad spectrum of abilities (see Figure 12.7).

13 Autobiographical memory: a biocultural relay between the individual and the environment

It may at first seem contradictory, but neuroscientific methods on their own cannot distinguish autobiographical memory from episodic memory[1] at all, whereas results from developmental psychology even demonstrate that autobiographical memory does not develop until after episodic memory has. Although this finding may appear somewhat contradictory, it can be explained by the fact that the neural substrate for episodic memory is in itself fully capable of developing the autobiographical component: at least, this is so if a coevolutionary developmental environment is in force that integrates the different demands of sociality and individuality, and of ontogenetic and phylogenetic development, so that they all function in a coordinated way. When a species is in principle capable of making use of such a developmental environment, it needs a relay station that makes its members "sociable" and ready for associating with expanding and diversifying social groups. The autobiographical memory is just such a relay, a psychosocial force that guarantees subjective coherency and continuity although the social environments and their demands on the individual fluctuate. It is precisely this function as a relay station that explains why we have evidence of historically different levels of autobiographical functioning as well as why, looking at different intercultural effects, we find that the origin of a continuous self-identity is initiated at widely different age groups. Autobiographical memory is therefore not a whole new additional memory system, but a biopsychosocial instance that represents the relay station between the individual and the environment, between the subject and culture.

---

1 The autobiographical memory system is occasionally distinguished not only from the other memory systems (procedural memory, priming, perceptual memory, semantic memory or system of knowledge; compare Figure 4.11, p. 69), but also from the episodic memory (see Conway, 2001; Conway & Pleydell-Pearce, 2000), although there is no convincing proof of such a distinction to date on either the level of brain anatomy (such as differences in the structures assumed to be involved) or differences in patterns of activity seen in functional imagery techniques. Based on such studies up to now (Fink et al., 1996), it is only possible to speculate that autobiographical recall more strongly activates emotional regions (for example, the amygdala) than the rather more neutral episodic recall does.

This is why the development of autobiographical memory progresses in parallel with the step-by-step synchronization of maturing individuals and their social environment. In this way, ontogeny becomes identical with the sociogenesis of a human being over the course of time.

Autobiographical memory not only makes it possible for us to mark memories as our own, but it also makes up the temporal feedback matrix of ourselves, with which we can evaluate where and how we have changed and where and how we have remained the same. And it makes an adjustable matrix possible in the face of the attributions, evaluations and judgments that the social environment makes on us practically at all times. It is hard not to experience at least a slight or even a terrible sense of insecurity if someone remarks, "You have really changed over the years!" The desire for personal continuity is in no way just an individual one. No social group or society could function without continuity in the identity of its members, and this is simply due to the fact that cooperation – the central, defining category of human existential technique – is only guaranteed when people are reliably the same today, tomorrow and yesterday.

We have already mentioned that autobiographical memory serves social synchronization, and the more complex societies become and the longer their chain of activities and intermediates becomes, the more time their members need for the proper formation of autobiography, and thus the individual autobiographical memory is an even more complex achievement in the final analysis.

One central problem of an interdisciplinary perspective on memory is the neuroscientific focus on the individual, because such an individualistic perspective cannot equally well treat the fact that memory is formed and structured within a social process. It is this social process which is the specifically human element in our life and enables information to become something much more complicated, namely, a memory.

The conflict between an individual perspective and social processes is already present in the basic approach of the social sciences as soon as an orientation in the direction of interaction is brought into discussions on developmental psychology and socialization research. Even in these two fields, the implicit assumption is usually that the individual and society are two different, separate entities, and as a result the cardinal question of all social science directly concerns how a social being develops from an asocial one, or, put alternatively, how a society that consists only of individuals can be more than the sum of its members and their behavior. But as many scientists before us have emphasized, each in his or her own way, this dichotomy in the long run is just as detrimental as the idea that autobiographical memory is essentially only something a single individual achieves. For example, the sociologist Norbert Elias (1939/1996) wrote 70 years ago that the psychogenesis and sociogenesis of a child can only be adequately understood if we view the basic process as being one that evolves within the configuration of humans who were there before the developing child. Its entire development after birth depends on the cultural and social activities and techniques that this configuration of people themselves developed in a coevolutionary manner.

This perspective has been pursued by such different developmental psychologists as Lev Wygotsky, Daniel Stern, and Michael Tomasello, all of whom showed that human beings do not "internalize" things during their development, but, rather, that they are involved in practically learning in cooperation with others (Stern) what they need in order to function properly in any one particular society and to become fully accepted members of that society. The fact that in this process the developing members become highly specific, individual personalities, when interpersonal relationships become intrapersonal psychic formations, is something we can see particularly well in the development of autobiographical memory.

The development of memory proceeds from the social level to the individual one: from (1) the infant and young child who exists only in a private universe of just living from day to day, without an episodic memory and without being able to distinguish the sources of his or her memories, on to (2) the preschool child who attains a self-positioning system in a time frame with the help of improvements in temporal differentiations and finally reaches an autobiographical self with the help of language acquisition and a cognitive self-awareness, which integrates the earlier and the coming experiences into a life history that is both social and individual at the same time.

References

Abu-Akel, A. (2003). A neurobiological mapping of theory of mind. *Brain Research Reviews, 43,* 29–40.

Ackerman, P. L. (2000). Domain-specific knowledge as the "dark matter" of adult intelligence: Gf/Gc, personality and interest correlates. *Journal of Gerontology: Psychological Sciences, 55B,* P69–P84.

Adair, J. C., Schwartz, R. L., Na, D. L., Fennell, E., Gilmore, R. L., & Heilman, K. M. (1997). Anosognosia: Examining the disconnection hypothesis. *Journal of Neurology, Neurosurgery, and Psychiatry, 63,* 798–800.

Aldenhoff, J. (1997). Überlegungen zur Psychobiologie der Depression. *Nervenarzt, 68,* 379–389.

Allaire, J. C., & Marsiske, M. (1999). Everyday cognition: Age and intellectual ability correlates. *Psychology and Aging, 14,* 627–644.

Anderson, B., & Rutledge, V. (1996). Age and hemisphere effects on dendritic structure. *Brain, 119,* 1983–1990.

Anderson, J. R. (1976). *Language, memory, and thought.* Hillsdale, NJ: Lawrence Erlbaum Associates, Inc.

Anderson, N. D., & Craik, F. I. M. (2000). Memory in the aging brain. In E. Tulving & F. I. M. Craik (Eds.), *The Oxford handbook of memory* (pp. 411–426). New York: Oxford University Press.

Anderson, N. D., Iidaka, T., Cabeza, R., Kapur, S., McIntosh, R., & Craik, F. I. M. (2000). The effects of divided attention on encoding- and retrieval-related brain activity: A PET study of younger and older adults. *Journal of Cognitive Neuroscience, 12,* 775–792.

Andy, O. J., & Stephan, H. (1976). Septum development in primates. In J. F. Defrance (Ed.), *The septal nuclei* (Vol. 20, pp. 3–36). New York: Plenum Press.

Anton, G., & Zingerle, H. (1902). *Bau, Leistung und Erkrankung des menschlichen Stirnhirnes.* Graz, Austria: Leuschner und Lubensky.

Aram, D. M., Ekelman, B. L., Rose, D. F., & Whitaker, H. A. (1985). Verbal and cognitive sequelae of unilateral lesions acquired in early childhood. *Journal of Clinical and Experimental Neuropsychology: Official Journal of the International Neuropsychological Society, 7,* 55–78.

Armstrong, E. (1982). Mosaic evolution in the primate brain: Differences and similarities in the hominoid thalamus. In E. Armstrong & D. Falk (Eds.), *Primate brain evolution* (pp. 131–161). New York: Plenum Press.

Armstrong, E. (1986). Enlarged limbic structures in the human brain: The anterior thalamus and medial mamillary body. *Brain Research, 362,* 394–397.

Armstrong, E., & Falk, D. (1982). *Primate brain evolution. Methods and concepts.* New York: Plenum Press.

Arnold, S. E., & Trojanowski, J. Q. (1996). Human fetal hippocampal development: 1. Cytoarchitecture, myeloarchitecture and morphologic features. *Journal of Comparative Neurology, 376,* 274–292.

Assmann, A. (2001). Wie wahr sind Erinnerungen? In H. Welzer (Ed.), *Das soziale Gedächtnis. Geschichte, Erinnerung, Tradierung* (pp. 103–122). Hamburg: Hamburger Edition.

Atkinson, R. C., & Shiffrin, R. M. (1968). Human memory: A proposed system and its control processes. In K. W. Spence & J. T. Spence (Eds.), *The psychology of learning and motivation: Advances in research in theory* (Vol. 2, pp. 89–195). New York: Academic Press.

Awh, E., & Jonides, J. (2001). Overlapping mechanisms of attention and spatial working memory. *Trends in Cognitive Sciences, 5,* 119–126.

Bachevalier, J. (1990). Ontogenetic development of habit and memory formation in primates. In A. Diamond (Ed.), The development and neural bases of higher cognitive functions. *Annals of the New York Academy of Sciences* (Vol. 608, pp. 457–477). New York: New York Academy of Sciences Press.

Bäckman, L., Almkvist, O., Andersson, J. L. R., Nordberg, A., Winblad, B., Reineck, R., et al. (1997). Brain activation in young and older adults during implicit and explicit retrieval. *Journal of Cognitive Neuroscience, 9,* 378–391.

Bäckman, L., & Larsson, M. (1992). Recall of organizable words and objects in adulthood: Influences of instructions, retention interval, and retrieval cues. *Journals of Gerontology, 47,* P273–P278.

Bäckman, L., Mäntylä, T., & Herlitz, A. (1990). The optimization of episodic remembering in old age. In P. B. Baltes & M. M. Baltes (Eds.), *Successful aging: Perspectives from the behavioral sciences* (pp. 118–163). New York: Cambridge University Press.

Bäckman, L., & Nilsson, L.-G. (1996). Semantic memory functioning across the adult life span. *European Psychologist, 1,* 27–33.

Bäckman, L., Small, B. J., & Wahlin, A. (2001). Aging and memory. In J. E. Birren & K. W. Shaie (Eds.), *The psychology of aging* (pp. 349–377). San Diego, CA: Academic Press.

Baddeley, A. (2000a). Short-term and working memory. In E. Tulving & F. I. M. Craik (Eds.), *The Oxford handbook of memory* (pp. 77–92). New York: Oxford University Press.

Baddeley, A. (2000b). The episodic buffer: A new component of working memory? *Trends in Cognitive Sciences, 4,* 417–423.

Baddeley, A. D. (1986). *Working memory.* Oxford: Oxford University Press.

Baddeley, A. D. (1992). Working memory. *Science, 255,* 556–559.

Baddeley, A. D. (1998). *Human memory: theory and practice* (Rev. ed.). Boston: Allyn and Bacon.

Baddeley, A. D. (1998). Recent developments in working memory. *Current Opinion in Neurobiology, 8,* 234–238.

Baddeley, A. D. (2002). Is working memory still working? *European Psychologist, 7,* 85–97.

Baddeley, A. D., & Hitch, G. (1974). Working memory. In G. H. Bower (Ed.), *The psychology of learning and motivation* (pp. 47–89). New York: Academic Press.

Bailey, C. H., & Kandel, E. R. (1995). Molecular and structural mechanisms underlying long-term memory. In M. S. Gazzaniga (Ed.), *The cognitive neurosciences* (pp. 19–36). Cambridge, MA: MIT Press.

Balota, D. A., Cortese, M. J., Duchek, J. M., Adams, D., Roediger, H. L. I., McDermott, K. B., et al. (1999). Veridical and false memories in healthy older adults and in dementia of the Alzheimer's type. *Cognitive Neuropsychology, 16*, 361–384.

Baltes, M. M., Lang, F. R., & Wilms, H.-U. (1998). Selektive Optimierung mit Kompensation: Erfolgreiches Altern in der Alltagsgestaltung. In A. Kruse (Ed.), *Psychosoziale Gerontologie. Band 1: Grundlagen* (pp. 188–202). Göttingen: Hogrefe.

Baltes, P. B. (1997). Die unvollendete Architektur der menschlichen Ontogenese: Implikationen für die Zukunft des vierten Lebensalters. *Psychologische Rundschau, 48*, 191–210.

Baltes, P. B. (1998). Theoretical propositions of life-span developmental psychology: On the dynamics between growth and decline. In M. P. Lawton & T. A. Salthouse (Eds.), *Essential papers on the psychology of aging* (pp. 86–123). New York: New York University Press.

Baltes, P. B., & Lindenberger, U. (1997). Emergence of a powerful connection between sensory and cognitive functions across the adult life span: A new window to the study of cognitive aging? *Psychology and Aging, 12*, 12–21.

Baltes, P. B., & Smith, J. (1997). A systemic-holistic view of psychological functioning in very old age: Introduction to a collection of articles from the Berlin Aging Study. *Psychology and Aging, 12*, 395–409.

Barr, R., Dowden, A., & Hayne, H. (1996). Developmental changes in deferred imitation by 6–24 months old infants. *Infant Behavior and Development, 19*, 159–170.

Barr, R., & Vieira, A. (1999, January). Piggyboarding the puppet onto the train. Associated memories form across experimental paradigms in 6-month-old infants. Paper presented at the New England Mini-Conference on Infant Studies. Providence, RI.

Barrera, M. E., & Maurer, D. (1981a). The perception of facial expression by the three-month-old. *Child Development, 52*, 203–206.

Barrera, M. E., & Maurer, D. (1981b). Discrimination of strangers by the three-month-old. *Child Development, 52*, 558–563.

Bartlett, F. C. (1932/1997). *Remembering: A study in experimental and social psychology*. London: Cambridge University Press.

Bartzokis, G., Beckson, M., Lu, P. H., Nuechterlein, K. H., Edwards, N., & Mintz, J. (2001). Age-related changes in frontal and temporal lobe volumes in men. *Archives of General Psychiatry, 58*, 461–465.

Bartzokis, G., Cummings, J. L., Sultzer, D., Henderson, V. W., Nuechterlein, K. H., & Mintz, J. (2003). White matter structural integrity in healthy aging adults and patients with Alzheimer disease. *Archives of Neurology, 60*, 393–398.

Bateson, P., Barker, D., Clutton-Brock, T., Deb, D., D'Udine, B., Foley, R. A., et al. (2004). Developmental plasticity and human health. *Nature, 430*, 419–421.

Bauer, J. (2002). *Das Gedächtnis des Körpers. Wie Beziehungen und Lebensstile unsere Gene steuern*. Frankfurt am Main: Eichborn.

Bauer, P. J., Hertsgaard, L. A., & Dow, G. A. (1994). After 8 months have passed: Long-term recall of events by 1- to 2-year-old children. *Memory, 2*, 353–382.

Bauer, P. J., & Wewerka, S. S. (1995). One- to two-year-olds' recall of events: The more expressed, the more impressed. *Journal of Experimental Child Psychology, 59*, 475–496.

238   *References*

Becker, A. M., & Sternbach, I. (1953). Über Zeitsinnstörung bei Thalamusherden. *Wiener Zeitschrift für Nervenheilkunde, 7*, 62–67.

Bednar, J. A., & Miikulainen, R. (2003). Learning innate face preferences. *Neural Computation, 15*, 1525–1557.

Benes, F. M. (1994). Development of the corticolimbic system. In G. Dawson & K. W. Fischer (Eds.), *Human behavior and the developing brain* (pp. 176–206). New York: Guilford Press.

Benes, F. M. (2001). The development of prefrontal cortex: The maturation of neuro-transmitter systems and their interactions. In C. A. Nelson & M. Luciana (Eds.), *Handbook of developmental cognitive neuroscience* (pp. 79–92). Cambridge, MA: MIT Press.

Berger, H. (1923). Klinische Beiträge zur Pathologie des Grosshirns. I. Mitteilung: Herderkrankungen der Präfrontalregion. *Archiv für Psychiatrie und Nerven-krankheiten, 69*, 1–46.

Beringer, K. (1927). *Der Meskalinrausch* (Monographien aus dem Gesamtgebiete der Neurologie und Psychiatrie, No. 49). Berlin: Springer.

Bernasconi, A., Bernasconi, N., Lassonde, M., Toussaint, P.-J., Meyer, E., Reutens, D. C., et al. (2000). Sensorimotor organization in patients who have undergone hemispherectomy: A study with ^{15}O-water PET and somatosensory evoked poten-tials. *NeuroReport, 11*, 3085–3090.

Bertenthal, B. I., & Fischer, K. W. (1978). Development of self-recognition in the infant. *Developmental Psychology, 14*, 44–50.

Bickerton, D. (1995). *Language and human behavior*. Seattle, WA: University of Washington Press.

Bigelow, H. J. (1850). Dr. Harlow's case of recovery from the passage of an iron bar through the head. *American Journal of the Medical Sciences, 39*, 13–22 (and one table).

Bird, C. M, Castelli, F., Malik, O., Frith, U., & Husain, M. (2004). The impact of extensive medial frontal lobe damage on "Theory of mind" and cognition. *Brain, 127*, 914–928.

Birren, J. E. (1960). Behavioral theories of aging. In N. W. Shock (Ed.), *Aging: Some social and biological aspects*. Washington, DC: American Association for the Advancement of Science.

Birren, J. E., & Fisher, L. M. (1995). Aging and speed of behavior: Possible con-sequences for psychological functioning. *Annual Review of Psychology, 46*, 329–353.

Black, S. E. (1999). Can SPECT predict the future for mild cognitive impairment? *Canadian Journal of Neurological Sciences, 26*, 4–6.

Blair, R. J. R. (2004). The roles of orbital frontal cortex in the modulation of antisocial behavior. *Brain and Cognition, 55*, 198–208.

Bloom, P. (2000). *How children learn the meanings of words*. Cambridge, MA: MIT Press.

Bloom, P. (2001). Précis of *How children learn the meanings of words. Behavioral and Brain Sciences, 24*, 1095–1103.

Boksa, P., & El-Khodor, B. F. (2003). Birth insult interacts with stress at adult-hood to alter dopaminergic function in animal models: Possible implications for schizophrenia and other disorders. *Neuroscience and Biobehavioral Reviews, 27*, 91–101.

Bonhoeffer, K. (1901). *Die akuten Geisteskrankheiten der Gewohnheitstrinker*. Jena: Fischer.

Bonin, G. von, & Bailey, P. (1961). Pattern of the cerebral isocortex. In H. Hofer, A. H. Schulz, & D. Starck (Eds.), *Primatologia II (2. Lieferung)* (pp. 1–42). Basel: Karger.

Botwinick, J. (1977). Intellectual abilities. In J. E. Birren & K. W. Schaie (Eds.), *Handbook of the psychology of aging* (pp. 580–605). New York: Van Nostrand Reinhold.

Bourgeois, J.-P., Goldman-Rakic, P. S., & Rakic, P. (2000). Formation, elimination, and stabilization of synapses in the primate cerebral cortex. In M. S. Gazzaniga (Ed.), *The new cognitive neurosciences* (2nd ed., pp. 45–53). Cambridge, MA: MIT Press.

Bowles, N. L., & Poon, L. W. (1985). Aging and retrieval of words in semantic memory. *Journal of Gerontology, 40*, 71–77.

Bozoki, A., Giordani, B., Heidebrink, J. L., Berent, S., & Foster, N. L. (2001). Mild cognitive impairments predict dementia in nondemented elderly patients with memory loss. *Archives of Neurology, 58*, 411–416.

Braak, H., & Braak, E. (1996). Evolution of the neuropathology of Alzheimer's disease. *Acta Neurologica Scandinavica, 165*, 3–12.

Braak, H., & Braak, E. (1997). Frequency of stages of Alzheimer-related lesions in different age categories. *Neurobiology of Aging, 18*, 351–357.

Braak, H., del Tredici, K., & Braak, E. (2003). Spectrum of pathology. In R. C. Peterson (Ed.), *Mild cognitive impairment. Aging to Alzheimer's disease* (pp. 149–189). Oxford: Oxford University Press.

Brand, M., Fujiwara, E., Kalbe, E., Steingass, H.-P., Kessler, J., & Markowitsch, H. J. (2003). Cognitive estimation and affective judgments in alcoholic Korsakoff patients. *Journal of Clinical and Experimental Neuropsychology, 25*, 324–334.

Brand, M., & Markowitsch, H. J. (2003). The bottleneck structures implicated in memory processing. In R. H. Kluwe, G. Lüer, & F. Rösler (Eds.), *Learning and memory* (pp. 171–184). Basel: Birkhäuser.

Brandimonte, M., Einstein, G. O., & McDaniel, M. A. (1996). *Prospective memory: Theory and applications*. Hillsdale, NJ: Lawrence Erlbaum Associates, Inc.

Braun, K., & Bock, J. (2003). Die Narben der Kindheit. *Gehirn & Geist, 1*, 50–53.

Brébion, G., Ehrlich, M.-F., & Tardieu, H. (1995). Working memory in older subjects: Dealing with ongoing and stored information in language comprehension. *Psychological Research, 58*, 225–232.

Brennan, M., Welsh, M. C., & Fischer, C. B. (1997). Aging and executive function skills – an examination of a community-dwelling older adult population. *Perceptual and Motor Skills, 84*, 1187–1197.

Brodmann, K. (1909). *Vergleichende Lokalisationslehre der Grosshirnrinde in ihren Prinzipien dargestellt auf Grund des Zellenbaues*. Leipzig: Barth.

Brodmann, K. (1912). Ergebnisse über die vergleichende histologische Lokalisation der Grosshirnrinde mit besonderer Berücksichtigung des Stirnhirns. *Anatomischer Anzeiger (Suppl.), 41*, 157–216.

Brody, B. A., Kinney, H. C., Kloman, A. S., & Gilles, F. H. (1987). Sequence of central nervous system myelination in human infancy. 1. An autopsy study of myelination. *Journal of Neuropathology and Experimental Neurology, 46*, 283–301.

Buonomano, D. V., & Merzenich M. M. (1998). Cortical plasticity: From synapses to maps. *Annual Review of Neuroscience, 21*, 149–186.

Burke, D. M. (1997). Language, aging and inhibitory deficits: Evaluation of a theory. *Journal of Gerontology: Psychological Sciences, 52B*, P254–P264.

Burke, D. M., MacKay, D. G., & James, L. E. (2000). Theoretical approaches to language and aging. In T. J. Perfect & E. A. Maylor (Eds.), *Models of cognitive aging* (pp. 204–237). New York: Oxford University Press.

Burns, J. M., & Swerdlow, R. H. (2003). Right orbitofrontal tumor with pedophilia symptom and constructional apraxia sign. *Archives of Neurology, 60*, 437–440.

Bushnell, I. W. R., Sai, F., & Mullin, J. T. (1989). Neonatal recognition of the mother's face. *British Journal of Developmental Psychology, 7*, 3–15.

Busse, A., Bischkopf, J., Riedel-Heller, S. G., & Angermeyer, M. C. (2003). Mild cognitive impairment: Prevalence and incidence according to different diagnostic criteria. *British Journal of Psychiatry, 182*, 449–454.

Butters, N., Pandya, D., Stein, D., & Rosen, J. (1972). A search for the spatial engram within the frontal lobes of monkeys. *Acta Neurobiologiae Experimentalis, 32*, 305–329.

Cabeza, R., McIntosh, A. R., Tulving, E., Nyberg, C., & Grady, C. L. (1997). Age-related differences in effective neural connectivity during encoding and recall. *NeuroReport, 8*, 3479–3483.

Cabeza, R., & Nyberg, L. (2000). Imaging cognition II: An empirical review of 275 PET and fMRI studies. *Journal of Cognitive Neuroscience, 12*, 1–47.

Cahill, L., Babinsky, R., Markowitsch, H. J., & McGaugh, J. L. (1995). Involvement of the amygdaloid complex in emotional memory. *Nature, 377*, 295–296.

Calabrese, P., Fink, G. R., Markowitsch, H. J., Kessler, J., Durwen, H., Liess, J., et al. (1994). Left hemispheric neuronal heterotopia. A PET, MRI, EEG, and neuropsychological investigation of a university student. *Neurology, 44*, 302–305.

Calarge, C., Andreasen, N. C., & O'Leary, D. S. (2003). Visualizing how one brain understands another: A PET study of theory of mind. *American Journal of Psychiatry, 160*, 1954–1964.

Callaway, C. W., Lydic, R., Baghdoyan, H. A., & Hobson, J. A. (1987). Pontogeniculooccipital waves: Spontaneous visual system activity during rapid eye movement sleep. *Cellular and Molecular Neurobiology, 7*, 105–149.

Calvin, W. H. (2004a). *Wie denkt das Gehirn*. Heidelberg: Elsevier.

Calvin, W. H. (2004b). *Evolving intellect during the last 1% of ape-to-human evolution*. Vortrag auf dem Neuro2004-Kongress, Düsseldorf (17.11.2004).

Canli, T., Desmond, J. E., Zhao, Z., & Gabrieli, J. D. E. (2002). Sex differences in the neural basis of emotional memories. *Proceedings of the National Academy of Sciences of the USA, 99*, 10789–10794.

Cappa, S. F., Binetti, G., Pezzini, A., Padovani, A., Rozzini, L., & Trabucchi, M. (1998). Object and action naming in Alzheimer's disease and frontotemporal dementia. *Neurology, 50*, 351–355.

Carpendale, J. I. M., & Lewis, C. (2004). Constructing an understanding of mind: The development of children's social understanding within social interaction. *Behavioral and Brain Sciences, 27*, 79–151.

Carpenter, M., Nagell, K., & Tomasello, M. (1998). *Social cognition, joint action and communicative competence at 15 months of age*. Chicago: University of Chicago Press.

Carpenter, P. A., Just, M. A., & Reichle, E. D. (2000). Working memory and executive function: Evidence from neuroimaging. *Current Opinion in Neurobiology, 10*, 195–199.

Carstensen, L. L., Pasupathi, M., Mayr, U., & Nesselroade, J. R. (2000). Emotional experience in everyday life across the adult life span. *Journal of Personality and Social Psychology, 79*, 644–655.

Cartwright, J. (2000). *Evolution and human behaviour*. New York: Palgrave.

Case, R. (1992). The role of the frontal lobes in the regulation of cognitive development. *Brain and Cognition, 20,* 51–73.

Cattell, R. B. (1963). Theory of fluid and crystallized intelligence: A critical experiment. *Journal of Educational Psychology, 54,* 1–22.

Cattell, R. B. (1987). *Intelligence: Its structure, growth and action.* Amsterdam: North Holland.

Cerella, J. (1990). Aging and information-processing rate. In J. E. Birren & K. W. Schaie (Eds.), *Handbook of the psychology of aging* (3rd ed., pp. 201–221). San Diego, CA: Academic Press.

Channon, S., & Crawford, S. (2000). The effects of anterior lesions on performance on a story comprehension test: Left anterior impairment on a theory of mind-type task. *Neuropsychologia, 38,* 1006–1017.

Cherry, K. E., & Pierre, C. S. T. (1998). Age-related differences in pictorial implicit memory: Role of perceptual and conceptual processes. *Experimental Aging Research, 24,* 53–62.

Chiron, C., Jambaque, I., Mabbout, R., Lounes, R., Dulac, O., & Syrota, A. (1997). The right brain hemisphere is dominant in human infants. *Brain, 120,* 1057–1066.

Chomsky, N. (1998 [1975]). *Reflexionen über die Sprache.* Frankfurt/M.: Suhrkamp. (Original title: *Reflections on language.* New York: Pantheon.)

Chow, K. L. (1967). Effects of ablation. In G. C. Quarton, T. Melnechuk, & F. O. Schmitt (Eds.), *The neurosciences* (pp. 705–713). New York: Rockefeller University Press.

Chugani, H. T. (1994). Development of regional brain glucose metabolism in relation to behavior and plasticity. In G. Dawson & K. W. Fischer (Eds.), *Human behavior and the developing brain* (pp. 153–175). New York: Guilford Press.

Chugani, H. T., & Phelps, M. E. (1986). Maturational changes in cerebral function in infants determined by [18]FDG positron emission tomography. *Science, 231,* 840–843.

Chugani, H. T., Phelps, M. E., & Mazziotta, J. C. (1987). Positron emission tomography study of human brain functional development. *Annals of Neurology, 22,* 487–497.

Cirulli, F., Berry, A., & Alleva, E. (2003). Early disruption of the mother–infant relationship: effects on brain plasticity and implications for psychopathology. *Neuroscience and Biobehavioral Reviews, 27,* 73–82.

Connelly, S. L., & Hasher, L. (1993). Aging and inhibition of spatial location. *Journal of Experimental Psychology: Human Perception and Performance, 19,* 1238–1250.

Conway, M., & Ross, M. (1984). Getting what you want by revising what you had. *Journal of Personality and Social Psychology, 47,* 738–748.

Conway, M. A. (2001). Sensory-perceptual episodic memory and its context: Autobiographical memory. *Philosophical Transactions of the Royal Society of London. Series B, Biological Sciences, 356,* 1375–1384.

Conway, M. A., & Pleydell-Pearce, C. W. (2000). The construction of autobiographical memories in the self-memory system. *Psychological Review, 107,* 261–288.

Conway, M. A., Pleydell-Pearce, C. W., & Whitecross, S. E. (2001). The neuroanatomy of autobiographical memory: A slow cortical potential study of autobiographical memory retrieval. *Journal of Memory and Language, 45,* 493–524.

Corey-Bloom, J., Wiederholt, W. C., Edelstein, S., Salmon, D. P., Cahn, D., & Barett-Connor, E. (1996). Cognitive and functional status of the oldest old. *Journal of the American Geriatrics Society, 44,* 671–674.

Corkin, S. (2002). What's new with the amnesic patient H.M.? *Nature Neuroscience, 3,* 153–160.

Corkin, S., Rosen, J., Sullivan, E. V., & Clegg, R. A. (1989). Penetrating head injury in young adulthood exacerbates cognitive decline in later years. *Journal of Neuroscience, 9,* 3876–3883.

Cowan, N. (2000). The magical number 4 in short-term memory: A reconsideration of mental storage capacity. *Behavioral and Brain Sciences, 24,* 87–185.

Craik, F. I. M. (1977). Age differences in human memory. In J. E. Birren & K. W. Schaie (Eds.), *Handbook of the psychology of aging* (pp. 384–420). New York: Van Nostrand Reinhold.

Craik, F. I. M., & Byrd, M. (1982). Aging and cognitive deficits: The role of attentional resources. In F. I. M. Craik & S. Trehub (Eds.), *Aging and cognitive processes* (pp. 191–211). New York: Plenum.

Cramon, D. Y. von, & Markowitsch, H. J. (2000). The septum and human memory. In R. Numan (Ed.), *The behavioral neuroscience of the septal region* (pp. 380–413). Berlin: Springer.

Cramon, D. Y. von, Markowitsch, H. J., & Schuri, U. (1993). The possible contribution of the septal region to memory. *Neuropsychologia, 31,* 1159–1180.

Creutzfeldt, O. D. (1995). *Cortex cerebri: Performance, structural and functional organization of the cortex.* Oxford: Oxford University Press.

Dahl, F. (1922). *Vergleichende Psychologie oder die Lehre von dem Seelenleben des Menschen und der Tiere.* Jena: Gustav Fischer.

Damasio, A. R. (1994). *Descartes' error: Emotion, reason, and the human brain.* New York: Grosset/Putnam.

Davatzikos, C., & Resnick, S. M. (1998). Sex differences in anatomic measures of interhemispheric connectivity: Correlations with cognition in women but not men. *Cerebral Cortex, 8,* 635–640.

Daw, M. (1996). *Visual development.* New York: Plenum Press.

Dawson, G., Panagiotides, H., Klinger, L. G., & Hill, D. (1992). The role of frontal lobe functioning in the development of infant self-regulatory behavior. *Brain and Cognition, 20,* 152–175.

De Bellis, M. D., & Keshavan, M. S. (2003). Sex differences in brain maturation in maltreatment-related pediatric posttraumatic stress disorder. *Neuroscience and Biobehavioral Reviews, 27,* 103–117.

De Bellis, M. D., & Thomas, L. A. (2003). Biologic findings of post-traumatic stress disorder and child maltreatment. *Current Psychiatry Reports, 5,* 108–117.

DeCasper, A. J., & Fifer, W. P. (1980). Of human bonding: Newborns prefer their mothers' voices. *Science, 208,* 1174–1176.

DeCasper, A. J., Lecanut, J.-P., Busnel, M.-C., Garnier-Deferre, C., & Maugeais, R. (1994). Fetal reactions to recurrent maternal speech. *Infant Behavior and Development, 17,* 159–164.

DeCasper, A. J., & Spence, M. J. (1986). Prenatal maternal speech influences newborns' perception of speech sounds. *Infant Behavior and Development, 9,* 133–150.

Deese, J. (1959). On the prediction of occurrence of particular verbal intrusions in immediate recall. *Journal of Experimental Psychology, 58,* 17–22.

Dehaene, S. (2003). Zum Lesen geboren. *Gehirn und Geist , 6,* 70–73.

De Keyser, J., De Backer, J. P., Vauquelin, G., & Ebinger, G. (1990). The effect of aging on the D_1 dopamine receptors in human frontal cortex. *Brain Research, 528,* 308–310.

De Keyser, J., De Backer, J. P., Vauquelin, G., & Ebinger, G. (1991). D_1 and D_2 dopamine receptors in human substantia nigra: Localization and the effect of aging. *Journal of Neurochemistry, 56*, 1130–1133.

DeLoache, J. S. (2000). Dual representation and young children's use of scale models. *Child Development, 71*, 329–338.

DeLoache, J. S., Uttal, D. H., & Rosengren, K. S. (2004). Scale errors offer evidence for a perception–action dissociation early in life. *Science, 304*, 1027–1029.

Dennis, M. (1991). Frontal lobe function in childhood and adolescence: A heuristic for assessing attention regulation, executive control, and the intentional states important for social discourse. *Developmental Neuropsychology, 7*, 327–358.

D'Esposito, M., & Grossmann, M. (1998). The physiological basis of executive function and working memory. *The Neuroscientist, 2*, 345–352.

De Volder, A. G., Bol, A., Blin, J., Robert, A., Arno, P., Grandin, C., et al. (1997). Brain energy metabolism in early blind subjects: Neural activity in the visual cortex. *Brain Research, 750*, 235–244.

Diamond, A. (1990). The development and neural bases of memory functions as indexed by the AB and DR tasks in human infants and infant monkeys. In A. Diamond (Ed.), *The development and neural bases of higher cognitive functions* (Vol. 608, pp. 267–309). *Annals of the New York Academy of Sciences*. New York: New York Academy of Sciences.

Dilling, H., Mombour, W., & Schmidt, M. H. (1999). *Internationale Klassifikation psychischer Störungen (ICD 10)* (3rd ed.). Bern: Verlag Hans Huber.

Dittmann, J. (2002). *Der Spracherwerb des Kindes. Verlauf und Störungen*. München: Beck.

Dolan, R. J., & Fletcher, P. C. (1999). Encoding and retrieval in human medial temporal lobes: An empirical investigation using functional magnetic resonance imaging (MRI). *Hippocampus, 9*, 25–34.

Dolcos, F., Rice, H. J, & Cabeza, R. (2002). Hemispheric asymmetry and aging: Right hemisphere decline or asymmetry reduction. *Neuroscience and Biobehavioral Reviews, 26*, 819–825.

Dolman, R., Roy, E. A., Dimeck, P. T., & Hall, C. R. (2000). Age, gesture span and dissociations among component subsystems of working memory. *Brain and Cognition, 43*, 164–168.

Donald, M. (1991). *Origins of the modern mind: Three stages in the evolution of culture and cognition*. Cambridge, MA: Harvard University Press.

Donald, M. (2001). *A mind so rare. The evolution of human consciousness*. New York: Norton.

Dong, Y., Fukuyama, H., Honda, M., Okada, T., Hanakawa, T., Nakamura, K., et al. (2000). Essential role of the right superior parietal cortex in Japanese *kana* mirror reading. An fMRI study. *Brain, 123*, 790–799.

Dornes, M. (1993). *Der kompetente Säugling*. Frankfurt/M.: Fischer.

Duchowny, M. (2004). Hemispherectomy for epilepsy. When is one half better than two. *Neurology, 62*, 1664–1665.

Earles, J. L., Connor, L. T., Frieske, D., Park, D. C., Smith, A. D., & Zwahr, M. (1997). Age differences in inhibition: Possible causes and consequences. *Aging, Neuropsychology, and Cognition, 4*, 45–57.

Eccles, J. C., Ito, M., & Szentagothai, J. (1967). *The cerebellum as a neuronal machine*. New York: Springer.

Edelman, G. M., & Tononi, G. (2002). *Gehirn und Geist. Wie aus Materie Bewußtsein entsteht.* München: Beck.

Edwards, D., & Middleton, D. (1988). Conversational remembering and family relationships: How children learn to remember. *Journal of Social and Personal Relationships, 5,* 3–25.

Einstein, G. O., & McDaniel, M. A. (1990). Normal aging and prospective memory. *Journal of Experimental Psychology: Learning, Memory, and Cognition, 16,* 717–726.

Eisenberg, A. R. (1985). Learning to describe past experiences in conversation. *Discourse Processes, 8,* 177–204.

Elias, N. (1969). *Über den Prozeß der Zivilisation.* Frankfurt/M.: Suhrkamp.

Elias, N. (1991). *The symbol theory.* London: Sage.

Elias, N. (1939/1996). *Die Gesellschaft der Individuen.* Frankfurt/M.: Suhrkamp.

Eliot, L. (2001). *Was geht da drinnen vor? Die Gehirnentwicklung in den ersten fünf Lebensjahren.* Berlin: Berlin Verlag.

Empelen, R., van, Jennekens-Schinkel, A., Buskens, E., Helders, P. J. M., & Nieuwenhuizen, O. van (2004). Functional consequences of hemispherectomy. *Brain, 127,* 2071–2079.

Engel, A. K., Fries, P., König, P., Brecht, M., & Singer, W. (1999). Does time help to understand consciousness? *Consciousness and Cognition, 8,* 260–268.

Esiri, M. (1994). Dementia and normal aging: Neuropathology. In F. A. Huppert, C. Brayne, & D. W. O'Connor (Eds.), *Dementia and normal aging* (pp. 385–436). Cambridge: Cambridge University Press.

Eslinger, P. J., Flaherty-Craig, C. V., & Benton, A. L. (2004). Developmental outcomes after early prefrontal cortex damage. *Brain and Cognition, 55,* 84–103.

Eslinger, P. J., & Grattan, L. M. (1991). Perspectives on the developmental consequences of early frontal lobe damage: introduction. *Developmental Neuropsychology 7,* 257–260.

Eslinger, P. J., Grattan, L. M., Damasio, H., & Damasio, A. R. (1992). Developmental consequences of childhood frontal lobe damage. *Archives of Neurology, 49,* 764–769.

Fabiani, M., & Wee, E. (2001). Age-related changes in working memory and frontal lobe function: A review. In C. A. Nelson & M. Luciana (Eds.), *Handbook of developmental cognitive neuroscience* (pp. 473–488). Cambridge, MA: MIT Press.

Farrar, M. J., Fasig, L. G., & Welch-Ross, M. K. (1997). Attachment and emotion in autobiographical memory development. *Journal of Experimental Child Psychology, 67,* 389–408.

Ferguson, S. A., Hashtroudi, S., & Johnson, M. K. (1992). Age differences in using source-relevant cues. *Psychology and Aging, 7,* 443–452.

Field, T. M., Woodson, R., Greenberg, R., & Cohen, D. (1982). Discrimination and imitation of facial expressions by term and preterm neonates. *Infant Behavior and Development, 6,* 485–489.

Fifer, W. P., & Moon, C. M. (1995). The effects of fetal experience with sound. In J. P. Lecanut, N. A. Krasnegor, W. P. Fifer, & W. P. Smotherman (Eds.), *Fetal development: A psychobiological perspective* (pp. 351–366). Hillsdale, NJ: Lawrence Erlbaum Associates, Inc.

Fine, C., Lumsden, J., & Blair, R. J. R. (2001). Dissociation between "theory of mind" and executive functions in a patient with early left amygdala damage. *Brain, 124,* 287–298.

Finger, S., & Almli, C. R. (1984). *Early brain damage. Vol. 2: Neurobiology and behavior.* Orlando, FL: Academic Press.

Finger, S., & Stein, D. G. (1982). *Brain damage and recovery. Research and clinical perspectives.* New York: Academic Press.

Fink, G. R., Markowitsch, H. J., Reinkemeier, M., Bruckbauer, T., Kessler, J., & Heiss, W.-D. (1996). Cerebral representation of one's own past: Neural networks involved in autobiographical memory. *Journal of Neuroscience, 16,* 4275–4282.

Fischer, R. (1946). Selbstbeobachtungen im Mezkalin-Rausch. *Schweizer Zeitschrift für Psychologie, 5,* 308–313.

Fisher, D. C., Ledbetter, M. F., Cohen, N. J., Marmor, D., & Tulsky, D. S. (2000). WAIS-III and WMS-III profiles of mildly to severely brain injured patients. *Applied Neuropsychology, 7,* 126–132.

Fisk, J. E., & Warr, P. (1996). Age and working memory: The role of perceptual speed, the central executive, and the phonological loop. *Psychology and Aging, 11,* 316–323.

Fivush, R. (1991). The social construction of personal narratives. *Merrill-Palmer Quarterly, 37,* 59–82.

Fivush, R. (1994). Constructing narrative, emotion and self in parent–child conversation about the past. In U. Neisser & R. Fivush (Eds.), *The remembering self: Construction and accuracy in the self-narrative* (pp. 136–157). New York: Cambridge University Press.

Fivush, R., Brotman, M., Bruckner, J. P., & Goodman, S. (2000). Gender differences in parent–child emotion narratives. *Sex Roles, 42,* 233–254.

Fivush, R., & Fromhoff, F.A. (1988). Style and structure in mother–child conversations about the past. *Discourse Processes, 11,* 337–355.

Fivush, R., Gray, J. T., & Fromhoff, F. A. (1987). Two-year-olds' talk about the past. *Cognitive Development, 3,* 393–409.

Flechsig, P. (1896a). *Die Lokalisation der geistigen Vorgänge, insbesondere der Sinnesempfindungen des Menschen.* Leipzig: Veit & Comp.

Flechsig, P. (1896b). *Gehirn und Seele.* Leipzig: Veit & Comp.

Fletcher, P. C., & Henson, R. N. A. (2001). Frontal lobes and human memory: Insights from functional neuroimaging. *Brain, 124,* 849–881.

Foster, J. K., Behrmann, M., & Stuss, D. T. (1995). Aging and visual search: Generalized cognitive slowing or selective deficit in attention? *Aging and Cognition, 2,* 279–299.

Fozard, J. L. (1990). Vision and hearing in aging. In J. E. Birren & K. W. Schaie (Eds.), *Handbook of the psychology of aging* (3rd ed., pp. 150–170). San Diego, CA: Academic Press.

Fraisse, P. (1985). *Psychologie der Zeit. Konditionierung, Wahrnehmung, Kontrolle, Zeitschätzung, Zeitbegriff.* München: E. Reinhardt.

Frank, M. G., Issa, N. P., & Stryker, M. P. (2001). Sleep enhances plasticity in the developing visual cortex. *Neuron, 30,* 275–287.

Freedman, M., Knoefel, J., Naeser, M., & Levine, H. (1984). Computerized axial tomography in aging. In M. L. Albert (Ed.), *Clinical neurology of aging* (pp. 139–148). New York: Oxford University Press.

Freud, S. (1919). Das Unheimliche. *Imago, 5,* 297–324.

Fried, J. (2004). *Der Schleier der Erinnerung. Grundzüge einer historischen Memorik.* München: C. H. Beck.

Friedman, A., & Pines, A. (1991). Sex differences in gender-related childhood memories. *Sex Roles, 25,* 25–32.

Fristoe N. M., Salthouse T. A., & Woodard J. L. (1997). Examination of age-related deficits on the Wisconsin Card Sorting Test. *Neuropsychology, 11,* 428–436.

Fujiwara, E., Brand, M., Kracht, L., Kessler, J., Diebel, A., Netz, J., & Markowitsch, H. J. (2008). Functional retrograde amnesia: A multiple case study. *Cortex, 44,* 29–45.

Fujiwara, E., Brand, M., & Markowitsch, H. J. (2002). Emotionale Bewertung und Gedächtnis bei Patienten mit alkoholbedingtem Korsakow-Syndrom. *Praxis Klinische Verhaltensmedizin und Rehabilitation, 60,* 275–281.

Fujiwara, E., & Markowitsch, H. J. (2003). Das mnestische Blockadesyndrom: Hirn-physiologische Korrelate von Angst und Stress. In G. Schiepek (Eds.), *Neurobiologie der Psychotherapie* (pp. 186–212). Stuttgart: Schattauer Verlag.

Fujiwara, E., Piefke, M., Lux, S., Fink, G. R., Kessler, J., Kracht, L., et al. (2004). Brain correlates of functional retrograde amnesia in three patients. *Brain and Cognition, 54,* 135–136.

Fuster, J. M. (1997a). Network memory. *Trends in Neurosciences, 20,* 451–459.

Fuster, J. M. (1997b). *The prefrontal cortex* (3rd ed.). Philadelphia: Lippincott-Raven,

Gabrieli, J. D. E., McGlinchey-Berroth, R., Carrillo, M. C., Gluck, M. A., Cermak, L. S., & Disterhoft, J. F. (1995). Intact delay-eyeblink classical conditioning in amnesia. *Behavioral Neuroscience, 109,* 819–827.

Gabrieli, J. D. E., Vaidya, C. J., Stone, M., Francis, W. S., Thompson-Schill, S. L., Fleischman, D. A., et al. (1999). Convergent behavioral and neuropsychological evidence for a distinction between identification and production forms of repetition priming. *Journal of Experimental Psychology: General, 128,* 479–498.

Gagnon, R., Hunse, C., Carmichael, L., Fellows, F., & Patrick, J. (1986). Effects of vibratory acoustic stimulation on human fetal breathing and gross body movements near term. *American Journal of Obstetrics and Gynecology, 155,* 1227–1230.

Galaburda, A. M., LeMay, M., Kemper, T. L., & Geschwind, N. (1978). Right–left asymmetries in the brain. *Science, 199,* 852–856.

Galaburda, A. M., & Pandya, D. N. (1982). Role of architectonics and connections in the study of primate brain evolution. In E. Armstrong & D. Falk (Eds.), *Primate brain evolution* (pp. 203–216). New York: Plenum Press.

Galasko, D., Bennett, D., Sano, M., Ernesto, C., Thomas, R., Grundman, M., et al. (1997). Alzheimer's Disease Cooperative Study. An inventory to assess activities of daily living for clinical trials in Alzheimer's disease. *Alzheimer Disease and Associated Disorders, 11,* 33–39.

Galvin, J. E., Palmer, J. L., & Morris, J. C. (2003). Mild cognitive impairment represents early Alzheimer's disease. *Research and Practice in Alzheimer's Disease, 6,* 38–42.

Ganis, G., Kosslyn, S. M., Stose, S., Thompson, W. L., & Yurgelun-Todd, D. A. (2003). Neural correlates of different types of deception: An fMRI investigation. *Cerebral Cortex, 13,* 830–843.

Gannon, P. J., Holloway, R. L., Broadfield, D. C., & Braun, A. R. (1998). Asymmetry of chimpanzee planum temporale: Humanlike pattern of Wernicke's brain language area homolog. *Science, 279,* 220–222.

Garde, E., Mortensen, E. L., Krabbe, K., Rostrup, E., & Larsson, H. B. (2000). Relation between age-related decline in intelligence and cerebral white-matter hyperintensities in healthy octogenarians: A longitudinal study. *Lancet, 19,* 628–634.

Geinisman, Y., Detoledo-Morrell, L., Morrell, F., & Heller, R. E. (1995). Hippocampal markers of age-related memory dysfunction: Behavioral, electrophysiological and morphological perspectives. *Progress in Neurobiology*, *45*, 223–252.

Gelman, R., & Gallistel, C. R. (2004). Language and the origin of numerical concepts. *Science*, *306*, 441–443.

Gelman, S. A. (2004). Psychological essentialism in children. *Trends in Cognitive Sciences*, *8*, 404–409.

Geschwind, N., & Galaburda, A. M. (1982). *Cerebral lateralization*. Cambridge, MA: MIT Press.

Giambra, L. M. (1993). Sustained attention in older adults: Performance and processes. In J. Cerella, J. Rybash, W. Hoyer, & M. L. Commons (Eds.), *Adult information processing: Limits on loss* (pp. 259–272). San Diego, CA: Academic Press.

Gibson, K. R. (1991). Myelination and behavioral development: A comparative perspective of neoteny, altriciality and intelligence. In K. R. Gibson & A. C. Peterson (Eds.), *Brain maturation and cognitive development: Comparative and cross-cultural perspectives* (pp. 29–63). New York: Aldine de Gruyter.

Gilbert, P. E., Kesner, R. P., & DeCoteau, W. E. (1998). Memory for spatial location: Role of the hippocampus in mediating spatial pattern separation. *Journal of Neuroscience*, *18*, 804–810.

Gilinsky, A. S., & Judd, B. B. (1994). Working memory and bias in reasoning across the adult life span. *Psychology and Aging*, *9*, 356–371.

Gilles, J. (2004). Change of mind. *Nature*, *430*, 14.

Glaser, B. G., & Strauss, A. L. (1998). *Grounded theory. Strategien qualitativer Forschung*. Bern: Huber.

Glezer, I. L., Jacobs, M. S., & Morgane, P. J. (1988). Implications of the "initial brain" concept for brain evolution in Cetacea. *Behavioral and Brain Sciences*, *11*, 75–116.

Glover, S. (2004). What causes scale errors in children? *Trends in Cognitive Sciences*, *8*, 440–442.

Goldman, P. S., & Galkin, T. W. (1978). Prenatal removal of frontal association cortex in the fetal rhesus monkey: Anatomical and functional consequences in postnatal life. *Brain Research*, *152*, 451–485.

Goldman-Rakic, P. S. (1987). Development of cortical circuitry and cognitive function. *Child Development*, *58*, 601–622.

Gordon, P. (2004). Numerical cognition without words: Evidence from Amazonia. *Science*, *306*, 496–499.

Götz, M. (2003). Brain development: Glial cells generate neurons – implications for neuropsychiatric disorders. In M. A. Ron & T. W. Robbins (Eds.), *Disorders of brain and mind* (Vol. 2, pp. 59–73). Cambridge: Cambridge University Press.

Grafman, J. (1999). Experimental assessment of adult frontal lobe function. In B. L. Miller & J. L. Cummings (Eds.), *The human frontal lobes: Functions and disorders* (pp. 321–344). New York: Guilford Press.

Grattan, L. M., & Eslinger, P. J. (1991). Frontal lobe damage in children and adults: A comparative review. *Developmental Neuropsychology*, *7*, 283–326.

Grattan, L. M., & Eslinger, P. J. (1992). Long-term psychological consequences of childhood. Frontal lobe lesion in patient DT. *Brain and Cognition*, *20*, 185–195.

Grégoire, J., & van der Linden, M. (1997). Effects of age on forward and backward digit span. *Aging, Neuropsychology, and Cognition*, *4*, 140–149.

Gregory, C., Lough, S., Stone, V., Erzinclioglu, S., & Martin, L. (2002). Theory of mind in patients with frontal variant frontotemporal dementia and Alzheimer's disease: Theoretical and practical implications. *Brain*, *125*, 752–764.

Grimm, H. (1998). Sprachentwicklung – allgemeintheoretisch und differentiell betrach-
tet. In R. Oerter & L. Montada (Eds.), *Entwicklungspsychologie. Ein Lehrbuch*
(4th ed., pp. 705–757). Weinheim: PVU.

Grimm, H., & Weinert, S. (2002). Sprachentwicklung. In R. Oerter & L. Montada
(Eds.), *Entwicklungspsychologie* (pp. 517–559). Weinheim: Beltz.

Gross, J. J., Carstensen, L. L., Pasupathi, M., Tsai, J., Götestam Skorpen, C.,
& Hsu, A. Y. C. (1997). Emotion and aging. *Psychology and Aging, 12*, 590–
599.

Grünthal, E. (1932). Die erworbenen Verblödungen (II: Klinik und Anatomie).
Fortschritte der Neurologie und Psychiatrie, 4, 306–320.

Grünthal, E. (1939). Ueber das Corpus mamillare und den Korsakowschen Symp-
tomenkomplex. *Confinia Neurologica, 2*, 64–95.

Grüsser, O.-J. (1988). Die phylogenetische Hirnentwicklung und die funktionelle
Lateralisation der menschlichen Großhirnrinde. In G. Oepen (Ed.), *Psychiatrie
des rechten und linken Gehirns: Neuropsychologische Ansätze zum Verständnis von
"Persönlichkeit", "Depression" und "Schizophrenie"* (pp. 34–50). Köln: Deutscher
Ärzte-Verlag.

Gunning-Dixon, F. M., & Raz, N. (2000). The cognitive correlates of white matter
abnormalities in normal aging: A quantitative review. *Neuropsychology, 14*,
224–232.

Gur, R. C., Gunning-Dixon, F., Bilker, W. B., & Gur, R. E. (2002). Sex differences in
temporo-limbic and frontal brain volumes of healthy adults. *Cerebral Cortex, 12*,
998–1003.

Gur, R. C., Turetsky, B. I., Matsui, M., Yan, M., Bilker, W., Hughett, P., et al. (1999).
Sex differences in brain gray and white matter in healthy young adults: Correlations
with cognitive performance. *Journal of Neuroscience, 19*, 4065–4072.

Habermas, T., & Bluck, S. (2000). Getting a life: The development of the lift story in
adolescence. *Psychological Bulletin, 126*, 748–769.

Habib, R., Nyberg, L., & Tulving, E. (2003). Hemispheric asymmetries of memory:
The HERA model revisited. *Trends in Cognitive Sciences, 7*, 241–245.

Haden, C., Haine, R., & Fivush, R. (1997). Developing narrative structure in parent–
child conversations about the past. *Developmental Psychology, 33*, 295–307.

Haden, C. A., Ornstein, P. A., Eckerman, C. O., & Didow, S. M. (2001). Mother–child
conversational interactions as events unfold: Linkages to subsequent remembering. *Child Development, 72*, 1016–1031.

Haist, F., Bowden Gore, J., & Mao, H. (2001). Consolidation of human memory over
decades revealed by functional magnetic resonance imaging. *Nature Neuroscience,
4*, 1139–1145.

Harley, K., & Reese, E. (1999). Origins of autobiographical memory. *Developmental
Psychology, 35*, 1338–1348.

Harlow, H. F., & Zimmerman, R. R. (1959). Affectional responses in the infant
monkey. *Science, 130*, 421–432.

Harlow, J. M. (1848). Passage of an iron rod through the head. *Boston Medical and
Surgical Journal, 39*, 389–393.

Harlow, J. M. (1869). *Recovery from the passage of an iron bar through the head.*
Boston: D. Clapp and Son.

Härting, C., & Markowitsch, H. J. (1996). Different degrees of impairment in recall/
recognition and anterograde/retrograde memory performance in a transient global
amnesic case. *Neurocase, 2*, 45–49.

Hartley, A. A. (1993). Evidence for the selective preservation of spatial selective attention in old age. *Psychology and Aging, 3*, 371–379.

Hasegawa, M., Houdou, S., Mito, T., Takashima, S., Asanuma, K., & Ohno, T. (1992). Development of myelination in the human fetal and infant cerebrum: A myelin basic protein immunohistochemical study. *Brain & Development, 14*, 1–6.

Hasher, L., & Zacks, R. T. (1988). Working memory, comprehension, and aging: A review and a new view. In G. H. Bower (Ed.), *The psychology of learning and motivation* (Vol. 22, pp. 193–225). Orlando, FL: Academic Press.

Hashtroudi, S., Parker, E. S., Luis, J. D., & Reisen, C. A. (1989). Generation and elaboration in older adults. *Experimental Aging Research, 15*, 73–78.

Hawkins, H. L., Kramer, A. F., & Capaldi, D. (1992). Aging, exercise, and attention. *Psychology and Aging, 7*, 643–653.

Hayne, H., Boniface, J., & Barr, R. (2000). The development of declarative memory in human infants: Age-related changes in deferred imitation. *Behavioral Neuroscience, 114*, 77–83.

Heinsen, H., Henn, R., Eisenmenger, W., Gotz, M., Bohl, J., Bethke, B., et al. (1994). Quantitative investigations on the human entorhinal area: Left–right asymmetry and age-related changes. *Anatomy and Embryology, 190*, 181–194.

Hell, W. (1998). Gedächtnistäuschungen. Fehlleistungen des Erinnerns im Experiment und im Alltag. In E. P. Fischer (Ed.), *Gedächtnis und Erinnerung* (pp. 233–277). Munich: Piper.

Heller, W. (1993). Gender differences in depression: Perspectives from neuropsychology. *Journal of Affective Disorders, 29*, 129–143.

Hellige, J. B., & Yamauchi, M. (1999). Quantitative and qualitative hemispheric asymmetry for processing Japanese kana. *Brain and Cognition, 40*, 453–463.

Hepper, P. G. (1992). Fetal psychology: An embryonic science. In J. G. Nijhuis (Ed.), *Fetal behavior: Developmental and perinatal aspects* (pp. 129–155). Oxford: Oxford University Press.

Hepper, P. G., & Shahidullah, S. B. (1994). Development of fetal hearing. *Archives of Disease in Childhood, 71*, 81–87.

Hering, E. (1870). *Ueber das Gedächtnis als eine allgemeine Funktion der organisierten Materie. Vortrag gehalten in der feierlichen Sitzung der Kaiserlichen Akademie der Wissenschaften in Wien am XXX. Mai MDCCCLXX*. Leipzig: Akademische Verlagsgesellschaft.

Hertz-Pannier, L., Chiron, C., Jambaqué, I., Renaux-Kieffer, V., Van der Moortele, P.-F., Delalande, O., et al. (2002). Late plasticity for language in a child's non-dominant hemisphere. A pre- and post-surgery fMRI study. *Brain, 125*, 361–372.

Hodges, J. R., Patterson, K., Graham, N., & Dawson, K. (1996). Naming and knowing in dementia of Alzheimer's type. *Brain and Language, 54*, 302–325.

Hodos, W. (1988). Comparative neuroanatomy and the evolution of intelligence. In H. J. Jerison & I. Jerison (Eds.), *Intelligence and evolutionary biology* (pp. 93–107). Berlin: Springer.

Hof, P. R., Vogt, B. A., Bouras, C., & Morrison, J. H. (1997). Atypical form of Alzheimer's disease with prominent posterior cortical atrophy: A review of lesion distribution and circuit disconnection in cortical visual pathways. *Vision Research, 37*, 3609–3625.

Hoff, H., & Pötzl, O. (1938). Anatomischer Befund eines Falles mit Zeitrafferphänomen. *Deutsche Zeitschrift für Nervenheilkunde, 145*, 150–178.

Hogan, D. B., & McKeith, I. G. (2001). Of MCI and dementia: Improving diagnosis and treatment. *Neurology, 56,* 1131–1132.

Hollup, S. A., Molden, S., Donnett, J. G., Moser, M.-B., & Moser, E. I. (2001). Place fields of rat hippocampal pyramidal cells and spatial learning in the watermaze. *European Journal of Neuroscience, 13,* 1197–1208.

Hopf, A. (1956). Volumetrische Untersuchungen zur vergleichenden Anatomie des Thalamus. *Journal für Hirnforschung, 8,* 25–38.

Hopkins, W. D., Marino, L., Rilling, J. K., & MacGregor, L. A. (1998). Planum temporale asymmetries in great apes as revealed by magnetic resonance imaging (MRI). *NeuroReport, 9,* 2913–2918.

Hopkins, W. D., Wesley, M. J., Izard, M. K., & Hook, M. (2004). Chimpanzees (*Pan troglodytes*) are predominantly right-handed: Replication in three populations of apes. *Behavioral Neuroscience, 11,* 659–663.

Horn, J. L. (1982). The theory of fluid and crystallized intelligence in relation to concepts of cognitive psychology and aging in adulthood. In F. I. M. Craik & S. Trehub (Eds.), *Aging and cognitive processes* (pp. 237–278). New York: Plenum Press.

Howe, M. L. (2000). *The fate of early memories.* Washington, DC: American Psychological Association.

Howe, M. L., & Courage, M. L. (1993). On resolving the enigma of infantile amnesia. *Psychological Bulletin, 113,* 305–326.

Howe, M. L., & Courage, M. L. (1997). The emergence and early development of autobiographical memory. *Psychological Review, 104,* 499–523.

Howe, M. L., Courage, M. L., & Edison, S. (2003). When autobiographical memory begins. *Developmental Review, 23,* 471–494.

Howes, M., Siegel, M., & Brown, F. (1993). Early childhood memories: Accuracy and affect. *Cognition, 47,* 95–115.

Howieson, D. B., Holm, L. A., Kaye, J. A., Oken, B. S., & Howieson, J. (1993). Neurologic function in the optimally healthy oldest old: Neuropsychological evaluation. *Neurology, 43,* 1882–1886.

Hudson, J. A. (1990). The emergence of autobiographical memory in mother–child conversation. In R. Fivush & J. A. Hudson (Eds.), *Knowing and remembering in young children* (pp. 166–196). Cambridge: Cambridge University Press.

Hudson, R. (1985). Do newborn rabbits learn the odor stimuli releasing nipple-suckling behavior? *Developmental Psychobiology, 18,* 575–585.

Huether, G., Adler, L., & Rüther, E. (1999). Die neurobiologische Verankerung psychosozialer Erfahrungen. *Zeitschrift für psychosomatische Medizin, 45,* 2–17.

Humphrey, D. G., & Kramer, A. F. (1997). Age differences in visual search for feature, conjunction, and triple-conjunction targets. *Psychology and Aging, 12,* 704–717.

Huschke, E. (1854). *Schaedel, Hirn und Seele des Menschen und der Thiere nach Alter, Geschlecht und Race.* Jena: F. Mauke.

Huttenlocher, P. R. (1979). Synaptic density in human frontal cortex: Developmental changes and effects of aging. *Brain Research, 163,* 195–205.

Huttenlocher, P. R. (1990). Morphometric study of human cerebral cortex development. *Neuropsychologia, 28,* 517–527.

Huttenlocher, P. R. (1994). Synaptogenesis in human cerebral cortex. In G. Dawson & K. W. Fischer (Eds.), *Human behavior and the developing brain* (pp. 137–152). New York: Guilford Press.

Huttenlocher, P. R. (1996). Morphometric study of human cerebral cortex development. In M. Johnson (Ed.), *Brain development and cognition: A reader* (pp. 112–124). Cambridge, MA: Blackwell.

Huttenlocher, P. R., & Dabholkar, A. S. (1997). Regional differences in synaptogenesis in human cerebral cortex. *Journal of Comparative Neurology, 387,* 167–178.

Huttenlocher, P. R., & deCourten, C. (1987). The development of synapses in striate cortex of man. *Human Neurobiology, 6,* 1–9.

Huttenlocher, P. R., deCourten, C., Garey, L. G., & Van der Loos, H. (1982). Synaptogenesis in human visual cortex: Evidence for synapse elimination during normal development. *Neuroscience Letters, 33,* 247–252.

Huxley, J. (1953). *Evolution in action.* Based on the Patten Foundation Lectures delivered at Indiana University in 1951. London: Chatto & Windus.

Hyman, I. E., Husband, T. H., & Billigs, F. J. (1995). False memories of childhood experiences. *Applied Cognitive Psychology, 9,* 181–197.

Insausti, R., Juottonen, K., Soininen, H., Insausti, A. M., Partanen, K., Vainio, P., et al. (1998). MR volumetric analysis of the human entorhinal, perirhinal, and temporopolar cortices. *American Journal of Neuroradiology, 19,* 659–671.

Irle, E., & Markowitsch, H. J. (1982). Connections of the hippocampal formation, mamillary bodies, anterior thalamus and cingulate cortex. A retrograde study using horseradish peroxidase in the cat. *Experimental Brain Research, 47,* 79–94.

Irle, E., & Markowitsch, H. J. (1987). Basal forebrain-lesioned monkeys are severely impaired in tasks of associative and recognition memory. *Annals of Neurology, 22,* 735–743.

Isaacowitz, D. M., Turk Charles, S., & Carstensen, L. L. (2000). Emotion and cognition. In F. I. M. Craik & T. A. Salthause (Eds.), *The handbook of aging and cognition* (pp. 593–631). Mahwah, NJ: Lawrence Erlbaum Associates, Inc.

Isaacson, R. L. (1975). The myth of recovery from early brain damage. In N. R. Ellis (Ed.), *Aberrant development in infancy* (pp. 1–25). Hillsdale, NJ: Lawrence Erlbaum Associates, Inc.

Isaacson, R. L. (1988). Brain lesion studies related to memory: A critique of strategies and interpretations. In H. J. Markowitsch (Ed.), *Information processing by the brain* (pp. 87–106). Toronto: Huber.

Isingrini, M., & Vazou, F. (1997). Relation between fluid intelligence and frontal lobe functioning in older adults. *International Journal of Aging and Human Development, 45,* 99–109.

Jacobsen, C. F., & Nissen, H. W. (1937). Studies of cerebral function in primates: IV. The effects of frontal lobe lesions on the delayed alternation habit in monkeys. *Journal of Comparative and Physiological Psychology, 23,* 101–112.

James, W. (1950 [1890]). *The principles of psychology.* New York: Dover Publications. (Original publication: *The principles of psychology* (2 vols). New York: Holt.)

Jenkins, L., Myerson, J., Hale, S., & Fry, A. F. (1999). Life span developmental differences in interference with verbal and spatial working memory. *Psychonomic Bulletin & Review, 6,* 28–40.

Jerison, H. J. (1973). *The evolution of the brain and intelligence.* New York: Academic Press.

Jin, K., Peel, A. L., Mao, X. O., Xie, L., Cottrell, B. A., Henshall, D. C., et al. (2004). Increased hippocampal neurogenesis in Alzheimer's disease. *Proceedings of the National Academy of Sciences of the USA, 101,* 343–347.

Johansson, B., & Berg, S. (1989). The robustness of the terminal decline phenomenon:

Longitudinal data from the digit-span memory test. *Journal of Gerontology; Psychological Sciences, 44*, 184–186.

Johnson, K. A., Jones, K., Holman, B. L., Becker, J. A., Spiers, P. A., Satlin, A., et al. (1998). Preclinical prediction of Alzheimer's disease using SPECT. *Neurology, 50*, 1563–1571.

Johnson, M. H. (2001). Functional brain development in humans. *Nature Reviews Neuroscience, 2*, 475–483.

Johnson, M. H. (2003). Development of human brain functions. *Biological Psychiatry, 54*, 1312–1316.

Johnson, M. K., Hashtroudi, S., & Lindsay, D. S. (1993). Source monitoring. *Psychological Bulletin, 114*, 3–28.

Johnson, S. C., Baxter, L. C., Wilder, L. S., Pipe, J. G., Heiserman, J. E., & Prigatano, G. P. (2002). Neural correlates of self-reflection. *Brain, 125*, 1808–1814.

Johnson, S. P. (2003). The nature of cognitive development. *Trends in Cognitive Sciences, 7*, 102–104.

Kaasinen, V., Nagren, K., Hietala, J., Farde, L., & Rinne, J. O. (2001). Sex differences in extrastriatal dopamine D_2-like receptors in the human brain. *American Journal of Psychiatry, 158*, 308–311.

Kamada, K., Kober, H., Saguer, M., Möller, M., Kaltenhäuser, M., & Vieth, J. (1998). Responses to silent kanji reading of the native Japanese and German in task subtraction magnetencephalography. *Cognitive Brain Research, 7*, 89–98.

Kaminski, J., Call, J., & Fischer, J. (2004). Word learning in a domestic dog: Evidence for "fast mapping". *Science, 304*, 1682–1683.

Kandel, E. R., Kupfermann, I., & Iversen, S. (2000). Learning and memory. In E. R. Kandel, J. H. Schwartz, & T. M. Jessell (Eds.), *Principles of neural science* (pp. 1227–1245). Amsterdam: Elsevier.

Kawano, M., Ichimiya, A., Ogomori, K., Kuwabara, Y., Sasaki, M., Yoshida, T., et al. (2001). Relationship between both IQ and Mini-Mental State Examination and the regional cerebral glucose metabolism in clinically diagnosed Alzheimer's disease: A PET study. *Dementia and Geriatric Cognitive Disorders, 12*, 171–176.

Keenan, J. P., McCutcheon, B., Sanders, G., Freund, S., Gallup, G. G., Jr., & Pascual-Leone, A. (1999). Left hand advantage in a self-face recognition task. *Neuropsychologia, 37*, 1421–1425.

Keenan, J. P., Wheeler, M., Gallup, G. G., Jr., & Pascual-Leone, A. (2000). Self-recognition and the right prefrontal cortex. *Trends in Cognitive Sciences, 4*, 338–344.

Kemper, S. (1986). Imitation of complex syntactic constructions by elderly adults. *Applied Psycholinguistics, 7*, 277–288.

Kemper, S. (1987a). Life span changes in syntactic complexity. *Journal of Gerontology, 42*, 323–328.

Kemper, S. (1987b). Syntactic complexity and elderly adults' prose recall. *Experimental Aging Research, 13*, 47–52.

Kemper, T. L. (1994). Neuroanatomical and neuropathological changes during aging and in dementia. In M. L. Albert & E. J. E. Knoepfel (Eds.), *Clinical neurology of aging* (pp. 3–67). New York: Oxford University Press.

Kemtes, K. A., & Kemper, S. (1997). Younger and older adults' on-line processing of syntactically ambiguous sentences. *Psychology and Aging, 12*, 362–371.

Kennard, M. A. (1938). Reorganization of motor function in the cerebral cortex of monkeys deprived of motor and premotor areas in infancy. *Journal of Neurophysiology, 1*, 477–496.

Kennard, M. A. (1940). Relation of age to motor impairment in man and sub-human primates. *A. M. A. Archives of Neurology and Psychiatry, 44*, 377–397.

Kennard, M. A. (1942). Cortical reorganization of motor function: Studies on a series of monkeys of various ages from infancy to maturity. *A. M. A. Archives of Neurology and Psychiatry, 48*, 227–240.

Kessels, R. P. C., de Haan, E. H. F., Kappelle, L. J., & Postma, A. (2001). Varieties of human spatial memory: A meta-analysis on the effects of hippocampal lesions. *Brain Research Reviews, 35*, 295–303.

Kessler, J., Denzler, P., & Markowitsch, H. J. (1999). *Altersprofil-Test*. Göttingen: Hogrefe.

Kessler, J., Irle, E., & Markowitsch, H. J. (1986). Korsakoff and alcoholic subjects are severely impaired in animal tasks of association memory. *Neuropsychologia, 24*, 671–680.

Kessler, J., & Kalbe, E. (1997). Gedächtnisstörungen im Alter: Prodrom einer Demenz? In S. Weis & G. Weber (Eds.), *Handbuch Morbus Alzheimer* (pp. 859–887). Weinheim: Psychologie Verlags Union.

Kessler, J., Markowitsch, H. J., & Bast-Kessler, C. (1987). Memory of alcoholic patients, including Korsakoff's, tested with a Brown–Peterson paradigm. *Archives of Psychology, 101*, 115–132.

Kessler, J., Markowitsch, H. J., & Denzler, P. (1990). *Der Mini-Mental-Status Test*. Weinheim: Beltz-Test-Verlag.

Kessler, J., Markowitsch, H. J., Guldin, W., Riess, R., Pritzel, M., Streicher, M., et al. (1980). Comparative analysis of delayed alternation learning in cats, mice, and guinea pigs. *Animal Learning and Behavior, 8*, 457–464.

Kihlstrom, J. F., & Harackiewicz, J. M. (1982). The earliest recollection: A new survey. *Journal of Personality, 50*, 134–148.

Kim, J. J., & Thompson, R. F. (1997). Cerebellar circuits and synaptic mechanisms involved in classical eyeblink conditioning. *Trends in Neurosciences, 20*, 177–181.

Kimberg, D. Y., D'Esposito, M., & Farah, M. J. (1998). Cognitive functions in the prefrontal cortex – working memory and executive control. *Current Directions in Psychological Science, 6*, 185–192.

Klein, M. (1997). *Cognitive aging, attention, and mild traumatic brain injury*. Maastricht: Neuropsych Publishers.

Kliegel, M., Moor, C., & Rott, C. (2004). Cognitive status and development in the oldest old: A longitudinal analysis from the Heidelberg Centenarian Study. *Archives of Gerontology and Geriatrics, 39*, 143–156.

Kliegel, M., Ramuschkat, G., & Martin, M. (2003). Exekutive Funktionen und prospektive Gedächtnisleistung im Alter. *Zeitschrift für Gerontologie und Geriatrie, 36*, 35–41.

Klingberg, T., Vaidya, C. J., Gabrieli, J. D. E., Moseley, M. E., & Hedehus, M. (1999). Myelination and organization of the frontal white matter in children: A diffusion tensor MRI study. *NeuroReport, 10*, 2817–2821.

Knecht, S., Henningsen, H., Höhling, C., Elbert, T., Flor, H., Pantev, C., et al. (1998). Plasticity of plasticity? Changes in the pattern of perceptual correlates of reorganization after amputation. *Brain, 121*, 717–724.

Koch, G. (2001). Affekt oder Effekt. Was haben Bilder, was Worte nicht haben. In H. Welzer (Ed.), *Das soziale Gedächtnis. Geschichte, Erinnerung, Tradierung* (pp. 123–133). Hamburg: Hamburger Edition.

Kolb, B. (1989). Brain development, plasticity, and behavior. *American Psychologist*, *44*, 1203–1212.

Kolb, B., & Whishaw, I. Q. (1998). *Neuropsychologie*. Heidelberg: Spektrum.

Kolb, B., Wilson, B., & Taylor, L. (1992). Developmental changes in the recognition and comprehension of facial expression: Implications for frontal lobe function. *Brain and Cognition*, *20*, 74–84.

Konner, M. (1991). Universals of behavioral development in relation to brain myelination. In K. R. Gibson & A. Petersen (Eds.), *Brain maturation and cognitive development* (pp. 181–222). New York: de Gruyter.

Kossoff, E. H., Buck, C., & Freeman, J. M. (2002). Outcomes of 32 hemispherectomies for Sturge–Weber syndrome worldwide. *Neurology*, *59*, 1735–1738.

Kotary, L., & Hoyer, W. (1995). Age and the ability to inhibit distractor information in visual selective attention. *Experimental Aging Research*, *21*, 159–171.

Koutstaal, W., Schacter, D. L., Galluccio, L., & Stofer, K. A. (1999). Reducing gist-based false recognition in older adults: Encoding and retrieval manipulations. *Psychology and Aging*, *14*, 220–237.

Kozel, F. A., & Padgett, T. M. (2004). A replication study of the neural correlates of deception. *Behavioral Neuroscience*, *118*, 852–856.

Kramer, A. F., Hahn, S., & Gopher, D. (1999a). Task coordination and aging: Explorations of executive control processes in the task switching paradigm. *Acta Psychologica*, *101*, 339–378.

Kramer, A. F., Larish, J. F., Weber, T. A., & Bardell, L. (1999b). Training for executive control: Task coordination strategies and aging. In D. Gopher & A. Koriat (Eds.), *Attention and performance: XVII* (pp. 617–652). Cambridge, MA: MIT Press.

Krasuski, J. S., Alexander, G. E., Horwitz, B., Daly, E. M., Murphy, D. G., Rapoport, S. I. et al. (1998). Volumes of medial temporal lobe structures in patients with Alzheimer's disease and mild cognitive impairment (and in healthy controls). *Biological Psychiatry*, *43*, 60–68.

Krauss, S. (1930). Untersuchungen über Aufbau und Störungen der menschlichen Handlung. I. Teil: Die Korsakowsche Störung. *Archiv für die gesamte Psychologie*, *77*, 649–692.

Kroll, N., Markowitsch, H. J., Knight, R., & Cramon, D. Y. von (1997). Retrieval of old memories – the temporo-frontal hypothesis. *Brain*, *120*, 1377–1399.

Kuhl, P. K., & Meltzoff, A. N. (1982). The bimodal perception of speech in infancy. *Science*, *218*, 1138–1141.

Laine, M., Vuorinen, E., & Rinne, J. O. (1997). Picture naming deficits in vascular dementia and Alzheimer's disease. *Journal of Clinical and Experimental Neuropsychology*, *19*, 126–140.

Larsson, M., & Bäckman, L. (1998). Modality memory across the adult life span: Evidence for selective olfactory deficits. *Experimental Aging Research*, *24*, 63–82.

Laver, G. D., & Burke, D. M. (1993). Why do semantic priming effects increase in old age? A meta-analysis. *Psychology and Aging*, *8*, 34–43.

La Voie, D., & Light, L. L. (1994). Adult age differences in repetition priming: A meta-analysis. *Psychology and Aging*, *9*, 539–553.

Lawrence, B., Myerson, J., & Hale, S. (1998). Differential decline of verbal and visuospatial processing speed across the adult life span. *Aging, Neuropsychology, and Cognition*, *5*, 129–146.

Lawton, M. P., & Brody, E. M. (1969). Assessment of older people: Self-maintaining and instrumental activities of daily living. *Gerontologist*, *9*, 179–186.

Lawton, M. P., Kleban, M. H., Rajagopal, D., & Dean, J. (1992). Dimensions of affective experience in three age groups. *Psychology and Aging, 7*, 171–184.

Leiner, H. C., Leiner, A. L., & Dow, R. S. (1991). The human cerebro-cerebellar system: Its computing, cognitive, and language skills. *Behavioural Brain Research, 44*, 113–128.

Leiner, H. C., Leiner, A. L., & Dow, R. S. (1993). Cognitive and language functions of the human cerebellum. *Trends in Neurosciences, 16*, 444–447.

LeMay, M. (1976). Morphological cerebral asymmetries of modern man, fossil man, and nonhuman primate. *Annals of the New York Academy of Sciences, 280*, 349–366.

Leonhardt, G., Bingel, U., Spiekermann, G., Kurthen, M., Müller, S., & Hufnagel, A. (2001). Cortical activation in patients with functional hemispherectomy. *Journal of Neurology, 248*, 881–888.

Lepage, M., Habib, R., & Tulving, E. (1998). Hippocampal PET activations of memory encoding and retrieval: The HIPER model. *Hippocampus, 8*, 313–322.

Levenson, R. W., Carstensen, L. L., Friesen, W. V., & Ekman, P. (1991). Emotion, physiology, and expression in old age. *Psychology and Aging, 6*, 28–35.

Levine, B., Black, S. E., Cabeza, R., Sinden, M., McIntosh, A. R., Toth, J. P., et al. (1998). Episodic memory and the self in a case of isolated retrograde amnesia. *Brain, 121*, 1951–1973.

Levine, B., Stuss, D. T., & Milberg, W. P. (1995). Concept generation: Validation of a test of executive functioning in a normal aging population. *Journal of Clinical and Experimental Neuropsychology, 17*, 740–758.

Lhermitte, F. (1983). 'Utilization behaviour' and its relation to lesions of the frontal lobes. *Brain, 106*, 237–255.

Li, S.-C. (2003). Biocultural orchestration of developmental plasticity across levels: The interplay of biology and culture in shaping the mind and behavior across the life span. *Psychological Bulletin, 129*, 171–194.

Libet, B., Pearl, D., Morledge, D.E., Gleason, C.A., Hosobuchi, Y., & Barbaro, N.M. (1991). Control of the transition from sensory detection to sensory awareness in man by the duration of thalamic stimulus: The cerebral "time-on" factor. *Brain, 114*, 1731–1757.

Liégeois, F., Connelly, A., Cross, J. H., Boyd, S. G., Gadian, D. G., Vargha-Khadem, F., et al. (2004). Language reorganization in children with early-onset lesions of the left hemisphere: An fMRI study. *Brain, 127*, 1229–1236.

Light, L. L. (1991). Memory and aging: Four hypotheses in search of data. *Annual Review of Psychology, 42*, 333–376.

Light, L. L. (1997). Memory and aging. In E. L. Björk & R. A. Björk (Eds.), *Memory* (pp. 443–490). San Diego, CA: Academic Press.

Light, L. L., & Albertson, S. A. (1989). Direct and indirect tests of memory for category exemplars in young and older adults. *Psychology and Aging, 4*, 487–492.

Light, L. L., & Capps, J. L. (1986). Comprehension of pronouns in young and older adults. *Developmental Psychology, 22*, 580–585.

Lindenberger, U., & Baltes, P. B. (1997). Intellectual functioning in old and very old age: Cross-sectional results from the Berlin Aging Study. *Psychology and Aging, 12*, 410–432.

Lindenberger, U., Mayr, U., & Kliegl, R. (1993). Speed and intelligence in old age. *Psychology and Aging, 8*, 207–220.

Liotti, M., Ryder, K., & Woldorff, M. G. (1998). Auditory attention in the congenitally blind: Where, when and what gets reorganized? *NeuroReport, 9,* 1007–1012.

Lipsitt, L. P. (1990). Learning processes in the human newborn: Sensitization, habituation and classical conditioning. In A. Diamond (Ed.), *Development and neural bases of higher cognitive functions* (pp. 113–127). New York: New York Academy of Sciences Press.

Loftus, E. F., Feldman, J., & Dashiell, R. (1995). The reality of illusory memories. In D. L. Schacter (Ed.), *Memory distortion: How minds, brains and societies reconstruct the past* (pp. 47–68). Cambridge: Cambridge University Press.

Loftus, E. F., & Pickrell, J. E. (1995). The formation of false memories. *Psychiatric Annals, 25,* 720–725.

Lorente de No, R. (1934). Studies on the structure of the cerebral cortex. II. Continuation of the study of the ammonic system. *Journal für Psychologie und Neurologie, 46,* 114–177.

Lowe, C., & Rabbitt, P. (1997). Cognitive models of ageing and frontal lobe deficits. In P. Rabbitt (Ed.), *Methodology of frontal and executive function* (pp. 39–59). Hove, UK: Psychology Press.

Lupien, S. J., & Wan, N. (2004). Successful ageing: From cell to self. *Philosophical Transactions of the Royal Society of London. Series B, Biological Sciences, 359,* 1413–1426.

Lurija, A. R. (1991). *Der Mann, dessen Welt in Scherben ging.* Reinbek bei Hamburg: Rowohlt.

Luzzi, S., Pucci, E., Di Bella, P., & Piccirilli, M. (2000). Topographical disorientation consequent to amnesia of spatial location in a patient with right parahippocampal damage. *Cortex, 36,* 427–434.

MacLean, P. D. (1970). The triune brain, emotion, and the scientific bias. In F. O. Schmitt (Ed.), *The neurosciences: Second study program* (pp. 336–349). New York: Rockefeller University Press.

Madden, D. J., Pierce, T. W., & Allen, P. A. (1996). Adult age differences in the use of distractor homogeneity during visual research. *Psychology and Aging, 11,* 454–474.

Madden, D. J., Turkington, T. G., Provenzale, J. M., Hawk, T. C., Hoffman, J. M., & Coleman, R. E. (1997). Selective and divided visual attention: Age-related changes in regional cerebral blood flow measured by $H_2{}^{15}O$-PET. *Human Brain Mapping, 5,* 389–409.

Maguire, E. A., Gadian, D. G., Johnsrude, I. S., Good, C. D., Ashburner, J., Frackowiak, R. S. J., et al. (2000). Navigation-related structural change in the hippocampi of taxi drivers. *Proceedings of the National Academy of Sciences of the USA, 97,* 4398–4403.

Mähler, C. (1999). Naive Theorien im kindlichen Denken. *Zeitschrift für Entwicklungspsychologie und Pädagogische Psychologie, 31,* 53–66.

Makin, J. W., & Porter, R. H. (1989). Attractiveness of lactating females' breast odors to neonates. *Child Development, 60,* 803–810.

Malloch, S. (1999). Mother and infants and communicative musicality. *Musicae Scientiae,* Special Issue. European Society for the Cognitive Sciences of Music, Liège, 13–28.

Mäntylä, T. (1994). Remembering to remember: Adult age differences in prospective memory. *Journal of Gerontology: Psychological Sciences, 49,* 276–282.

Markman, E. M., & Abelev, M. (2004). Word learning in dogs? *Trends in Cognitive Sciences, 8,* 479–481.

Markowitsch, H. J. (1985). Der Fall H.M. im Dienste der Hirnforschung. *Naturwissenschaftliche Rundschau, 38*, 410–416.

Markowitsch, H. J. (1988). Anatomical and functional organization of the primate prefrontal cortical system. In H. D. Steklis & J. Erwin (Eds.), *Comparative primate biology*, Vol. IV: *Neurosciences* (pp. 99–153). New York: Alan R. Liss.

Markowitsch, H. J. (1992). *Intellectual functions and the brain. An historical perspective*. Toronto: Hogrefe & Huber.

Markowitsch, H. J. (1995). Which brain regions are critically involved in retrieval of old episodic memory? *Brain Research Reviews, 21*, 117–127.

Markowitsch, H. J. (1998/99). Differential contribution of the right and left amygdala to affective information processing. *Behavioural Neurology, 11*, 233–244.

Markowitsch, H. J. (1999a). *Gedächtnisstörungen*. Stuttgart: Kohlhammer.

Markowitsch, H. J. (1999b). Functional neuroimaging correlates of functional amnesia. *Memory, 7*, 561–583.

Markowitsch, H. J. (2000a). Amnésie psychogène et autres troubles dissociatifs. In M. Van der Linden, J.-M. Danion, & A. Agniel (Eds.), *La psychopathologie: une approche cognitive et neuropsychologique* (pp. 265–280). Paris: Éditions Solal.

Markowitsch, H. J. (2000b). Memory and amnesia. In M.-M. Mesulam (Eds.), *Principles of behavioral and cognitive neurology* (pp. 257–293). New York: Oxford University Press.

Markowitsch, H. J. (2001a). Mnestische Blockaden als Stress- und Traumafolgen. *Zeitschrift für Klinische Psychologie und Psychotherapie, 30*, 204–211.

Markowitsch, H. J. (2001b). Die Erinnerung von Zeitzeugen aus der Sicht der Gedächtnisforschung. *BIOS: Zeitschrift für Biographieforschung und Oral History, 13*, 30–50.

Markowitsch, H. J. (2002a). *Dem Gedächtnis auf der Spur: Vom Erinnern und Vergessen*. Darmstadt: Wissenschaftliche Buchgesellschaft und PRIMUS-Verlag.

Markowitsch, H. J. (2002b). Autobiographisches Gedächtnis aus neurowissenschaftlicher Sicht. *BIOS: Zeitschrift für Biographieforschung und Oral History, 15*, 187–201.

Markowitsch, H. J. (2003a). Autonoëtic consciousness. In A. S. David & T. Kircher (Eds.), *The self in neuroscience and psychiatry* (pp. 180–196). Cambridge: Cambridge University Press.

Markowitsch, H. J. (2003b). Memory: Disturbances and therapy. In T. Brandt, L. Caplan, J. Dichgans, H. C. Diener, & C. Kennard (Eds.), *Neurological disorders: Course and treatment* (2nd ed.) (pp. 287–302). San Diego, CA: Academic Press.

Markowitsch, H. J. (2004a). Das Bewusstsein – Formen, Modelle, Beschreibungsmöglichkeiten. *Anästhesiologie & Intensivmedizin, 39*, 627–633.

Markowitsch, H. J. (2004b). Warum wir keinen freien Willen haben. Der sogenannte freie Wille aus Sicht der Hirnforschung. *Psychologische Rundschau, 55*, 162–168.

Markowitsch, H. J. (2004c). Gehirn und Bewusstsein: Der Mensch als Maschine? In G. Kaiser (Ed.), *Wissenschaftszentrum Nordrhein-Westfalen Jahrbuch 2003/2004* (pp. 44–50). Düsseldorf: Wissenschaftszentrum NRW.

Markowitsch, H. J. (2005). The neuroanatomy of memory. In P. Halligan & P. Wade (Eds.), *The effectiveness of rehabilitation for cognitive deficits* (pp. 105–114). Oxford: Oxford University Press.

Markowitsch, H. J., & Borsutzky, S. (2004). Gedächtnis und Hippocampus des Menschen. In C. G. Lipinski & D.F. Braus (Eds.), *Hippocampus. Klinisch relevante Schlüsselfunktionen* (p. 73–100). Bad Honnef: Hippocampus Verlag.

Markowitsch, H. J., Calabrese, P., Fink, G. R., Durwen, H. F., Kessler, J., Härting, C., et al. (1997a). Impaired episodic memory retrieval in a case of probable psychogenic amnesia. *Psychiatry Research: Neuroimaging Section, 74*, 119–126.

Markowitsch, H. J., Calabrese, P., Neufeld, H., Gehlen, W., & Durwen, H. F. (1999). Retrograde amnesia for famous events and faces after left fronto-temporal brain damage. *Cortex, 35*, 243–252.

Markowitsch, H. J., Cramon, D. Y. von, & Schuri, U. (1993). Mnestic performance profile of a bilateral diencephalic infarct patient with preserved intelligence and severe amnesic disturbances. *Journal of Clinical and Experimental Neuropsychology, 15*, 627–652.

Markowitsch, H. J., Fink, G. R., Thöne, A. I. M., Kessler, J., & Heiss, W.-D. (1997b). Persistent psychogenic amnesia with a PET-proven organic basis. *Cognitive Neuropsychiatry, 2*, 135–158.

Markowitsch, H. J., Kalbe, E., Kessler, J., Stockhausen H.-M. von, Ghaemi, M., & Heiss, W.-D. (1999a). Short-term memory deficit after focal parietal damage. *Journal of Clinical and Experimental Neuropsychology, 21*, 784–796.

Markowitsch, H. J., & Kessler, J. (2000). Massive impairment in executive functions with partial preservation of other cognitive functions: The case of a young patient with severe degeneration of the prefrontal cortex. *Experimental Brain Research, 133*, 94–102.

Markowitsch, H. J., Kessler, J., & Denzler, P. (1986). Recognition memory and psychophysiological responses towards stimuli with neutral and emotional content. A study of Korsakoff patients and recently detoxified and long-term abstinent alcoholics. *International Journal of Neuroscience, 29*, 1–35.

Markowitsch, H. J., Kessler, J., Russ, M. O., Frölich, L., Schneider, B., & Maurer, K. (1999b). Mnestic block syndrome. *Cortex, 35*, 219–230.

Markowitsch, H. J., Kessler, J., Van der Ven, C., Weber-Luxenburger, G., & Heiss, W.-D. (1998). Psychic trauma causing grossly reduced brain metabolism and cognitive deterioration. *Neuropsychologia, 36*, 77–82.

Markowitsch, H. J., Kessler, J., Weber-Luxenburger, G., Van der Ven, C., & Heiss, W.-D. (2000). Neuroimaging and behavioral correlates of recovery from 'mnestic block syndrome' and other cognitive deteriorations. *Neuropsychiatry, Neuropsychology, and Behavioral Neurology, 13*, 60–66.

Markowitsch, H. J., & Pritzel, M. (1979). The prefrontal cortex: Projection area of the thalamic mediodorsal nucleus? *Physiological Psychology, 7*, 1–6.

Marlowe, W. B. (1992). The impact of a right prefrontal lesion on the developing brain. *Brain and Cognition, 20*, 205–213.

Marshall, J. C. (2000). Planum of the apes: A case study. *Brain and Language, 71*, 145–148.

Martin, W. R., Ye, F. Q., & Allen, P. S. (1998). Increasing striatal iron content associated with normal aging. *Movement Disorders, 13*, 281–286.

Matano, S., Baron, G., Stephan, H., & Frahm, H. D. (1985). Volume comparisons in the cerebellar complex of primates. II. Cerebellar nuclei. *Folia Primatologia, 44*, 182–203.

Matsuo, K., Nakai, T., Kato, C., Moriya, T., Isoda, H., Takehara, Y., et al. (2000). Dissociation of writing processes: Functional magnetic resonance imaging during writing of Japanese ideographic characters. *Cognitive Brain Research, 9*, 281–286.

Matthes-von Cramon, G., & Cramon, D. Y. von (2000). Störungen exekutiver

Funktionen. In W. Sturm, M. Herrmann, & C.-W. Wallesch (Eds.), *Lehrbuch der Klinischen Neuropsychologie* (pp. 392–410). Lisse: Swets & Zeitlinger.

Maylor, E. A. (1993). Aging and forgetting in prospective and retrospective memory tasks. *Psychology and Aging, 8*, 420–428.

McDowd, J. M. (1997). Inhibition in attention and aging. *Journal of Gerontology: Psychological Sciences, 52B*, P265–P273.

McDowd, J. M., & Craik, F. J. M. (1988). Effects of aging and task difficulty on divided attention performance. *Journal of Experimental Psychology: Human Perception and Performance, 14*, 267–280.

McGlinchey-Berroth, R., Brawn, C., & Disterhoft, J. F. (1999). Temporal discrimination learning in severe amnesic patients reveals an alteration in the timing of eyeblink conditioned responses. *Behavioral Neuroscience, 113*, 10–18.

McGlinchey-Berroth, R., Carrillo, M. C., Gabrieli, J. D. E., Brawn, C. M., & Disterhoft, J. F. (1997). Impaired trace eyeblink conditioning in bilateral, medial-temporal lobe amnesia. *Behavioral Neuroscience, 111*, 873–882.

McGlinchey-Berroth, R., Cermak, L. S., Carrillo, M. C., Armfield, S., Gabrieli, S., & Disterhoft, J. F. (1995). Impaired delay eyeblink conditioning in amnesic Korsakoff's patients and recovered alcoholics. *Alcoholism: Clinical and Experimental Research, 19*, 1127–1132.

McKee, R. D., & Squire, L. R. (1993). On the development of declarative memory. *Journal of Experimental Psychology: Learning, Memory and Cognition, 19*, 397–404.

McKelvey, R., Bergman, H., Stern, J., Rush, C., Zahirney, G., & Chertkow, H. (1999). Lack of prognostic significance of SPECT abnormalities in non-demented elderly subjects with memory loss. *Canadian Journal of Neurological Sciences, 26*, 23–28.

Mehler, J., Juscyk, P. W., Lambertz, G., Halsted, G., Bertoncini, J., & Amiel-Tison, C. (1988). A precursor of language acquisition in young infants. *Cognition, 29*, 143–178.

Meltzoff, A. N. (1988). Infant imitation and memory: Nine-month-olds in immediate and deferred tests. *Child Development, 59*, 217–225.

Meltzoff, A. N. (1995). What infant memory tells us about infantile amnesia: Long-term recall and deferred imitation. *Journal of Experimental Child Psychology, 59*, 497–515.

Meltzoff, A. N. (1999). Origins of theory of mind, cognition and communication. *Journal of Communication Disorders, 32*, 251–269.

Meltzoff, A. N., & Moore, M. H. (1977). Imitation of facial and manual gestures by human neonates. *Science, 198*, 75–78.

Meltzoff, A. N., & Moore, M. H. (1989). Imitation in newborn infants: Exploring the range of gestures imitated and the underlying mechanisms. *Developmental Psychology, 25*, 954–962.

Menzel, R., Brandt, R., Gumbert, A., Komischke, B., & Kunze, J. (2000). Two spatial memories for honeybee navigation. *Proceedings of the Royal Society of London. Series B, Biological Sciences, 267*, 961–968.

Menzel, R., & Giurfa, M. (2001). Cognitive architecture of a mini-brain: The honeybee. *Trends in Cognitive Sciences, 5*, 62–71.

Meyer, K. U., & Baltes, P. B. (1996). *Die Berliner Altersstudie*. Berlin: Akademie Verlag.

Middleton, D., & Edwards, D. (Eds.) (1990). Conversational remembering: A social psychological approach. In D. Middleton & D. Edwards (Eds.), *Collective remembering* (pp. 23–45). London: Sage.

Miller, B. L., Seeley, W. W., Mychack, P., Rosen, H. J., Mena, I., & Boone, K. (2001). Neuroanatomy of the self. Evidence from patients with frontotemporal dementia. *Neurology, 57*, 817–821.

Miller, P. (1993). *Theorien der Entwicklungspsychologie*. Heidelberg: Spektrum.

Mills, D. L., Coffey-Corina, S. A., & Neville, H. J. (1991). Variability in cerebral organization during primary language acquisition. In G. Dawson & K. W. Fischer (Eds.), *Human behavior and the developing brain* (pp. 427–455). New York: Guilford Press.

Mirescu, C., Peters, J. D., & Gould, E. (2004). Early life experience alters response of adult neurogenesis to stress. *Nature Neuroscience, 7*, 841–846.

Mishkin, M. (1957). Effects of small frontal lesions on delayed alternation in monkeys. *Journal of Neurophysiology, 20*, 615–622.

Montanes, P., Goldblum, M. C., & Boller, F. (1995). The naming impairment of living and nonliving items in Alzheimer's disease. *Journal of the International Neuropsychological Society, 1*, 39–48.

Morris, J. C., Storandt, M., Miller, P., McKeel, D. W., Price, J. L., Rubin, E. H., et al. (2001). Mild cognitive impairment represents early-stage Alzheimer disease. *Archives of Neurology, 58*, 397–405.

Moscovitch, M., & Winocur, G. (1995). Frontal lobes, memory, and aging. *Annals of the New York Academy of Sciences, 769*, 119–150.

Moscovitch, M., Winocur, G., & McLachlan, D. (1986). Memory as assessed by recognition and reading time in normal and memory-impaired people with Alzheimer's disease and other neurological disorders. *Journal of Experimental Psychology: General, 115*, 331–347.

Mullen, M. K. (1994). Earliest recollections of childhood: A demographic analysis. *Cognition, 52*, 55–79.

Murphy, D. G., DeCarli, C., McIntosh, A. R., Daly, E., Mentis, M. J., Pietrini, P., et al. (1996). Sex differences in human brain morphometry and metabolism: An *in vivo* quantitative magnetic resonance imaging and positron emission tomography study on the effect of aging. *Archives of General Psychiatry, 53*, 585–594.

Musso, M., Weiller, C., Kiebel, S., Müller, S. P., Bülau, P., & Rijntjes, M. (1999). Training-induced brain plasticity in aphasia. *Brain, 122*, 1781–1790.

Nadel, L., & Zola-Morgan, S. (1984). Infantile amnesia: A neurobiological perspective. In M. Moscovitch (Ed.), *Infant memory* (pp. 145–172). New York: Plenum Press.

Nagy, Z., Westerberg, H., & Klingberg, T. (2004). Maturation of white matter is associated with the development of cognitive functions during childhood. *Journal of Cognitive Neuroscience, 16*, 1227–1233.

Nauta, W. J. H. (1979). Expanding borders of the limbic system concept. In T. Rasmussen & R. Marino (Eds.), *Functional neurosurgery* (pp. 7–23). New York: Raven Press.

Naveh-Benjamin, M., & Craik, F. I. M. (1995). Memory for context and its use in item memory: Comparisons of younger and older persons. *Psychology and Aging, 10*, 284–293.

Nebes, R. D., & Brady, C. B. (1989). Focused and divided attention in Alzheimer's disease. *Cortex, 25*, 305–315.

Neisser, U. (1991). Two perceptually given aspects of the self and their development. *Developmental Review, 11*, 197–209.

Nelson, C. A., Monk, C. S., Lin, J., & Carver, L. J. (2000). Functional neuroanatomy of spatial working memory in children. *Developmental Psychology, 36*, 109–116.

Nelson, H. E. (1976). A modified card sorting test sensitive to frontal lobe defects. *Cortex*, *12*, 313–324.

Nelson, K. (1973). Structure and strategy in learning to talk. *Monographs of the Society for Research in Child Development*, *38*, (whole issue).

Nelson, K. (1974). Concept, word and sentence: Interrelations in acquisition and development. *Psychological Review*, *81*, 267–285.

Nelson, K. (1989). *Narratives from the crib*. Cambridge, MA: Harvard University Press.

Nelson, K. (1993). The psychological and social origins of autobiographical memory. *Psychological Science*, *4*, 7–14.

Nelson, K. (1995). The ontogeny of human memory: A cognitive neuroscience perspective. *Developmental Psychology*, *31*, 723–738.

Nelson, K. (1998). *Language in cognitive development*. Cambridge: Cambridge University Press.

Nelson, K. (2002). Erzählung und Selbst, Mythos und Erinnerung: Die Entwicklung des autobiographischen Gedächtnisses und des kulturellen Selbst. *Zeitschrift für Biographieforschung und Oral History*, *15*, 241–263.

Nelson, K. (2003). Self and social functions: Individual autobiographical memory and collective narrative. *Memory*, *11*, 125–136.

Nelson, K. (2005). Narrative and self, myth and memory: Emergence of the cultural self. In R. Fivush & C. Haden (Eds.), *The development of autobiographical memory and self-understanding* (pp. 3–28). Hillsdale, NJ: Lawrence Erlbaum Associates, Inc.

Nelson, K., & Fivush, R. (2000). Socialisation of memory. In E. Tulving & F. I. M. Craik (Eds.), *The Oxford handbook of memory* (pp. 283–295). Oxford: Oxford University Press.

Nelson, K., & Fivush, R. (2004). The emergence of autobiographical memory: A social cultural developmental theory. *Psychological Review*, *111*, 486–511.

Nelson, K., Skwerer, D., Goldman, S., Henseler, S., Presler, N., & Walkenfeld, F. F. (2002). Entering a community of minds: An experiential approach to "theory of mind". *Human Development*, *191*, 1–23.

Neumann, O. (1996). Theories of attention. In O. Neumann & A. F. Sanders (Eds.), *Handbook of perception and action* (Vol. 3, pp. 389–446). New York: Academic Press.

Neville, H. J., & Bavelier, D. (2000). Specificity and plasticity in neurocognitive development in humans. In M. S. Gazzaniga (Ed.), *The new cognitive neurosciences* (2nd ed., pp. 83–98). Cambridge, MA: MIT Press.

Newport, E. L. (1990). Maturational constraints on language learning. *Cognitive Science*, *14*, 11–28.

Nicholas, M., Obler, L. K., Au, R., & Albert, M. L. (1996). On the nature of naming errors in aging and dementia: A study of semantic relatedness. *Brain and Language*, *54*, 184–195.

Nieuwenhuys, R. (1996). The greater limbic system, the emotional motor system and the brain. In G. Holstege, R. Bandler, & C. B. Saper (Eds.), *The emotional motor system* (pp. 551–580). (Progress in Brain Research, Vol. 107). Amsterdam: Elsevier.

Nilsson, L.-G., Bäckman, L., Erngrund, K., Nyberg, L., Adolfsson, R., Bucht, G., et al. (1997). The Betula prospective cohort study: Memory, health, and aging. *Aging, Neuropsychology, and Cognition*, *4*, 1–32.

Njiokiktjien, C., de Sonnevill, L., & Vaal, J. (1994). Callosal size in children with learning disabilities. *Behavioural Brain Research*, *64*, 213–218.

Nobre, A. C., & Plunkett, K. (1997). The neural system of language: Structure and development. *Current Opinion in Neurobiology, 7*, 262–268.

Norman, D. A., & Shallice, T. (1986). Attention to action: Willed and automatic control of behavior. In R. J. Davidson, G. E. Schwartz, & D. Shapiro (Eds.), *Consciousness and self-regulation: Advances in research and theory* (pp. 1–18). New York: Plenum Press.

Norman, S., Kemper, S., & Kynette, D. (1992). Adults' reading comprehension: Effects of syntactic complexity and working memory. *Journal of Gerontology: Psychological Sciences, 47*, P258–P265.

Nottebohm, F. (1981). Origins and mechanisms in the establishment of cerebral dominance. In M. S. Gazzaniga (Ed.), *Handbook of behavioral neurology, Vol. 2: Neuropsychology* (pp. 295–344). New York: Plenum Press.

Ojemann, G. A. (1998). Neurology of language. In G. Adelman & B. Smith (Eds.), *The encyclopedia of neuroscience* (2nd ed.) (pp. 1009–1013). Amsterdam: Elsevier.

Olton, D. S., Branch, M., & Best, P. J. (1978). Spatial correlates of hippocampal unit activity. *Experimental Neurology, 58*, 387–409.

Ovtscharoff, W., & Braun, K. (2001). Maternal separation and social isolation modulate the postnatal development of synaptic composition in the infralimbic cortex of *Octodon degus. Neuroscience, 104*, 33–40.

Owsley, C., Ball, K., Sloane, M. E., Roenker, D. L., & Bruni, J. R. (1991). Visual/cognitive correlates of vehicle accidents in older drivers. *Psychology and Aging, 6*, 403–415.

Owsley, C., Berry, B., Sloane, M., Stalvey, B., & Wells J. (1998). Improved vision enhances explicit memory capabilities in older adults. Poster session presented at the Cognitive Aging Conference, Atlanta, GA.

Palombo, S. R. (1978). *Dreaming and memory. A new information-processing model.* New York: Basic Books.

Pantev, C., & Lütkenhöner, B. (2000). Magnetencephalographic studies of functional organization and plasticity of the human auditory cortex. *Journal of Clinical Neurophysiology, 17*, 130–142.

Papathanasiou, I. (2003). Nervous system mechanisms of recovery and plasticity following injury. *Acta Neuropsychologica, 1*, 345–354.

Papousek, M. (1994). Melodies in caregiver's speech: A specific guidance towards language. *Early Development and Parenting, 3*, 5–17.

Papousek, M., Papousek, H., & Symmes, D. (1991). The meanings and melodies in motherese in tone and stress languages. *Infant Behavior and Development, 14*, 415–440.

Park, D. C., & Gutchess, A. H. (2002). Aging, cognition, and culture: A neuroscientific perspective. *Neuroscience and Biobehavioral Reviews, 26*, 859–867.

Park, D. C., & Puglisi, J. T. (1985). Older adults' memory for the color of pictures and words. *Journal of Gerontology, 40*, 198–204.

Parkin, A. J. (1997). Normal age-related memory loss and its relation to frontal lobe dysfunction. In P. Rabbitt (Ed.), *Methodology of frontal and executive function* (pp. 177–190). Hove, UK: Psychology Press.

Parkin, A. J., & Java, R. L. (1999). Deterioration of frontal lobe function in normal aging: Influences of fluid intelligence versus perceptual speed. *Neuropsychology, 13*, 539–545.

Pascalis, O., & de Schonen, S. (1994). Recognition memory in 3- to 4-year-old human neonates. *NeuroReport, 5*, 1721–1724.

Pawlow, I. P. (1953). *Sämtliche Werke*. Berlin: Akademie-Verlag.

Perner, J. (2000). Memory and theory of mind. In E. Tulving & F. I. M. Craik (Eds.), *The Oxford handbook of memory* (pp. 297–314). New York: Oxford University Press.

Perner, J., & Dienes, Z. (2003). Developmental aspects of consciousness: How much theory of mind do you need to be consciously aware? *Consciousness and Cognition, 12*, 63–82.

Perner, J., Lang, B., & Kloo, D. (2002). Theory of mind and self-control: More than a common problem of inhibition. *Child Development, 73*, 752–767.

Perner, J., & Ruffman, T. (1995). Episodic memory and autonoetic consciousness: Developmental evidence and a theory of childhood amnesia. *Journal of Experimental Child Psychology, 59*, 516–548.

Petersen, R. C., Doody, R., Kurz, A., Mohs, R. C., Morris, J. C., Rabins, P. V., et al. (2001). Current concepts in mild cognitive impairment. *Archives of Neurology, 58*, 1985–1992.

Petersen, R. C., Smith, G. E., Waring, S. C., Ivnik, R. J., Tangalos, E. G., & Kokmen, E. (1999). Mild cognitive impairment: Clinical characterization and outcome. *Archives of Neurology, 56*, 303–308.

Peterson, C., Jesso, B., & McCabe, A. (1999). Encouraging narratives in preschoolers: An intervention study. *Journal of Child Language, 26*, 49–67.

Petrides, M., & Pandya, D. N. (1994). Comparative architectonic analysis of the human and the macaque frontal cortex. In F. Boller & J. Grafman (Eds.), *Handbook of neuropsychology* (Vol. 9, pp. 17–58). Amsterdam: Elsevier, 1994.

Piaget, J. (1926). *Language and thought of the child*. New York: Harcourt, Brace.

Piaget, J. (1962). *Play, dreams, and imitation in childhood*. New York: W. W. Norton.

Piaget, J. (1972). Intellectual evolution from adolescence to adulthood. *Human Development, 15*, 1–12.

Piaget, J. (1974). *Die Bildung des Zeitbegriffs beim Kinde*. Frankfurt/M.: Suhrkamp.

Piaget, J. (1981). Time perception in children. In J. T. Fraser (Ed.), *The voices of time* (pp. 202–216). Cambridge, MA: University of Massachusetts Press.

Pillemer, D. B. (1992). Remembering personal circumstances. A functional analysis. In E. Winograd & U. Neisser (Eds.), *Affect and accuracy in recall. Studies of "flashbulb" memories* (pp. 236–264). New York: Cambridge University Press.

Pillemer, D. B., Picariello, M. L., & Pruett, J. C. (1994). Very long-term memories of a salient preschool event. *Applied Cognitive Psychology, 8*, 95–106.

Pillow, B.-H. (1989). Early understanding of perception as a source of knowledge. *Journal of Experimental Child Psychology, 47*, 116–129.

Pinker, S. (1994). *The language instinct: How the mind creates language*. New York: HarperCollins.

Plude, D. J., & Hoyer, W. J. (1985). Attention and performance: Identifying and localizing age deficits. In N. Charness (Ed.), *Aging and performance* (pp. 47–99). New York: Wiley.

Poeggel, G., Helmeke, C., Abraham, A., Schwabe, T., Friedrich, P., & Braun, K. (2003). Juvenile emotional experience alters synaptic composition in the rodent cortex, hippocampus, and lateral amygdala. *Proceedings of the National Academy of Sciences of the USA, 100*, 16137–16142.

Pontius, A. A., & Yudowitz, B. S. (1980). Frontal lobe system dysfunction in some criminal actions as shown in the narratives test. *Journal of Nervous and Mental Disease, 168*, 111–117.

Portmann, A. ([1956] 1995). *Biologie und Geist*. Frankfurt/Main: Suhrkamp.

Posner, M. I., & Rafal, R. D. (1987). Cognitive theories of attention and the rehabilitation of attentional deficits. In R. J. Meier, A. C. Benton, & L. Diller (Eds.), *Neuropsychological rehabilitation* (pp. 182–201). Edinburgh: Churchill Livingstone.

Povinelli, D. J. (1995). The unduplicated self. In P. Rochat (Ed.), *The self in early infancy* (pp. 162–192). Amsterdam: North Holland-Elsevier.

Povinelli, D. J., Landau, K. R., & Perilloux, H. C. (1996). Self-recognition in young children using delayed versus live feedback: Evidence of a developmental asynchrony. *Child Development, 67*, 1540–1554.

Pratt, M. W., & Robbins, S. L. (1991). That's the way it was: Age differences in the structure and quality of adults' personal narratives. *Discourse Processes, 14*, 73–85.

Preuss, T. M. (1995). The argument from animals to humans in cognitive neuroscience. In M. S. Gazzaniga (Ed.), *The cognitive neurosciences* (pp. 1227–1241). Cambridge, MA: MIT Press.

Preuss, T. M., & Kaas, J. H. (1999). Human brain evolution. In M. J. Zigmond, F. E. Bloom, S. C. Landis, J. L. Roberts, & L. R. Squire (Eds.), *Fundamental neuroscience* (pp. 1283–1311). San Diego, CA: Academic Press.

Pribram, K. H., & Tubbs, W. E. (1967). Short-term memory, parsing and the primate frontal cortex. *Science, 156*, 1765–1767.

Price, B. H., Daffner, K. R., Stowe, R. M., & Mesulam, M. M. (1990). The compartmental learning disabilities of early frontal lobe damage. *Brain, 113*, 1383–1393.

Price, J. L., & Morris, J. C. (1999). Tangles and plaques in nondemented aging and "preclinical" Alzheimer's disease. *Annals of Neurology, 45*, 358–368.

Pritzel, M., Brand, M., & Markowitsch, H. J. (2003). *Gehirn und Verhalten*. Heidelberg: Spektrum Akademischer Verlagsanstalt.

Pritzel, M., & Markowitsch, H. J. (1997). Sexueller Dimorphismus: Inwieweit bedingen Unterschiede im Aufbau des Gehirns zwischen Mann und Frau auch Unterschiede im Verhalten? *Psychologische Rundschau, 48*, 16–31.

Proust, M. (1953 [1913]). Auf der Suche nach der verlorenen Zeit. In *Swanns Welt* (vol. 1). Frankfurt/M.: Suhrkamp.

Prull, M. W., Gabrieli, J. D. E., & Bunge, S. A. (2000). Age-related changes in memory: A cognitive neuroscience perspective. In F. I. M. Craik & T. A. Salthouse (Eds.), *The handbook of aging and cognition* (2nd ed., pp. 91–153). Mahwah, NJ: Lawrence Erlbaum Associates, Inc.

Pushkar, D., Arbuckle, T., Conway, M., Chaikelson, J., & Maag, U. (1997). Everyday activity parameters and competence in older adults. *Psychology and Aging, 12*, 600–609.

Qin, Y., Carter, C. S., Silk, E. M., Stenger, V. A., Fissell, K., Goode, A., et al. (2004). The change of the brain activation patterns as children learn algebra equation solving. *Proceedings of the National Academy of Sciences of the USA, 101*, 5686–5691.

Quine, W. (1969). *Set theory and its logic*. Cambridge, MA: Belknap.

Rabbitt, P. (1997). *Methodology of frontal and executive function* (pp. 135–153). Hove, UK: Psychology Press.

Raine, A., Lencz, T., Bihrle, S., LaCasse, L., & Colletti, P. (2000). Reduced prefrontal gray matter volume and reduced autonomic activity in antisocial personality disorder. *Archives of General Psychiatry, 57*, 119–127.

Raine, A., Lencz, T., Taylor, K., Hellige, J. B., Bihrle, S., Lacasse, L., et al. (2003). Corpus callosum abnormalities in psychopathic antisocial individuals. *Archives of General Psychiatry, 60*, 1134–1142.

Raine, A., Meloy, J. R., Bihrle, S., Stoddard, J., LaCasse, L., & Buchsbaum, M.S. (1998a). Reduced prefrontal and increased subcortical brain functioning assessed using positron emission tomography in predatory and affective murderers. *Behavioral Sciences and the Law*, *16*, 319–332.

Raine, A., Stoddard, J., Bihrle, S., & Buchsbaum, M. (1998b). Prefrontal glucose in murderers lacking psychosocial deprivation. *Neuropsychiatry, Neuropsychology, and Behavioral Neurology*, *11*, 1–7.

Rakic, P. (2002a). Neurogenesis in adult primate neocortex: An evaluation of the evidence. *Nature Reviews Neuroscience*, *3*, 65–71.

Rakic, P. (2002b). Adult neurogenesis in mammals: an identity crisis. *Journal of Neuroscience*, *22*, 614–618.

Rakic, P., & Yakovlev, P. I. (1968). Development of the corpus callosum and cavum septi in man. *Journal of Comparative Neurology*, *132*, 45–72.

Rakic, S., & Zecevic, N. (2000). Programmed cell death in the developing human telencephalon. *European Journal of Neuroscience*, *12*, 2721–2734.

Rapoport, S. I. (1990). Integrated phylogeny of the primate brain, with special reference to humans and their diseases. *Brain Research Reviews*, *15*, 267–294.

Raz, N. (1996). Neuroanatomy of aging brain: Evidence from structural MRI. In E. D. Bigler (Ed.), *Neuroimaging II: Clinical applications* (pp. 153–182). New York: Academic Press.

Raz, N. (2000). Aging of the brain and its impact on cognitive performance: Integration of structural and functional findings. In F. I. M. Craik & T. A. Salthouse (Eds.), *The handbook of aging and cognition* (pp. 1–90). Mahwah, NJ: Lawrence Erlbaum Associates, Inc.

Raz, N., Gunning, F. M., Head, D., Dupuis, J. H., McQuain, J. M., Briggs, S. D., et al. (1997). Selective aging of human cerebral cortex observed *in vivo*: Differential vulnerability of the prefrontal gray matter. *Cerebral Cortex*, *7*, 268–282.

Reese, E. (2002). Social factors in the development of autobiographical memory: The state of the art. *Social Development*, *11*, 124–142.

Reese, E., & Fivush, R. (1993). Parental styles of talking about the past. *Developmental Psychology*, *29*, 596–606.

Reese, E., Haden, C. A., & Fivush, R. (1993). Mother–child conversations about the past: Relationships of style and memory over time. *Cognitive Development*, *8*, 403–430.

Reese, E., Haden, C. A., & Fivush, R. (1996). Mothers, fathers, daughters, sons: Gender differences in reminiscing. *Research on Language and Social Interaction*, *29*, 27–56.

Roberts, T. P. L., Disbrow, E. A., Roberts, H. C., & Rowley, H. A. (2000). Quantification and reproducibility of tracking cortical extent of activation by use of functional MR imaging and magnetencephalography. *American Journal of Neuroradiology*, *21*, 1377–1387.

Rochat, P. (2001). Origins of self-concept. In G. Brenner & A. Fogel (Eds.), *Blackwell handbook of infant development* (pp. 191–212). Malden, MA: Blackwell.

Rochat, P., Querido, J.-G., & Striano, T. (1999). Emerging sensitivity to the timing and structure of protoconversation in early infancy. *Developmental Psychology*, *35*, 950–957.

Röder, B., Teder-Sälejärvi, W., Sterr, A., Rösler, F., Hillyard, S. A., & Neville, H. J. (1999). Improved auditory spatial tuning in blind humans. *Nature*, *400*, 162–166.

Roediger, H. L. I., & McDermott, K. B. (1995). Creating false memories: Remembering words not presented in lists. *Journal of Experimental Psychology: Learning, Memory, and Cognition, 21*, 803–814.

Rogers, W. A. (2000). Attention and aging. In D. Park & N. Schwarz (Eds.), *Cognitive aging: A primer* (pp. 57–73). Philadelphia: Psychology Press.

Rolls, E. T. (1996). The orbitofrontal cortex. *Philosophical Transactions of the Royal Society of London. Series B, 351*, 1433-1444.

Rolls, E. T., Stringer, S. M., & Trappenberg, T. P. (2002). A unified model of spatial and episodic memory. *Proceedings of the Royal Society of London. Series B, Biological Sciences, 269*, 1087–1093.

Romeo, R. D., Richardson, H. N., & Sisk, C. L. (2002). Puberty and the maturation of the male brain and sexual behaviour: Recasting a behavioural potential. *Neuroscience and Biobehavioral Reviews, 26*, 381–391.

Rose, J. E., & Woolsey, C. N. (1948). The orbitofrontal cortex and its connections with the mediodorsal nucleus in rabbit, sheep, and cat. In J. F. Fulton, C. D. Aring, & S. B. Wortis (Eds.), *Research publications for research in nervous and mental disease: The frontal lobes* (Vol. 27, pp. 210–232). Baltimore, MD: Williams & Wilkins.

Rose, S. (1998). *Gehirn, Gedächtnis, Bewusstsein. Eine Reise zum Mittelpunkt des Menschseins.* Bergisch Gladbach: Bastei Lübbe.

Rosen, J. T. (1990). "Age-associated memory impairment": A critique. *European Journal of Cognitive Psychology, 2*, 275–287.

Rosenkilde, C. (1978). Delayed alternation behavior following ablations of the medial or dorsal prefrontal cortex in dogs. *Physiology and Behavior, 20*, 397–402.

Rosenzweig, M. R., & Bennett, E. L. (1996). Psychobiology of plasticity: Effects of training and experience on brain and behavior. *Behavioural Brain Research, 78*, 57–65.

Rosenzweig, M. R., Bennett, E. L., & Diamond, M. C. (1972). Brain changes in response to experience. *Scientific American, 26*, 21–29.

Ross, M., & Holmberg, D. (1990). Recounting the past: Gender differences in the recall of events in the history of close relationships. *The Ontario Symposium: Self-Inference Processes, 6*, 135–152.

Rovee-Collier, C. (1997). Dissociations in infant memory: Rethinking the development of implicit and explicit memory. *Psychological Review, 104*, 467–498.

Rovee-Collier, C. (1999). The development of infant memory. *Current Directions in Psychological Science, 8*, 80–85.

Rovee-Collier, C., & Hartshorn, K. (1999). Long-term memory in human infants: Lessons in psychobiology. *Advances in the Study of Behavior, 28*, 175–245.

Rovee-Collier, C., & Hayne, H. (1987). Reactivation of infant memory: Implications for cognitive development. In H. W. Reese (Ed.), *Advances in child development and behavior* (Vol. 20, pp. 185–238). New York: Academic Press.

Rovee-Collier, C., & Hayne, H. (2001). Memory in infancy and early childhood. In E. Tulving & F. I. M. Craik (Eds.), *The Oxford handbook of memory* (pp. 267–282). New York: Oxford University Press.

Rovee-Collier, C., Hayne, H., & Colombo, M. (2000). *The development of implicit and explicit memory* (Advances in Consciousness Research, Vol. 24). Amsterdam: John Benjamins.

Rowe, A. D., Bullock, P. R., Polkey, C. E., & Morris, R. G. (2001). "Theory of mind" impairments and their relationship to executive functioning following frontal lobe excisions. *Brain, 124*, 600–616.

Rubens, A. B. (1977). Asymmetries of human cerebral cortex. In S. Harnad, R. W. Doty, L. Goldstein, J. Jaynes, & G. Krauthamer (Eds.), *Lateralization in the nervous system* (pp. 503–516). New York: Academic Press.

Rudinger, G., & Rietz, C. (1995). Intelligenz – Neuere Ergebnisse aus der Bonner Längsschnittstudie des Alterns (BOLSA). In A. Kruse & R. Schmitz-Scherzer (Eds.), *Psychologie der Lebensalter* (pp. 185–199). Darmstadt: Steinkopff.

Salat, D. H., Kaye, J. A., & Janowsky, J. S. (1999). Prefrontal gray and white matter volumes in healthy aging and Alzheimer disease. *Archives of Neurology, 56,* 338–344.

Salk, L. (1962). Mothers' heartbeat as an imprinting stimulus. *Transactions of the New York Academy of Sciences, 24,* 753–763.

Salthouse, T. A. (1994a). The aging of working memory. *Neuropsychology, 8,* 535–543.

Salthouse, T. A. (1994b). How many causes are there of age-related decrements in cognitive functioning? *Developmental Review, 14,* 413–437.

Salthouse, T. A. (1996a). Constraints on theories of cognitive aging. *Psychonomic Bulletin & Review, 3,* 287–299.

Salthouse, T. A. (1996b). The processing-speed theory of adult age differences in cognition. *Psychological Review, 103,* 403–428.

Salthouse, T. A. (1998). Independence of age-related influences on cognitive abilities across the life span. *Developmental Psychology, 34,* 851–864.

Salthouse, T. A. (2000). Steps toward the explanation of adult age differences in cognition. In T. J. Perfect & E. A. Maylor (Eds.), *Models of cognitive aging* (pp. 19–49). New York: Oxford University Press.

Salthouse, T. A., & Babcock, R. L. (1991). Decomposing adult age differences in working memory. *Developmental Psychology, 27,* 763–776.

Salthouse, T. A., Fristoe, N., McGuthry, K. E., & Hambrick, D. Z. (1998). Relation of task switching to speed, age, and fluid intelligence. *Psychology and Aging, 13,* 445–461.

Saß, H., Wittchen, H.-U., & Zaudig, M. (1996). *Diagnostisches und statistisches Manual psychischer Störungen (DSM-IV).* Göttingen: Hogrefe.

Saxe, R., Carey, S., & Kanwisher, N. (2004). Understanding other minds: Linking developmental psychology and functional neuroimaging. *Annual Review of Psychology, 55,* 87–124.

Schaal, B., & Orgeur, P. (1992). Olfaction *in utero*: Can the rodent model be generalized? *Quarterly Journal of Experimental Psychology, B44,* 345–378.

Schacter, D. L. (1996). *Searching for memory. The brain, the mind, and the past.* New York: Basic Books.

Schacter, D. L. (1999). The seven sins of memory. *American Psychologist, 54,* 182–201.

Schacter, D. L., & Moscovitch, M. (1984). Infants, amnesiacs and dissociable memory systems. In M. Moscovitch (Ed.), *Infant memory: Its relation to normal and pathological memory in humans and other animals* (pp. 173–216). New York: Plenum Press.

Schaie, K. W. (1990). Intellectual development in adulthood. In J. E. Birren & K. W. Schaie (Eds.), *Handbook of the psychology of aging* (3rd ed., pp. 291–309). San Diego, CA: Academic Press.

Schaie, K. W. (1996). *Intellectual development in adulthood: The Seattle Longitudinal Study.* Cambridge: Cambridge University Press.

Schlaug, G., Jäncke, L., Huang, Y., Staiger, J., & Steinmetz, H. (1995). Increased corpus callosum size in musicians. *Neuropsychologia, 33,* 1047–1055.

Schneider, B. A., & Pichora-Fuller, M. K. (2000). Implications of perceptual deterioration for cognitive aging research. In F. I. M. Craik & T. A. Salthouse (Eds.), *The handbook of aging and cognition* (2nd ed., pp. 155–219). Mahwah, NJ: Lawrence Erlbaum Associates, Inc.

Schneider, G. E. (1979). Is it really better to have your brain lesion early? A revision of the "Kennard principle". *Neuropsychologia, 17*, 557–583.

Schore, A. N. (2000). The self-organization of the right brain and the neurobiology of emotional development. In M. Lewis & I. Granic (Eds.), *Emotion, development, and self-organization: Dynamic systems approaches to emotional development* (pp. 155–185). Cambridge: Cambridge University Press.

Schore, A. N. (2001). The effects of a secure attachment relationship on right brain development, affect regulation and infant mental health. *Infant Mental Health Journal, 22*, 1–66.

Schretlen, D., Pearlson, G. D., Anthony, J. C., Aylward, E. H., Augustine, A. M., Davis, A., et al. (2000). Elucidating the contributions of processing speed, executive ability, and frontal lobe volume to normal age-related differences in fluid intelligence. *Journal of the International Neuropsychological Society, 6*, 52–61.

Schugens, M. M., & Daum, I. (1999). Long-term retention of classical eyeblink conditioning in amnesia. *NeuroReport, 10*, 149–152.

Schugens, M. M., Daum, I., Spindler, M., & Birbaumer, N. (1997). Differential effects of aging on explicit and implicit memory. *Aging, Neuropsychology, and Cognition, 4*, 33–44.

Sekuler, A. B., Bennett, P. J., & Mamelak, M. (2000). Effects of aging on the useful field of view. *Experimental Aging Research, 26*, 103–120.

Serres, L. (2001). Morphological changes of the human hippocampal formation from midgestation to early childhood. In C. A. Nelson & M. Luciana (Eds.), *Handbook of developmental cognitive neuroscience* (pp. 45–58). Cambridge, MA: MIT Press.

Shallice, T. (1982). Specific impairments of planning. *Philosophical Transactions of the Royal Society of London. Series B, Biological Sciences, 298*, 199–209.

Shallice, T. (2001). "Theory of mind" and the prefrontal cortex. *Brain, 124*, 247–248.

Shallice, T., & Burgess, P. (1993). Supervisory control of action and thought selection. In A. Baddeley & L. Weiskrantz (Eds.), *Attention: Selection, awareness and control* (pp. 171–187). New York: Oxford University Press.

Shallice, T., Burgess, P. W., Schon, F., & Baxter, D. M. (1989). The origins of utilization behaviour. *Brain, 112*, 1587–1598.

Shastri, L. (2002). Episodic memory and cortico-hippocampal interactions. *Trends in Cognitive Sciences, 6*, 162–168.

Shaw, P., Lawrence, E. J., Radbourne, C., Bramham, J., Polkey, C. E., & David, A. S. (2004). The impact of early and late damage to the human amygdala on "theory of mind" reasoning. *Brain, 127*, 1535–1548.

Siebert, M., Markowitsch, H. J., & Bartel, P. (2003). Amygdala, affect, and cognition: Evidence from ten patients with Urbach–Wiethe disease. *Brain, 126*, 2627–2637.

Siegal, M., & Varley, R. (2002). Neural systems involved in "theory of mind". *Nature Reviews Neuroscience, 3*, 463–471.

Siegler, I. C. (1975). The terminal drop hypothesis: Fact or artifact? *Experimental Aging Research, 1*, 169–185.

Simic, G., Kostovic, I., Winblad, B., & Bogdanovic, N. (1997). Volume and number of neurons of the human hippocampal formation in normal aging and Alzheimer's disease. *Journal of Comparative Neurology, 379*, 482–494.

Simons, D. J., & Levin, D. T. (1998). Failure to detect changes to people during a real-world interaction. *Psychonomic Bulletin and Review*, *5*, 644–649.

Singer, W. (1999). Time as coding space? *Current Opinion in Neurobiology*, *9*, 189–194.

Singer, W. (2002). *Der Beobachter im Gehirn*. Frankfurt/M.: Suhrkamp.

Sinz, R. (1979). *Neurobiologie und Gedächtnis*. Stuttgart: Gustav Fischer.

Skinner, B. F. (1938). *The behavior of organisms: An experimental analysis*. New York: Appleton-Century.

Sliwinski, M., Lipton, R. B., Buschke, H., & Stewart, W. (1996). The effects of pre-clinical dementia on estimates of normal cognitive functioning in aging. *Journals of Gerontology: Series B. Psychological Sciences and Socal Sciences*, *51 B*, 217–225.

Small, S. A. (2001). Age-related memory decline. *Archives of Neurology*, *58*, 360–364.

Spearman, C. (1904). "General intelligence": Objectively determined and measured. *American Journal of Psychology*, *15*, 201–292.

Spence, C., Shore, D. I., Gazzaniga, M. S., Soto-Faraco, S. E., & Kingstone, A. (2001). Failure to remap visuotactile space across the midline in the split-brain. *Canadian Journal of Experimental Psychology*, *55*, 133–141.

Spiro, R. J. (1980). Constructive processes in prose comprehension and recall. In R. J. Spiro, B. C. Bruce, & W. F. Brewer (Eds.), *Theoretical issues in reading comprehension: Perspectives from cognitive psychology, linguistics, artificial intelligence, and education* (pp. 245–278). Hillsdale, NJ: Lawrence Erlbaum Associates, Inc.

Springer, S., & Deutsch, G. (1989). *Left brain, right brain* (3rd ed.). New York: W. H. Freeman.

Stein, D. G., Rosen, J. J., & Butters, N. (1974). *Plasticity and recovery of function in the nervous system*. New York: Academic Press.

Stephan, H. (1975). *Allocortex. Handbuch der mikroskopischen Anatomie des Menschen* (Vol. 4, Part 9). Berlin: Springer.

Stern, D. N. (1985). *The interpersonal world of the infant. A view from psychoanalysis and developmental psychology*. New York: Basic Books.

Stern, D. N. (1998). *Die Mutterschaftskonstellation. Eine vergleichende Darstellung verschiedener Formen der Mutter-Kind-Psychotherapie*. Stuttgart: Klett-Cotta.

Stern, D. N. (1999). Vitality contours: The temporal contour of feelings as a basic unit for constructing the infant's social experience. In P. Rochat (Ed.), *Early social cognition: Understanding others in the first months of life* (pp. 67–80). Mahwah, NJ: Lawrence Erlbaum Associates, Inc.

Stone, V. E., Baron-Cohen, S., Calder, A., Keane, J., & Young, A. (2003). Acquired theory of mind impairments in individuals with bilateral amygdala lesions. *Neuropsychologia*, *41*, 209–220.

Stone, V. E., Baron-Cohen, S., & Knight, R. T. (1998). Frontal lobe contributions to theory of mind. *Journal of Cognitive Neuroscience*, *10*, 640–656.

Strouse, A., Ashmead, D. H., Ohde, R. N., & Grantham, D. W. (1998). Temporal processing in the aging auditory system. *Journal of the Acoustical Society of America*, *104*, 2385–2399.

Sturm, W., & Zimmermann, P. (2000). Aufmerksamkeitsstörungen. In W. Sturm, M. Hermann & C.-W. Wallesch (Eds.), *Lehrbuch der Klinischen Neuropsychologie* (pp. 345–365). Lisse: Swets & Zeitlinger.

Stuss, D. T., Gallup, G. G., Jr., & Alexander, M. P. (2001). The frontal lobes are necessary for "theory of mind". *Brain*, *124*, 279–286.

Tanapat, P., Hastings, N. B., & Gould, E. (2001). Adult neurogenesis in the hippocampal formation. In C. A. Nelson & M. Luciana (Eds.), *Handbook of developmental cognitive neuroscience* (pp. 93–105). Cambridge, MA: MIT Press.

Taylor, M. (1988). The development of children's understanding of the seeing–knowing distinction. In J. W. Astington, P. L. Harris, & D. R. Olson (Eds.), *Developing theories of mind* (pp. 207–225). New York: Cambridge University Press.

Tessler, M., & Nelson, K. (1994). Making memories: The influence of joint encoding on later recall. *Consciousness and Cognition*, *3*, 307–326.

Thierry, G., Vihman, M., & Roberts, M (2003). Familiar words capture the attention of 11-month-olds in less than 250 ms. *NeuroReport*, *14*, 2307–2310.

Thompson, E. P. (1987). *Die Entstehung der englischen Arbeiterklasse*. Frankfurt/M.: Suhrkamp. (Original title: *The making of the English working class*. London: Gollancz.)

Thöne-Otto, A. I. M., & Markowitsch, H. J. (2004). *Gedächtnisstörungen nach Hirnschäden. Serie Klinische Neuropsychologie*. Göttingen: Hogrefe.

Thorndike, E. L., & Woodworth, R. S. (1901). Influence of improvement in one mental function upon the efficiency of other mental functions. *Psychological Review*, *8*, 247–261, 384–395, 553–564.

Thurstone, L. L. (1938). *Primary mental abilities*. Chicago: University of Chicago Press.

Tisserand, D. J., Bosma, H., Van Boxtel, M. P. J., & Jolles, J. (2001). Head size and cognitive ability in nondemented older adults are related. *Neurology*, *56*, 969–971.

Tomasello, M. (1999). *The cultural origins of human cognition*. Cambridge, MA: Harvard University Press.

Tomasello, M. (2002). *Die kulturelle Entwicklung des menschlichen Denkens*. Frankfurt/M.: Suhrkamp.

Tomasello, M., Call, J., & Hare, B. (2003a). Chimpanzees understand psychological states – the question is which ones and to what extent. *Trends in Cognitive Science*, *7*, 153–56.

Tomasello, M., Call, J., & Hare, B. (2003b). Chimpanzees versus humans: It's not that simple. *Trends in Cognitive Sciences*, *7*, 239–240.

Trevarthen, C. (1998). Language development: Mechanisms in the brain. In G. Adelman & B. Smith (Eds.), *Encyclopedia of neuroscience* (2nd ed.) (pp. 1018–1026). Amsterdam: Elsevier.

Trevarthen, C. (2002). Frühe Kommunikation und autobiographisches Gedächtnis. *Zeitschrift für Biographieforschung und Oral History*, *15*, 213–240.

Tsang, P. S., & Shaner, T. L. (1998). Age, attention, expertise, and time-sharing performance. *Psychology and Aging*, *13*, 323–347.

Tulving, E. (1983). *Elements of episodic memory*. Oxford: Clarendon Press.

Tulving, E. (1995). Organization of memory: Quo vadis? In M. S. Gazzaniga (Ed.), *The cognitive neurosciences* (pp. 839–847). Cambridge, MA: MIT Press.

Tulving, E. (1999). Study of memory: Processes and systems. In J. K. Foster & M. Jelicic (Eds.), *Memory: Systems, process, or function? Debates in psychology* (pp. 11–30). New York: Oxford University Press.

Tulving, E. (2002). Episodic memory: From mind to brain. *Annual Review of Psychology*, *53*, 1–25.

Tulving, E. (2005). Episodic memory and autonoesis: Uniquely human? In H. Terrace & J. Metcalfe (Eds.), *The missing link in cognition: Evolution of self-knowing consciousness*. New York: Oxford University Press.

Tulving, E., Kapur, S., Craik, F. I. M., Moscovitch, M., & Houle, P. (1994). Hemispheric encoding/retrieval asymmetry in episodic memory: Positron emission tomography findings. *Proceedings of the National Academy of Sciences of the USA*, *91*, 2016–2020.

Tulving, E., & Markowitsch, H. J. (1994). Why should animal models of memory model human memory? *Behavioral and Brain Sciences*, *17*, 498–499 (Commentary).

Tulving, E., & Markowitsch, H. J. (1997). Memory beyond hippocampus. *Current Opinion in Neurobiology*, *7*, 209–216.

Tulving, E., & Markowitsch, H. J. (1998). Episodic and declarative memory: Role of the hippocampus. *Hippocampus*, *8*, 198–204.

Tun, P. A., & Wingfield, A. (1995). Does dividing attention become harder with age? Findings from the Divided Attention Questionnaire. *Aging and Cognition*, *2*, 39–66.

Usher, J.A., & Neisser, U. (1993). Childhood amnesia and the beginnings of memory for four early life events. *Journal of Experimental Psychology: General*, *122*, 155–165.

Van der Horst, L. (1928). Over de psychologie van het syndroom van Korsakow. *Psychiatric en Neurologic Bladen*, *32* (Wiersam-Festschrift), 59–77.

Van der Horst, L. (1932). Über die Psychologie des Korsakowsyndroms. *Monatsschrift für Psychiatrie*, *83*, 65–84.

van Wolffelaar, P., Brouwer, W. H., & van Zoemeren, A. H. (1990). Driving ability 5 to 10 years after severe head injury. In T. Benjamin (Ed.), *Driving behaviour in a social context* (pp. 564–574). Caen: Paradigme.

van Zoemeren, A. H., & Brouwer, W. H. (1994). *Clinical neuropsychology of attention*. New York: Oxford University Press.

Vargha-Khadem, F., Isaacs, E. B., Papaleoudi, H., Polkey, C. E., & Wilson, J. (1991). Development of language in 6 hemispherectomized patients. *Brain*, *114*, 473–495.

Vargha-Khadem, F., Salmond, C. H., Watkins, K. E., Friston, K. J., Gadian, D. G., & Mishkin, M. (2003). Developmental amnesia: Effect of age at injury. *Proceedings of the National Academy of Sciences of the USA*, *100*, 10055–10060.

Walton, G. E., Armstrong, E. S., & Bower, T. G. R. (1997). Faces as forms in the world of the newborn. *Infant Behavior and Development*, *20*, 537–543.

Wang, G. J., Volkow, N. D., Logan, J., Fowler, J. S., Schlyer, D., MacGregor, R. R., et al. (1995). Evaluation of age-related changes in serotonin 5-HT$_2$ and dopamine D$_2$ receptor availability in healthy human subjects. *Life Sciences*, *56*, 249–253.

Watson, L. (2001). *Der Duft der Verführung: Das unbewusste Riechen und die Macht der Lockstoffe*. Frankfurt/M.: Fischer.

Webb, S. J., Monk, C. S., & Nelson, C. A. (2001). Mechanisms of postnatal neuro-biological development: Implications for human development. *Developmental Psychology*, *19*, 147–171.

Wechsler, D. (1981). *Wechsler Adult Intelligence Scale – Revised (WAIS-R)*. New York: Psychological Corporation.

Welch-Ross, M. K. (1997). Mother–child participation in conversation about the past: Relationship to preschoolers' theory of mind. *Developmental Psychology*, *33*, 618–629.

Welch-Ross, M. K. (2001). Personalizing the temporally extended self: Evaluative self-awareness and the development of autobiographical memory. In C. Moore & K. Skene (Eds.), *The self in time: Developmental issues* (pp. 97–120). Hillsdale, NJ: Lawrence Erlbaum Associates, Inc.

Welford, A. T. (1965). Performance, biological mechanisms and age: A theoretical sketch. In A. T. Welford & J. E. Birren (Eds.), *Behavior, aging and the nervous system* (pp. 3–20). Springfield, IL: Charles C. Thomas.

Welzer, H. (2002). *Das kommunikative Gedächtnis. Eine Theorie der Erinnerung.* München: Beck.

Welzer, H., & Markowitsch, H. J. (2001). Umrisse einer interdisziplinären Gedächtnisforschung. *Psychologische Rundschau, 4*, 205–214.

Welzer, H., & Markowitsch, H. J. (2002). Die Entwicklung des autobiographischen Gedächtnisses. *Zeitschrift für Biographieforschung und Oral History Schwerpunktheft, 15*, 2.

Welzer, H., Moller, S., & Tschuggnall, K. (2002). *"Opa war kein Nazi." Nationalsozialismus und Holocaust im Familiengedächtnis. Frankfurt/M.: Fischer.*

Welzer, H., Montau, R., & Plass, C. (1997). *Was wir für böse Menschen sind! Der Nationalsozialismus im Gespräch zwischen den Generationen.* Tübingen: Edition Diskord.

Werker, J. F., & Tees, R. C. (1992). The organization and recognition of human speech perception. *Annual Review of Neuroscience, 15*, 377–402.

West, M. J. (1993). Regionally specific loss of neurons in the aging human hippocampus. *Neurobiology of Aging, 14*, 287–293.

West, R., & Baylis, G. C. (1998). Effects of increased response dominance and contextual disintegration on the Stroop interference effect in older adults. *Psychology and Aging, 13*, 206–217.

West, R., Jakubek, K., & Wymbs, N. (2002). Age-related declines in prospective memory: Behavioral and electrophysiological evidence. *Neuroscience and Biobehavioral Reviews, 26*, 827–833.

West, R. L. (1996). An application of prefrontal cortex function theory to cognitive aging. *Psychological Bulletin, 120*, 272–292.

Wheeler, M. A., Stuss, D. T., & Tulving E. (1997). Toward a theory of episodic memory: The frontal lobes and autonoetic consciousness. *Psychological Bulletin, 121*, 331–354.

Wiegersma, S., Scheer, E., & van der Hijman, R. (1990). Subjective ordering, short term memory, and the frontal lobes. *Neuropsychologia, 28*, 95–98.

Williams, D., & Mateer, C. A. (1992). Developmental impact of frontal lobe injury in middle childhood. *Brain and Cognition, 20*, 196–204.

Williams, J. M. G. (1997). Depression. In D. M. Clark & D. G. Fairburn (Eds.), *Science and practice of cognitive behaviour therapy* (pp. 259–284). Oxford: Oxford University Press.

Williams, M., & Zangwill, O. L. (1950). Disorders of temporal judgement associated with amnesic states. *Journal of Mental Science, 96*, 484–493.

Wimmer, H., & Perner, J. (1983). Beliefs about beliefs: Representation and constraining function of wrong beliefs in young children's understanding of deception. *Cognition, 13*, 103–128.

Wingfield, A., & Stine-Morrow, E. A. L. (2000). Language and speech. In F. I. M. Craik & T. A. Salthause (Eds.), *Handbook of aging and cognition* (pp. 359–416). Mahwah, NJ: Lawrence Erlbaum Associates, Inc.

Winkler, I., Kushnerenko, E., Horváth, J., Ceponiene, R., Fellman, V., Huotilainen, M., et al. (2003). Newborn infants can organize the auditory world. *Proceedings of the National Academy of Sciences of the USA, 100*, 11812–11815.

Winocur, G., Moscovitch, M., & Stuss, D. T. (1996). Explicit and implicit memory in the elderly: Evidence for double dissociation involving medial temporal- and frontal-lobe functions. *Neuropsychology, 10*, 57–65.

Wolf, H., Grunwald, M., Ecke, G. M., Zedlick, D., Bettin, S., Dannenberg, C., et al. (1998). The prognosis of mild cognitive impairment in the elderly. *Journal of Neural Transmission (Suppl.), 54*, 31–50.

Woodrow, H. (1914). The measurement of attention. *Psychological Monographs*, XVII (whole no. 76).

Woodruff-Pak, D. S. (1997). *The neuropsychology of aging.* Malden, MA: Blackwell.

Woodruff-Pak, D. S., & Papka, M. (1999). Theories of neuropsychology and aging. In V. L. Bengtson & K. W. Schaie (Eds.), *Handbook of theories of aging* (pp. 113–132). New York: Springer.

Woodruff-Pak, D. S., Romano, S., & Papka, M. (1996). Training to criterion in eyeblink classical conditioning in Alzheimer's disease, Down's syndrome with Alzheimer's disease, and healthy elderly. *Behavioral Neuroscience, 110*, 22–29.

Yakovlev, P., & Lecours, A. (1967). The myelinogenetic cycles of regional maturation of the brain. In A. Minkowski (Ed.), *Regional development of the brain* (pp. 3–70). Oxford: Blackwell.

Yamaguchi, S., Tsuchiya, H., & Kobayashi, S. (1995). Electrophysiologic correlates of age effects on visuospatial attention shift. *Cognitive Brain Research, 3*, 41–49.

Yantis, S., & Jonides, J. (1990). Abrupt visual onsets and selective attention: Voluntary versus automatic allocation. *Journal of Experimental Psychology: Human Perception and Performance, 16*, 121–134.

Ylikoski, R., Salonen, O., Mäntylä, R., Ylikoski, A., Keskivaara, P., & Erkinjuntti, T. (2000). Hippocampal and temporal lobe atrophy and age-related decline in memory. *Acta Neurologica Scandinavica, 101*, 273–278.

Young, J. Z. (1981). *The life of vertebrates.* Oxford: Clarendon Press.

Yuodelis, C., & Hendrickson, A. (1986). A qualitative and quantitative analysis of human fovea during development. *Vision Research, 26*, 847–855.

Zacks, R. T., & Hasher, L. (1997). Cognitive gerontology and attentional inhibition: A reply to Burke (1997) and McDowd (1997). *Journal of Gerontology: Psychological Sciences, 52B*, P274–P283.

Zacks, R. T., Hasher, L., & Li, K. Z. H. (2000). Human memory. In F. I. M. Craik & T. A. Salthouse (Eds.), *The handbook of aging and cognition* (2nd ed.) (pp. 293–357). Mahwah, NJ: Lawrence Erlbaum Associates, Inc.

Zaidel, E. (1989). Hemispheric independence and interaction in word recognition. In C. von Euler, J. Lundberg, & G. Lennerstand (Eds.), *Brain and reading* (Wenner-Gren International Symposium Series 54) (pp. 77–79). New York: M. Stockton Press.

Zelazo, P. D. (2004). The development of conscious control in childhood. *Trends in Cognitive Sciences, 8*, 12–17.

Zelinski, E. M., & Burnight, K. P. (1997). Sixteen-year longitudinal and time lag changes in memory and cognition in older adults. *Psychology and Aging, 12*, 503–513.

Zilles, K., Kawashima, R., Dabringhaus, A., Fukuda, H., & Schormann, T. (2001). Hemispheric shape of European and Japanese brains: 3D MRI analysis of inter-subject variability, ethnical, and gender differences. *NeuroImage, 13*, 262–271.

Zimprich, D. (1998). Geschwindigkeit der Informationsverarbeitung und fluide Intelligenz im höheren Erwachsenenalter. Eine Sekundäranalyse des Datenmaterials der Bonner Längsschnittstudie des Alterns anhand von "latent growth curve models". *Zeitschrift für Gerontologie und Geriatrie, 31*, 89–96.

Zuccarello, M., Facco, E., Zampieri, P., Zanardi, L., & Andrioli, G. C. (1985). Severe head injury in children: Early prognosis and outcome. *Child's Nervous System, 1*, 158–162.

Zulley, J., & Geisler, P. (2004). Der Schlaf – Ruhe und Aktivität. *Anästhesiologie & Intensivmedizin, 45*, 634–641.

Index